Mastering CSS

A guided journey through modern CSS

Rich Finelli

BIRMINGHAM - MUMBAI

Mastering CSS

First published: October 2017

Production reference: 2171117

Published by Packt Publishing Ltd.
Livery Place
35 Livery Street
Birmingham
B3 2PB, UK.

ISBN 978-1-78728-158-5

www.packtpub.com

Credits

Author
Rich Finelli

Commissioning Editor
Dominic Shakeshaft

Acquisition Editor
Ben Renow Clarke

Content Development Editor
Monika Sangwan

Technical Editor
Nidhisha Shetty

Copy Editor
Tom Jacob

Project Editor
Suzanne Coutinho

Proofreader
Safis Editing

Indexer
Pratik Shirodkar

Graphics
Kirk D'Penha

Production Coordinator
Arvindkumar Gupta

About the Author

Rich Finelli, is a front end developer and a CS video trainer. He is truly passionate and excited about front end technologies and enjoys learning about web development. Rich writes about what he's learning on his blog, richfinelli.com.

Thanks to my friends at Packt, Ben Renow-Clarke and Nidhisha Shetty for walking me through how to write a book. They must have thought I was George R. R. Martin with how many times I missed our target dates. Sorry for that. Thanks to Dominic Shakeshaft for reaching out to me and believing that my Mastering CSS video course should be the basis for a book.

Speaking of the video course, thanks to Nitee Shetty for editing and collaborating on the video course, which this book is largely based on.

Thanks to my mentors at Merrill Lynch: Pratik Mehta and my manager, Paresh Deshmukh, and everyone on the Front-end Engineering team whose relentless desire to learn pushes me to keep learning and honing my craft.

And most of all, I'd like to thank my wife, Renee, for all her support while writing this book. Many, many evenings were spent writing this book after work. Her support and encouragement helped me hang in there to get this book written. Love you, Renee!

www.PacktPub.com

For support files and downloads related to your book, please visit www.PacktPub.com.

Did you know that Packt offers eBook versions of every book published, with PDF and ePub files available? You can upgrade to the eBook version at www.PacktPub.com and as a print book customer, you are entitled to a discount on the eBook copy. Get in touch with us at service@packtpub.com for more details.

At www.PacktPub.com, you can also read a collection of free technical articles, sign up for a range of free newsletters and receive exclusive discounts and offers on Packt books and eBooks.

https://www.packtpub.com/mapt

Get the most in-demand software skills with Mapt. Mapt gives you full access to all Packt books and video courses, as well as industry-leading tools to help you plan your personal development and advance your career.

Why subscribe?

- Fully searchable across every book published by Packt
- Copy and paste, print, and bookmark content
- On demand and accessible via a web browser

Customer Feedback

Thanks for purchasing this Packt book. At Packt, quality is at the heart of our editorial process. To help us improve, please leave us an honest review on this book's Amazon page at `https://www.amazon.com/dp/1787281582`.

If you'd like to join our team of regular reviewers, you can email us at `customerreviews@packtpub.com`. We award our regular reviewers with free eBooks and videos in exchange for their valuable feedback. Help us be relentless in improving our products!

Table of Contents

Preface   1

Chapter 1: CSS Foundations   11

    The anatomy of a rule set and the three types of style sheets   12
        Dissecting a rule set   12
        External style sheets   13
        Embedded style sheets   15
        Inline style sheets   15
    The box model and block versus inline elements   17
        The box model   17
        Block level elements versus inline elements   21
    Summary   27

Chapter 2: Ramping Up   29

    Text editors   29
        Snippets   30
        Multiple cursors   33
        Syntax highlighting   34
        Code suggestion   35
    CSS reset   36
        Loading Eric Meyer's CSS reset   36
        Examining the CSS reset   40
        Customizing the CSS reset   42
    Chrome DevTools   46
        How to open developer tools   46
        Changing CSS inside the inspector   50
        Using the console to find errors   53
    Renaming elements — classes and IDs   56
        Classes   57
            Classifying multiple elements   60
        IDs   61
        Should we use classes or IDs?   63
    Descendant selectors   63
        Parent, child, and sibling elements   64
        Creating descendant selectors   65
        Calculating the weight of selectors   70

BEM   71
Summary   72
Chapter 3: Creating a Page Layout with Floats   73
  Float introduction–flowing text around images   73
    The Shark movies page   74
    The original purpose of floats   75
    Using the clear property to solve basic problems with floats   79
  Creating a multicolumn layout   82
    Centering an element   84
    Floating columns   86
    Targeting .column using a pseudo class   89
    Collapsed containers   91
  Solving the problems of floats   93
    Using the clear method   93
    Using overflow property with hidden value   95
    The float method   97
    Clearfix hack   98
  Summary   100
Chapter 4: Creating Buttons with Modular, Reusable CSS Classes, and CSS3   101
  Creating buttons with modular CSS   102
    Different button types   102
    Building standard buttons   104
  Multiple classes   110
    Changing the width of the buttons   112
    Changing the border and font colors of the buttons   113
    Positioning the button   115
  Specificity rules   119
    The weights of different selectors   119
    The !important declaration   123
    The universal selector   125
    Reality of the point system   127
  Transitions   128
    Creating a hover state   128
    Using the transition property   130
    Vendor prefixes   133
  Transforms   133
    Applying a scale to our button   134

Using the translate function	135
Using the rotate value	136
Adding vendor prefixes and :focus states	142
Styling the call-to-action button	**144**
Adding the HTML	145
Positioning using CSS	147
Styling the button	151
Gradients	**155**
Using the ultimate CSS gradient generator	156
The CSS output of the ultimate gradient generator	161
Summary	**164**
Chapter 5: Creating the Main Navigation and Drop-Down Menu	165
Starting the navigation	**165**
The semantic HTML for building a menu	166
Using CSS to style the navigation	168
Using pseudo classes	**175**
The first child	176
The last child	179
nth-child pseudo class	179
nth-of-type pseudo class	181
Absolute positioning	**183**
Absolutely positioning the shark	183
Using fixed positioning for the nav bar	187
Building the drop-down menu	**189**
Creating the basic HTML list	189
Styling the dropdown	191
Fixing the hover state	196
Hiding the drop-down menu using the off-screen hidden technique	199
CSS animations (part 1)	**201**
Defining the animation name, duration, and timing function	201
Setting additional keyframes	205
Vendor prefixes	208
CSS animations (part 2)	**209**
Animation delay, iteration-count, and fill-mode	209
animation-fill-mode	213
Using the animation shorthand	215
Vendor prefixes	216
Additional info on animations	217
Finalizing the navigation	**218**
Fixing the Z index issue	218

Adding box-shadow	221
Summary	225
Chapter 6: Becoming Responsive	227
Fluid grids	227
Converting pixels to percentages	228
Calculating percentage widths	230
Changing padding to a percentage	237
A fluid grid on the shark movies page	237
Flexible images	239
The octopus, crab, and whale images	240
The shark image	244
Shrinking images on the shark movies page	246
Media queries	250
Anatomy of a media query	253
Considering iPads and other tablet dimensions	258
Adding our three columns to the media query	259
The mobile-first approach	265
Solving the navigation problem	266
Mobile menu	270
Styling the mobile nav in its open state	270
Adding the hamburger menu icon	279
Hiding the menu	282
Using jQuery to trigger the menu on a click	283
Viewport meta tag	290
Testing our responsive design on a mobile device	290
The anatomy of the viewport meta tag	293
Summary	293
Chapter 7: Web Fonts	295
The @font-face property	295
Adding font files directly to the site	296
Defining and applying new fonts in our CSS	296
@font-face: a little tricky business	299
Making it work in all browsers	299
Google Web Fonts	301
Finding Google Fonts	301
Applying fonts in CSS	308
Adobe Typekit	311
Selecting fonts from Typekit	312
Adding fonts to the site	316

Icon fonts	321
Building the footer	321
Downloading a free icon font from the ZURB Foundation	324
Adding the icon font to our website	326
Styling icon fonts	332
Summary	336
Chapter 8: Workflow for HiDPI Devices	337
2x images	337
Creating a retina size image (2x)	338
Sizing down the 2x image using CSS	340
Checking the image quality on a retina device	344
Background images	346
Targeting the seaweed in the footer	346
Media query for device pixel ratio	348
Serving the 2x image only to retina devices	350
Scalable Vector Graphic (SVG)	352
Saving an Illustrator file as an SVG	355
Adding the SVG file as a background image	358
Adding the SVG as a regular ol' <img>	359
You can't stop SVG's, you can only hope to constrain them!	362
Using an inline SVG	364
Source set attribute (srcset)	370
What is srcset?	370
Adding a set of images to srcset	371
Testing the image set	372
Simplifying the srcset attribute	376
Browser support	377
Using the W descriptor and sizes attribute of the srcset attribute	379
Summary	380
Chapter 9: Flexbox, Part 1	381
Overview of the flexible box layout module	383
Flex terminology	383
Flex container and flex items	384
Main size and cross size	384
Main axis and cross axis	385
Justify-content and align-items	385
From floats to flexbox	385
Removing float-related properties from the columns section	386
Turning on flexbox using display: flex	391

Changing the flex-direction   395
   Browser shrinking   401
Understanding flex-grow, flex-basis, flex-shrink, and flex   403
Using flex-grow   403
Using flex-basis   408
Using flex-shrink   413
Using the flex shorthand   417
More layout, more positioning   420
Using the justify-content property   421
Nesting Flexboxes   428
Using automatic margins   431
Summary   434

Chapter 10: Flexbox, Part 2   435
Building the product listing   436
Using align-items   436
Using the align-self Flexbox property   451
Using flex-wrap and align-content   455
Using flex-wrap   455
Using align-content   460
Using the flex-flow shorthand   466
Changing the display order of flex items   467
Accessibility impact   480
Vendor prefixes   480
Autoprefixer   481
Gulp   483
Flexbox homework assignment   484
Summary   485

Chapter 11: Wrapping Up   487
The next steps   487
CSS preprocessors   487
   Variables   488
   Mixins   489
   SASS nesting   490
   Creating and importing partial files with SASS   490
JavaScript and jQuery   492
Conclusion and links   496
The box model and block versus inline elements   496
Floats   496
Modular CSS   497

CSS3   497
Creating the navigation   498
Making the site responsive   500
Web fonts   501
HiDPI devices   502
Flexbox   502
Final tidbit of advice: Audio Podcasts are terrific   502
Summary   502
Index   503

Preface

HTML, CSS, and JavaScript are the three core languages of the web. The more you know about all three of them, the better off you'll be. Of these three, the role of CSS is as the presentation language of the web. It describes things such as the colors, fonts, and layout of your pages.

There are some basic prerequisites for this book. I expect you understand how to write HTML, and understand basic CSS including styling fonts, adding margins, padding and background colors, and other things, such as what a hexadecimal color code is. In the coming chapters, I'll cover some of the basic concepts such as the box model, display properties, and types of style sheet. I'll also touch on a small amount of JavaScript and jQuery. You don't need any prior knowledge of these, but you will be getting a taste of them in this book.

Now, take a look at the final site we're going to build. In order to learn CSS, we'll finish building the following HTML5 website, which is all about sharks. I say *finish* building this site because the basic HTML and CSS will already be in place, and you can download them from the download package for this book. We'll add all the things that I will show you, and more. This site features modular and reusable CSS, which you will learn about as we move through the book. The site will first be built with floats for layout, before we rewrite the layout using flexbox. And we use web fonts for our text:

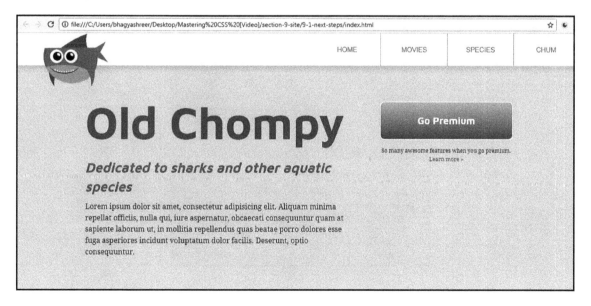

The navigation features a drop-down menu that uses CSS animations:

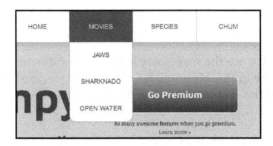

The site also features a call-to-action button with a CSS gradient:

The site is fully responsive. When we resize the browser, you can see that our two-column layout shifts into a single-column layout:

Also, our menu turns into a menu designed for mobile devices:

If we scroll down a little bit, we can see that we have ghost buttons that use CSS transitions. It's ready for HiDPI devices such as Apple's retina displays:

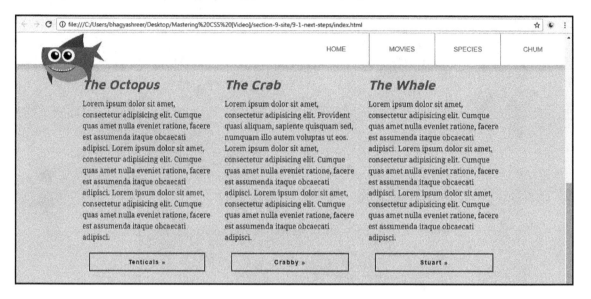

Most of the imagery on the site uses SVG:

At the very bottom of the page, we are using an icon font:

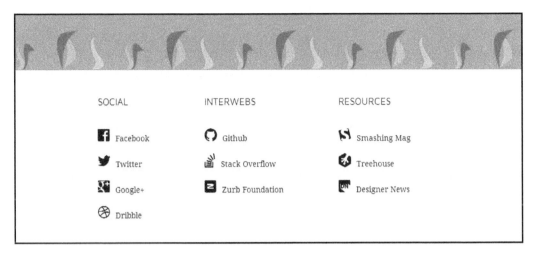

So, as you can see, you'll learn some really cool stuff in this book. To get the most out of it, I recommend that you follow along with me as I code.

What this book covers

Chapter 1, *CSS Foundations*, covers the fundamental concepts necessary to master CSS.

Chapter 2, *Ramping Up*, talks about the Sublime text editor; CSS reset, which resets the default styles in the browser; and descendant selectors.

Chapter 3, *Creating a Page Layout with Floats*, deep dives into floats. We'll cover the basic usage of floats, followed by creating the layout with floats, and understanding the common headaches caused by floats and how to solve for them .

Chapter 4, *Creating Buttons with Modular, Reusable CSS Classes, and CSS3*, covers modular CSS and multiple classes, and uses CSS3 to add transitions, hover states, transforms, and gradients to our buttons.

Chapter 5, *Creating the Main Navigation and Drop-Down Menu*, explains the functionality and presentation of our primary navigation.

Chapter 6, *Becoming Responsive*, covers the foundations of responsive web design and explains how to implement it to transform our static website into a mobile website.

Chapter 7, *Web Fonts*, discusses the basic syntax of the @font-face rule, font services, usage scenarios, and providers of web fonts and icon fonts.

Chapter 8, *Workflow for HiDPI Devices*, covers techniques for preparing images to account for Retina using SVG and techniques like the srcset attribute.

Chapter 9, *Flexbox, Part 1*, introduces the Flexbox module covering the basic implementation and properties.

Chapter 10, *Flexbox, Part 2*, covers more depth on Flexbox, building a new product listing and more advanced properties.

Chapter 11, *Wrapping Up*, wraps up the concepts of CSS that we covered in this book and provides some information on other CSS features that you can explore.

What you need for this book

Throughout the book, I've used Chrome as my browser because of its DevTools, among other things, but other browsers have similar tools. We'll use DevTools to explore code directly in the browser.

I've also used macOS throughout. If you're a Windows user and I refer to the command (*cmd*) key anywhere in the book, you should pretend that I am referring to the *Ctrl* key. Other than that, I don't think this will be an issue.

I have used the text editor *Sublime Text 3*. I should say that Sublime isn't the only good one out there. There are others like Atom and Visual Studio Code that do many of the same things.

Even though this book is on mastering CSS, we can't do much with CSS without HTML. So, we'll be working in HTML quite a bit. The goal is to use very clean, semantic HTML; that's what we want to aim for.

Who this book is for

This book is for web designers and developers who wish to master the best practices of CSS in their web projects. You should already know how to work with a web page, and be ready to use CSS to master website presentation.

Conventions

In this book, you will find a number of text styles that distinguish between different kinds of information. Here are some examples of these styles and an explanation of their meaning.

Code words in text, database table names, folder names, filenames, file extensions, path names, dummy URLs, user input, and Twitter handles are shown as follows: "To change the size of text use the `font-size` property."

A block of code is set as follows:

```
h2 {
  font-size: 26px;
  font-style: italic;
  color: #eb2428;
  margin-bottom: 10px;
}
```

When we wish to draw your attention to a particular part of a code block, the relevant lines or items are set in bold:

```
h2 {
  font-size: 26px;
  font-style: italic;
  color: #eb2428;
  margin-bottom: 10px;
}
```

Any command-line input or output is written as follows:

```
# cp /usr/src/asterisk-
addons/configs/cdr_mysql.conf.sample/etc/asterisk/cdr_mysql.conf
```

New terms and **important words** are shown in bold. Words that you see on the screen, for example, in menus or dialog boxes, appear in the text like this: "Clicking on the **Next** button moves you to the next screen."

Warnings or important notes appear in a box like this.

Tips and tricks appear like this.

Reader feedback

Feedback from our readers is always welcome. Let us know what you think about this book—what you liked or disliked. Reader feedback is important for us as it helps us develop titles that you will really get the most out of.

To send us general feedback, simply email `feedback@packtpub.com`, and mention the book's title in the subject of your message.

If there is a topic that you have expertise in and you are interested in either writing or contributing to a book, see our author guide at `www.packtpub.com/authors`.

Customer support

Now that you are the proud owner of a Packt book, we have a number of things to help you to get the most from your purchase.

Downloading the example code

You can download the example code files from your account at `http://www.packtpub.com` for all the Packt Publishing books you have purchased. If you purchased this book elsewhere, you can visit `http://www.packtpub.com/support` and register to have the files emailed directly to you. You can download the code files by following these steps:

1. Log in or register to our website using your email address and password.
2. Hover the mouse pointer on the **SUPPORT** tab at the top.
3. Click on **Code Downloads & Errata**.
4. Enter the name of the book in the **Search** box.
5. Select the book for which you're looking to download the code files.
6. Choose from the drop-down menu where you purchased this book from.
7. Click on **Code Download**.

Once the file is downloaded, please make sure that you unzip or extract the folder using the latest version of:

- WinRAR / 7-Zip for Windows
- Zipeg / iZip / UnRarX for Mac
- 7-Zip / PeaZip for Linux

The code bundle for the book is also hosted on GitHub at `https://github.com/PacktPublishing/Mastering-CSS`. We also have other code bundles from our rich catalog of books and videos available at `https://github.com/PacktPublishing/`. Check them out!

Downloading the color images of this book

We also provide you with a PDF file that has color images of the screenshots/diagrams used in this book. The color images will help you better understand the changes in the output. You can download this file from `https://www.packtpub.com/sites/default/files/downloads/MasteringCSS_ColorImages.pdf`.

Errata

Although we have taken every care to ensure the accuracy of our content, mistakes do happen. If you find a mistake in one of our books—maybe a mistake in the text or the code—we would be grateful if you could report this to us. By doing so, you can save other readers from frustration and help us improve subsequent versions of this book. If you find any errata, please report them by visiting `http://www.packtpub.com/submit-errata`, selecting your book, clicking on the **Errata Submission Form** link, and entering the details of your errata. Once your errata are verified, your submission will be accepted and the errata will be uploaded to our website or added to any list of existing errata under the Errata section of that title.

To view the previously submitted errata, go to `https://www.packtpub.com/books/content/support` and enter the name of the book in the search field. The required information will appear under the **Errata** section.

Piracy

Piracy of copyrighted material on the internet is an ongoing problem across all media. At Packt, we take the protection of our copyright and licenses very seriously. If you come across any illegal copies of our works in any form on the internet, please provide us with the location address or website name immediately so that we can pursue a remedy.

Please contact us at `copyright@packtpub.com` with a link to the suspected pirated material.

We appreciate your help in protecting our authors and our ability to bring you valuable content.

Questions

If you have a problem with any aspect of this book, you can contact us at `questions@packtpub.com`, and we will do our best to address the problem.

1
CSS Foundations

In this first chapter, *CSS Foundations,* we're going to take a look at the fundamental concepts necessary to master CSS. You're going to learn about the best practices in web development.

In the world of web development, things change often. For instance, in the past, tables were the technique of choice when laying out a webpage. Today, using a table for layout is definitely not what you want to do. Floats have been the most common way to create a layout for a while and will be what we learn about first. In the last year or so, flexbox has started to overtake floats for layout and we'll learn about flexbox towards the end of this book. CSS is progressing with other new layout modules that are designed to supplant floats for laying out a page. Grid layout, and CSS regions may be the way of the future. Since things rapidly evolve in the world of frontend web development, our key takeaway is that we can't stop learning CSS. In general, once you stop learning, your knowledge will becomes outdated very quickly. My intent is to teach the concepts and techniques that will benefit you for a long time.

In the two sections of this chapter, we'll review core concepts that are fundamental to web design and CSS. We'll start by reviewing how to create the most fundamental thing in CSS–the rule set-and go over the different places we can write those rule sets.

The anatomy of a rule set and the three types of style sheets

We're now a little more familiar with the content of the book and the website we're going to build. Before we start delving into more advanced topics, let's review a few CSS foundations. Going forward in this book, I'll use terms such as selector, property, and value, and you'll need to understand exactly what these terms mean in order to follow along. Here's what we'll do: we'll review a rule set first, and then we'll look at the three different places we can write those rule sets. So let's get started.

Dissecting a rule set

Let's jump into a CSS file and look at one of the rule sets in the following code block. It's targeting an h2-a level two headline. It's setting a `font-size` of `26px`, a `font-style` of `italic`, a `color` to a shade of red, and a `margin-bottom` of `10px`:

```
h2 {
    font-size: 26px;
    font-style: italic;
    color: #eb2428;
    margin-bottom: 10px;
}
```

So nothing too scary here! Let's dissect this a little bit though:

```
selector {
    property: value;
    property: value;
    property: value;
}
```

In the preceding code, `h2` is the *selector*. We are selecting an element on the page to target our style rules. The `h2` selector could be a `p`, an `li`, a `div`, an `a`, or any HTML element we want to target. It can also be a class, an ID, or an element attribute, which I'll talk about later. Next, we have properties and values inside the curly braces. From the opening curly brace to the closing curly brace is the *declaration block*. You can have as many properties as you want inside the curly braces, or declaration block. `font-size`, `color`, `font-style`, and `margin` are just a few of the many different properties that you can use. Each property has a corresponding value. Between each property and value, you must have a colon. Following the value is a semi colon, which is also mandatory. Each property and value is called a declaration. So the declaration block is everything inside the curly braces and a declaration is a single line that includes a property and a value. But really, there are three important things to remember in the anatomy of a rule set: the selector, the property, and the value. Now let's look at where we can write these rule sets.

External style sheets

Currently, we write our rule sets in an external style sheet. You can see it's literally its own file:

In the folder structure on the left-hand side of the screen, you can see that it's in a folder called `css`:

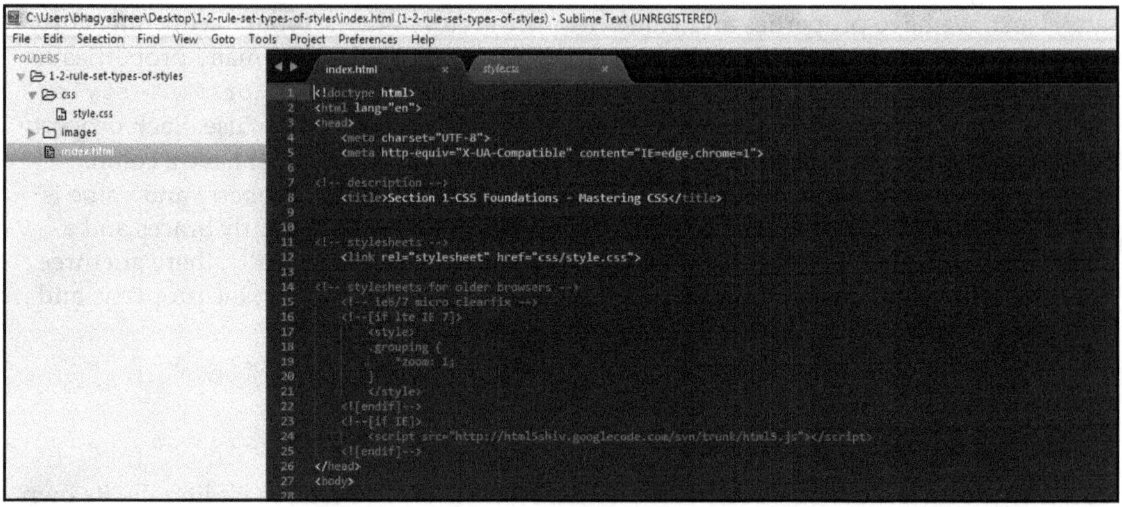

Besides **external** style sheets, there are also **inline** and **embedded** style sheets. The external style sheet is by far the best place to write your styles; it's a separate file that is linked to each HTML page. An external style sheet can control a whole website, which is the main reason why this is the preferred type of style sheet. Anywhere in between the `<head></head>` tags of your `index.html` file; this is where you can link to your external style sheet:

```
<head>
  <link rel="stylesheet" href="css/style.css">
</head>
```

The `href` attribute points to the location of the file. Here it's pointing to the `css` folder and then a file called `style.css`. There's also a `rel` attribute that just basically says that this is a `stylesheet`. In the past, you might have seen `text/css` as the value for the `type` attribute, as shown in the following code block, but that is no longer necessary in HTML5:

```
<head>
  <link rel="stylesheet" href="css/style.css" type="text/css">
</head>
```

You may have also seen a closing forward slash on a self-closing tag like the `link` element, but in HTML5 that forward slash is no longer necessary. So including it or excluding it won't have any impact on your site.

Embedded style sheets

Instead of using the best type of style sheet, the external style sheet, we can also write our rule sets in the head of HTML documents. This is called an **embedded style sheet**. There are plenty of reasons for not doing it this way. The main two reasons are that it hampers the workflow, and it only controls a single page of the site. What we would do is simply create somewhere in the head tag, these open and close <style> tags:

```
<head>
  <style>

  </style>
</head>
```

Anywhere inside this open <style> tag we can start adding our rule sets, which will only affect this one page:

```
<head>
  <style>
    h2 {
       font-size: 50px;
    }
  </style>
</head>
```

Again, this isn't the most preferred place to write your styles. Keeping them in an external style sheet will, 99 percent of the time, be the best place, but you do have the option of embedding styles in the head tag of your document.

Inline style sheets

Finally, the third type of style sheet is the inline style sheet. And its not really a style sheet - more like just an *inline style*. What we could do is write a style attribute actually inside an element in our HTML:

```
<h2 style="">
```

Inline styles are a little different from external and embedded style sheets that use the traditional rule set; here there's no selector and there's no complete rule set because you're writing it inside an HTML tag. We can enter a font-size of 10px. We write that property and value the same way we do in a rule set and we should cap it with a semicolon:

```
<h2 style="font-size: 10px;">
```

We can also change the color and cap that with a semicolon:

```
<h2 style="font-size: 10px; color: deeppink;">
```

Save this, refresh the website, and you can see the result:

This is by far the most inefficient way to write styles. However, writing CSS directly in an HTML element gives it the most weight and will overrule all embedded styles and all external styles that target the same element, unless the `!important` keyword is used. In `Chapter 4`, *Creating Buttons with Modular, Reusable CSS Classes, and CSS3* in the *Specificity Rules* section, I dive into cascades and other factors that make certain rules weigh more and override other rules.

Okay, so we have now created a rule set and learned what each part of a rule set is called, specifically, the selector, property, and value. This information will be helpful for you to retain, as I'll use this terminology often. We also reviewed the three different places you can create a style sheet: externally, embedded within the `<head>` tag, and inline, directly inside of an element. Again, external style sheets are the most efficient because they can control an entire website. This is the only place I write CSS if I can help it. Next, we'll review two more core concepts: the box model and the `display` property.

The box model and block versus inline elements

In this section, we'll review two more foundations of CSS: the box model and block versus inline elements. Fully grasping these two concepts is key in laying the ground work for CSS mastery later. First, we will review the box model and then we'll look at how that relates to block level elements. We'll follow that up with the characteristics of inline elements.

The box model

The **box model** defines how wide and tall elements on a page will be. To determine the horizontal space an element occupies, you add up the `content` + `padding-left` + `padding-right` + `border-left` + `border-right` + `margin-left` + `margin-right`:

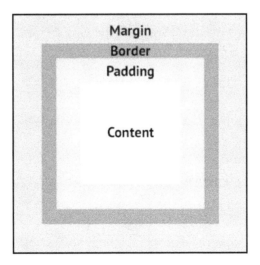

So let's take a look at this in practice by looking at the `h1` on our site, which is the blue text that says, "Old Chompy".

Here is the ruleset that makes this headline look the way it does:

```
h1 {
    font-size: 40px;
    line-height:1.4;
    font-weight: bold;
    color: #0072ae
}
```

Let's add in the following properties to give it a `width`, `padding`, `border`, and `margin`. As well as a noticeable `background-color`:

```
h1 {
    font-size: 40px;
    line-height:1.4;
    font-weight: bold;
    color: #0072ae
    background-color: black;
```

```
    width: 300px;
    padding: 50px;
    border: 10px solid blue;
    margin: 50px;
}
```

Here's what our headline looks like now. One big box:

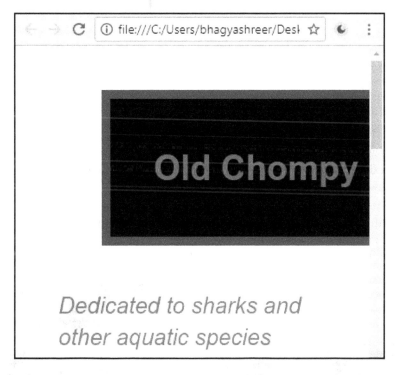

So those 5 properties that contribute to this element's box model are now in place; looking at the browser in the preceding screenshot, this h1 really looks like a box. We can see the border of 10px, the margin, which is outside the border, is 50px, and the padding, which is between the border and the text, is 50px. Then the width inside the padding is 300px. So this element's width is actually *300 + 20 + 100 + 100*, which adds up to a total size of 520px. So even though we said the width is 300px by defining the width property in our CSS file, the true space this element occupies is 520px.

Now, that is the traditional box model. I can modify this traditional box model using the `box-sizing` property with the `border-box` value. So let's use the `box-sizing` property and see how that affects the site. Add the property and value to the bottom of the `h1` declaration block, as shown here:

```
h1 {
    font-size: 40px;
    line-height:1.4;
    font-weight: bold;
    color: #0072ae
    background-color: black;
    width: 300px;
    padding: 50px;
    margin: 50px;
    border: 10px solid blue;
    box-sizing: border-box;
}
```

As illustrated in the following screenshot, `border-box` will include essentially subtract the `padding` and `border` from the `width` and `height` calculation. If I use `300px` as my `width`, the border of `20px` and the padding of `100px` will be subtracted from the `300px` I specified. This is a more intuitive box model and it is compatible with Internet Explorer 8 and higher, as well as all other major browsers. The final horizontal space this element now occupies goes from `520px` to `400px`.

Block level elements versus inline elements

Let's talk a little bit about block level elements. The heading 1 (h1), heading 2 (h2), paragraphs (p), list items (li), and divs (div) are all examples of natural block level elements. Block level elements have two defining traits: they expand the full width available, and they force elements that come after them to appear on the next line, meaning they stack on top of each other. So let's remove the box-sizing property from our declaration block as well as the width property to demonstrate how they take up the full width available if no width is specified:

```
h1 {
    font-size: 40px;
    line-height:1.4;
    font-weight: bold;
    color: #0072ae
    background-color: black;
    padding: 50px;
    margin: 50px;
    border: 10px solid blue;
}
```

Save this and refresh the site. You can see in the following screenshot that, as you make your browser window larger, it takes up the full width available, apart from the margin that we set of 50px on all sides:

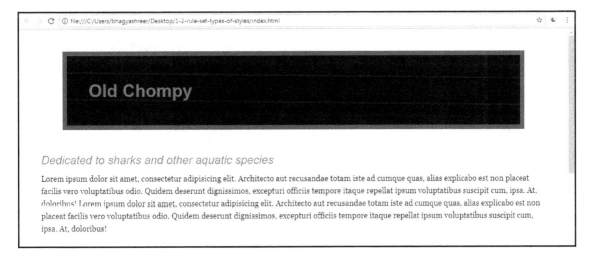

Now let's go into the HTML file, add two more of these h1 tags into the HTML, and save it:

```
<section>
    <h1>Old Chompy</h1>
    <h1>Old Chompy</h1>
    <h1&gt;Old Chompy</h1>
```

Here's what that looks like:

Now you can see how these block level elements stack on top of each other: good ol' block level elements.

Inline elements, on the other hand, behave differently. They sit next to each other horizontally and they don't take up the full width available. They only take up as much width as they need. A few elements that are naturally inline elements are the anchor (<a>), <span>, <i>, <b>, <strong>, and <em> tags.

Alright, so let me go into the HTML and add three `span` tags to the page:

```
<section>
  <h1>Old Chompy</h1>
  <h1>Old Chompy</h1>
  <h1>Old Chompy</h1>
  <span>Inline</span>
  <span>Inline</span>
  <span>Inline</span>
```

What I'll also do is generally target those `span` elements in a rule set and give them a green background, just to kind of see that they're distinct:

```
span {
  background-color: green;
}
```

Here's how that looks:

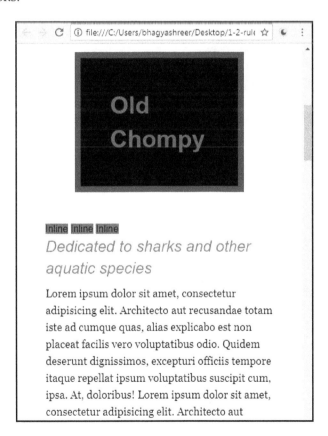

You can notice how the green inline elements sit next to each other horizontally instead of stacking vertically. Nothing special, but we can see how they do not take up the full width available, they only take as much as they need.

There are some things that inline elements do not do. They don't respond to `width` or `margin-top` or `margin-bottom`. So if an element is naturally inline and you give it a `width` and a `margin-top` or `margin-bottom`, as shown in the following code, it's going to do absolutely nothing:

```
span {
  background-color: green;
  width: 1000px;
  margin-top: 1000px;
}
```

Nothing changes:

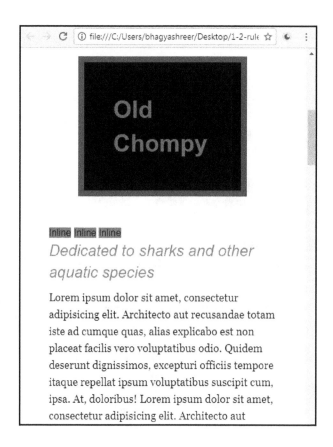

Inline elements just don't respect those properties, and those properties don't have an impact on them, so we'll remove those.

There's one last interesting thing you can do. There's a `display` property that allows you to change a natural block level element to inline and vice versa. So let's add a `display` property with the `block` value to our `span` selector and view that in the browser. So, I can just say `display: block` and also add some `margin-top`:

```
span {
  background-color: green;
  display: block;
  margin-top: 10px;
}
```

We can see that these elements now stack on top of each other and now respect the `margin-top` and `margin-bottom` values:

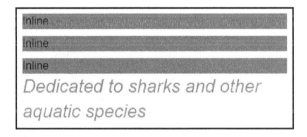

Elements with the `display` property set to `block` would respect any `width` value I give it, but it also takes up the full width available. You can see that it extends all the way to the edge of our screen. We could've just as easily used the `display: inline` property on our `h1` selector to change the nature of the display from block to inline. Lastly though, we can use `display: none`, which totally hides the element from the page and is often used for various reasons. So let's go to our `h1` declaration and say `display: none`:

```
h1 {
  font-size: 40px;
  line-height:1.4;
  font-weight: bold;
  color: #0072ae;
  background-color: black;
  padding: 50px;
  margin: 50px;
  border: 10px solid blue;
  display: none;
}
```

Now, if we look at our site, that `h1` is invisible. It's no longer something that the browser is going to show us:

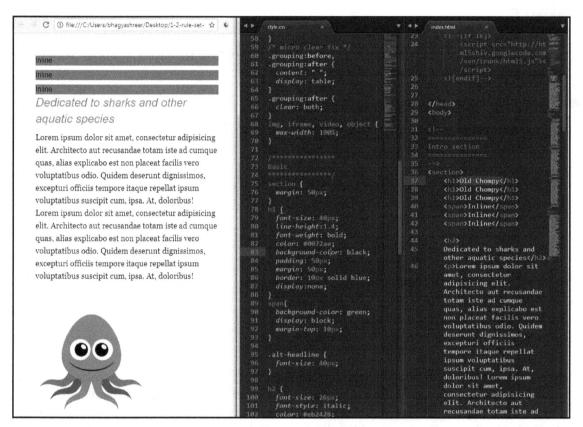

To sum up, all elements conform to a box model. The box model changes a little depending on how the `box-sizing` property is used, if used at all. Also, the box model changes based on whether the element is block or inline, the two most common display properties.

Summary

We have accomplished a lot in this first chapter. We've talked about how CSS is the presentation language of the web and really makes your website look like a website. We're now familiar with the site we'll be building and tools we'll be using in the upcoming chapters. We have covered core concepts such as rule sets, linking to an external style sheet, and the box model and display properties, all of which are vital in order to master CSS.

In the next chapter, we'll get into some tools that are necessary to write CSS, such as a good text editor, a CSS reset, and Chrome's Developer tools.

2
Ramping Up

In order to be a great coder, you need to ramp up and learn about things that will help you become a better developer. In this chapter, we're going to look at text editors that will speed up our workflow. We'll then look at a *CSS reset*, which resets the default browser such that its styling is reduced to nothing, and the built-in browser developer tools to help us troubleshoot our code. Then, we'll look at how to rename elements with classes and IDs as well as qualify our selectors using descendant selectors.

Text editors

HTML, CSS, and JavaScript can be written in any text-editing application. This is one of the great things about the three core web languages. The problem is that writing HTML, CSS, and JavaScript is extremely error-prone. For CSS, commas, semicolons, and curly braces need to be typed in the right spots. A specific syntax needs to be adhered to perfectly in most cases, else your page won't render as expected. The following is an illustration of TextEdit for Mac. It's similar in nature to Notepad for Windows, in that it doesn't have many features that make writing code easy:

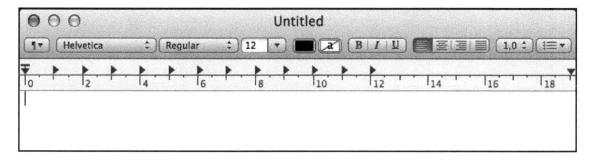

Let's write some code in TextEdit anyway. We start with the HTML doc type. Post this, we add an HTML opening and closing tag and then the `head` tag and inside that the `title` tag. You'll soon realize that it's a pretty tedious process, that is, writing code in TextEdit. We can write code here, but we're really getting nothing out of it, no syntax highlighting, and no other assistance whatsoever:

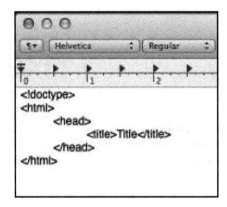

Luckily, a good text editor can really do the hard work for you. In this chapter, we'll look at such a text editor, namely Sublime Text 3, and some of the nice features it has to help you write HTML and CSS even better. First, we'll look at snippets, then we'll look at syntax highlighting, followed by code suggestions and multiple cursors. Sublime Text 3 is my text editor of choice as it is fast and easy to use. One of the things I love is how easy and natural it allows me to write code.

Snippets

In Sublime Text 3, you simply need to type in `html:5` in your HTML file and hit the *Tab* key to get a basic boilerplate for your HTML. So, all of the code that we had to type in TextEdit can be quickly written for us:

```
<!DOCTYPE html>
<html>
<head>
        <title></title>
</head>
<body>

</body>
</html>
```

Another thing is when you type in `div` and hit the *Tab* key, you can have `div` expanded with the closing tag created automatically and the cursor right in between the opening and closing `div` tag:

We can do this for any HTML element; just type in something like `p` and hit *Tab* and get your cursor right in between:

That is beautiful! It's really nice to have something that simple.

We can take this one step further and install the Emmet package. I highly encourage you to do so. This will provide you with even better code snippets. In fact, the `html:5` code snippet that produced the basic HTML boilerplate before, is actually an Emmet snippet; it doesn't come standard with Sublime:

```html
<!DOCTYPE html>
<html>
<head>
    <meta charset="UTF-8">
    <title>Document</title>
</head>
<body>

</body>
</html>
```

The ability to install packages, which are basically plugins, in Sublime is another reason why it's so powerful. There's a package for everything you need that doesn't come out of the box with Sublime. So let's say you need syntax highlighting for ColdFusion code; there's a package available that will do this for you. I have an article on my site that covers package installation, which is pretty simple. Just check it out at `richfinelli.com/installing-sublime-package-manager/`:

By far, this is the best package, and the first thing you should install is Emmet. With Emmet, say you go to your HTML and type in something like this:

```
div>ul>li*5>a{link$}
```

This will expand to the following:

```
<div>
  <ul>
    <li><a href="">link1</a></li>
    <li><a href="">link2</a></li>
    <li><a href="">link3</a></li>
    <li><a href="">link4</a></li>
    <li><a href="">link5</a></li>
  </ul>
</div>
```

Notice that the $ expanded in to 1 for the first a, and 2 for second, and so on, which can be very useful. Writing HTML quickly using a CSS selector-like syntax is just one of the nice things that Emmet allows you to do.

Multiple cursors

Keeping the div tag we just expanded with Emmet, let's look at Sublime's multiple cursors feature. Since we had five lists, we may need to type in the same thing in each one. If you hold down your *cmd* key and click on separate lines of code, you can actually create multiple cursors. As illustrated, you can now type the same thing in five different spots:

```html
<div>
    <ul>
        <li><a href="">link1</a></li>
        <li><a href="">link2</a></li>
        <li><a href="">link3</a></li>
        <li><a href="">link4</a></li>
        <li><a href="">link5</a></li>
    </ul>
</div>
```

Now, let's say you want to type in some placeholder text where you will have multiple cursors. First, type in "lorem5", or "lorem" followed by any other number, and you'll get than many words of placeholder "lorem ipsum" text:

```html
<div>
    <ul>
        <li><a href="">link1</a> lorem5</li>
        <li><a href="">link2</a> lorem5</li>
        <li><a href="">link3</a> lorem5</li>
        <li><a href="">link4</a> lorem5</li>
        <li><a href="">link5</a> lorem5</li>
    </ul>
</div>
```

Then, just hit *Tab*, and it will automatically expand to, in our case, 5 words of lorem ipsum text, as illustrated here:

```
<div>
    <ul>
        <li><a href="">link1</a> Lorem ipsum dolor sit amet.</li>
        <li><a href="">link2</a> Lorem ipsum dolor sit amet.</li>
        <li><a href="">link3</a> Lorem ipsum dolor sit amet.</li>
        <li><a href="">link4</a> Lorem ipsum dolor sit amet.</li>
        <li><a href="">link5</a> Lorem ipsum dolor sit amet.</li>
    </ul>
</div>
```

Syntax highlighting

Let's switch over to our CSS for a second. Another feature that will make our job much easier is syntax highlighting. Notice how the rule sets all follow a color scheme. The selectors are red, properties are blue, and the values are purple. They will start getting embedded into your subconscious mind:

```
1 p {
2       font-size: 30px;
3 }
4 div {
5       width: 240px;
6 }
```

What Sublime Text does for you is it subtly points out your mistakes. I often type in a semicolon where a colon is required. This will cause your CSS to not work. Syntax highlighting, though, tells me that something is wrong because, as shown in the following screenshot, the color scheme changes:

```
1 p {
2       font-size: 30px;
3 }
4 div {
5       width; 240px;
6 }
```

It's easy to spot a color difference but difficult to see the difference between a colon and a semicolon if you are not looking for it:

Code suggestion

There are some cool features available, such as code completion and code suggestion. So if you start typing in something like `border-`, you'll get all the different properties that start with `border`:

```
div {
    width; 240px;
    border|
}   border-top
    border-style
    border-width
    border-bottom
    border-color
    border-radius
    border-right
    border-image
```

In this case, I'm looking for `border radius`, so I can just go to that suggestion and hit *Tab* and it automatically completes the task for me:

```
div {
    width; 240px;
    border-radius: |
}
```

There are so many other reasons why I love this text editor that I won't go into. It comes at a cost of $70 but has an unlimited free trial that you can use to determine whether or not you like it—trust me, you will. Now I'm not saying that Sublime is the only text editor you should use or try. There are other good editors as well, like Visual Studio Code, Atom, Adobe Brackets, and others. If you're using something else that does most of the things I'm talking about and it works for you, then stick with it. Just make sure that you don't use Notepad or TextEdit to write your code as that will be very painful and unproductive.

A good text editor is essential for writing good HTML and CSS and will make our lives much easier. Next, you're going to learn about CSS resets and how they help us create a very good starting point for writing CSS.

CSS reset

In the last section, you learned about the power of a good text editor. In this section, we're going to use that text editor to explore something called a *CSS reset*. There's a lot of pieces to starting a website that need to be in place and are typically part of your website boilerplate. I call these pieces your "base layer". A big part of this *base layer* is the CSS reset. A reset allows you to eliminate browser inconsistencies with regard to default browser styling and eliminate all default browser styles in general. It allows *you* to more easily provide *your* handcrafted styles using CSS. In this section, we're going to first load in a CSS reset, then examine that reset and see what it's doing. Finally, we'll add to and customize the reset to fit our needs.

Loading Eric Meyer's CSS reset

There are a few different resets to choose from, but I've been hooked to the CSS guru Eric Meyer's reset. Let's go grab it from `meyerweb.com/eric/tools/css/reset/`:

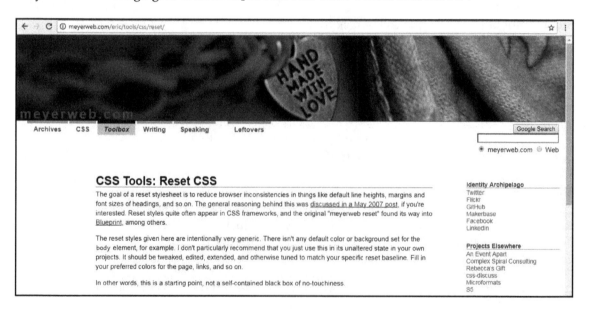

So, scroll down a little bit to find the top of the reset, then just highlight all of the code until you get to the closing curly brace:

```
ⓘ meyerweb.com/eric/tools/css/reset/

/* http://meyerweb.com/eric/tools/css/reset/
   v2.0 | 20110126
   License: none (public domain)
*/

html, body, div, span, applet, object, iframe,
h1, h2, h3, h4, h5, h6, p, blockquote, pre,
a, abbr, acronym, address, big, cite, code,
del, dfn, em, img, ins, kbd, q, s, samp,
small, strike, strong, sub, sup, tt, var,
b, u, i, center,
dl, dt, dd, ol, ul, li,
fieldset, form, label, legend,
table, caption, tbody, tfoot, thead, tr, th, td,
article, aside, canvas, details, embed,
figure, figcaption, footer, header, hgroup,
menu, nav, output, ruby, section, summary,
time, mark, audio, video {
        margin: 0;
        padding: 0;
        border: 0;
        font-size: 100%;
        font: inherit;
        vertical-align: baseline;
}
/* HTML5 display-role reset for older browsers */
article, aside, details, figcaption, figure,
footer, header, hgroup, menu, nav, section {
        display: block;
}
body {
        line-height: 1;
}
ol, ul {
        list-style: none;
}
blockquote, q {
        quotes: none;
}
blockquote:before, blockquote:after,
q:before, q:after {
        content: '';
        content: none;
}
table {
        border-collapse: collapse;
        border-spacing: 0;
}
```

Switch over to Sublime, open your style sheet, and paste it in there:

```css
/* http://meyerweb.com/eric/tools/css/reset/
   v2.0 | 20110126
   License: none (public domain)
*/
html, body, div, span, applet, object, iframe,
h1, h2, h3, h4, h5, h6, p, blockquote, pre,
a, abbr, acronym, address, big, cite, code,
del, dfn, em, img, ins, kbd, q, s, samp,
small, strike, strong, sub, sup, tt, var,
b, u, i, center,
dl, dt, dd, ol, ul, li,
fieldset, form, label, legend,
table, caption, tbody, tfoot, thead, tr, th, td,
article, aside, canvas, details, embed,
figure, figcaption, footer, header, hgroup,
menu, nav, output, ruby, section, summary,
time, mark, audio, video {
    margin: 0;
    padding: 0;
    border: 0;
    font-size: 100%;
    font: inherit;
    vertical-align: baseline;
}
/* HTML5 display-role reset for older browsers */
article, aside, details, figcaption, figure,
footer, header, hgroup, menu, nav, section {
    display: block;
}
body {
    line-height: 1.4;
    font-family: Arial, Helvetica, sans-serif;
}
ol, ul {
    list-style: none;
}
blockquote, q {
    quotes: none;
}
blockquote:before, blockquote:after,
q:before, q:after {
    content: '';
    content: none;
}
table {
    border-collapse: collapse;
    border-spacing: 0;
}
```

Before we save this, let's open the `index.html` file for our site. One of the things you can do with Sublime is this: if you right-click on your HTML file, you can select **Open in Browser** and it will open your default browser:

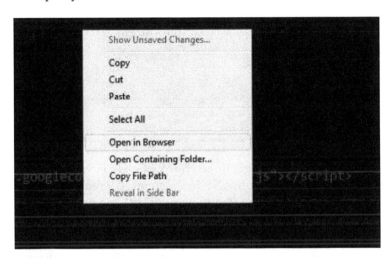

In my case, it's Chrome. So this is what the site will look like without the reset:

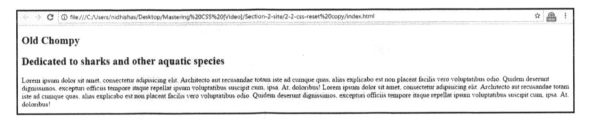

As you can see in the next screenshot, all of the CSS we added actually removed the little bit of styling we had. This is why we call it a reset. All text looks the same—no margin, no padding, no nothing.

Old Chompy
Dedicated to sharks and other aquatic species
Lorem ipsum dolor sit amet, consectetur adipisicing elit. Architecto aut recusandae totam iste ad cumque quas, alias explicabo est non placeat facilis vero voluptatibus odio. Quidem deserunt dignissimos, excepturi officiis tempore itaque repellat ipsum voluptatibus suscipit cum, ipsa. At, doloribus! Lorem ipsum dolor sit amet, consectetur adipisicing elit. Architecto aut recusandae totam iste ad cumque quas, alias explicabo est non placeat facilis vero voluptatibus odio. Quidem deserunt dignissimos, excepturi officiis tempore itaque repellat ipsum voluptatibus suscipit cum, ipsa. At, doloribus!

Examining the CSS reset

Up at the very top of our style sheet, there is a CSS comment that credits Eric Meyer for the reset. We'll leave that in there:

```
1   /* http://meyerweb.com/eric/tools/css/reset/
2      v2.0 | 20110126
3      License: none (public domain)
4   */
5
6   html, body, div, span, applet, object, iframe,
7   h1, h2, h3, h4, h5, h6, p, blockquote, pre,
8   a, abbr, acronym, address, big, cite, code,
```

Next, we have the bulk of the reset. This huge chunk of code is vaguely a reminder of the rule set you learned about in Chapter 1, *CSS Foundations*. It's really just a rule set with a very long selector. The selector has just about every HTML element separated by commas:

```
6   html, body, div, span, applet, object, iframe,
7   h1, h2, h3, h4, h5, h6, p, blockquote, pre,
8   a, abbr, acronym, address, big, cite, code,
9   del, dfn, em, img, ins, kbd, q, s, samp,
10  small, strike, strong, sub, sup, tt, var,
11  b, u, i, center,
12  dl, dt, dd, ol, ul, li,
13  fieldset, form, label, legend,
14  table, caption, tbody, tfoot, thead, tr, th, td,
15  article, aside, canvas, details, embed,
16  figure, figcaption, footer, header, hgroup,
17  menu, nav, output, ruby, section, summary,
18  time, mark, audio, video {
19      margin: 0;
20      padding: 0;
21      border: 0;
22      font-size: 100%;
23      font: inherit;
24      vertical-align: baseline;
25  }
```

This means that all these elements are going to receive the same styles from the declaration block:

```
... {
  margin: 0;
  padding: 0;
  border: 0;
  font-size: 100%;
  font: inherit;
  vertical-align: baseline;
}
```

As you can see in the first three declarations of this declaration block, margin, padding, and border are set to 0. Using the value of 0 is the same as using 0px just with two less characters. You just don't need to specify pixels if the value is zero. This removes the default margin, padding, and border from all the elements. Right below those declarations, we have the font-size property, which is 100%. This line is an instruction to make all the fonts browser-default, which basically means 16px since the default browser font size for most desktop browsers is 16px.

Below this declaration block, we have the new HTML5 elements whose display we set to block. This allows some older browsers that don't recognize these new elements to now consider them block-level elements. This allows HTML5 to work in some older browsers:

```
/* HTML5 display-role reset for older browsers */
article, aside, details, figcaption, figure,
footer, header, hgroup, menu, nav, section {
    display: block;
}
```

Next, we have a new selector and declaration that sets the line-height to 1:

```
body {
  line-height: 1;
}
```

The line-height property cascades downward, meaning if we set it on an element, for example, body, it will be inherited down to all the other elements it contains. The value of 1 is a unit-less value, so 1 will be equal to the size of the font. The value of 1.2 would be 1.2 times the size of the font. So, if the font-size is 16px and line-height is 1, then the line-height will be equivalent to 16px. If line-height is set to 2 and your font size is 16px, then line-height will be equivalent to 32px.

Next in the style sheet are the ordered and unordered lists, where we remove the bullet point and numbers from ul, ol and by way of cascade, li:

```
ol, ul {
    list-style: none;
}
```

Beneath this, you will see that the reset has set some defaults for the blockquote and q elements. I find myself rarely using block quotes, and this reset is kind of long, so typically I get delete this section of the reset. But if you find yourself using these elements often, then keep it in there:

```
blockquote, q {
    quotes: none;
}
blockquote:before, blockquote:after,
q:before, q:after {
    content: '';
    content: none;
}
```

Next, we have 2 table properties being reset: border-collapse and border-spacing: which I've never dug into too deeply but ultimately handle some nuanced table inconsistencies that you'll never see in any modern desktop browser.

```
table {
    border-collapse: collapse;
    border-spacing: 0;
}
```

This is pretty much the anatomy of a CSS reset. This reset should be a part of your base layer of CSS that gets you started. We'll now look at how we can add to this and customize it.

Customizing the CSS reset

Let's update the line-height and font-family property on the body element, which will establish what is called "vertical rhythm" and make Arial the default font-family for all the elements:

```
body {
    line-height: 1.4;
    font-family: Arial, Helvetica, sans-serif;
}
```

You will then see how it affects the text, chiefly adding some vertical space between rows lines of text:

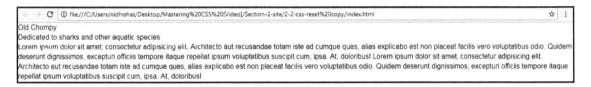

Establishing these defaults early for everything is nice; that way, you don't have to describe `line-height` and `font-family` over and over again for each element throughout your CSS. Note that not all properties act like `font-family` and `line-height` and are inherited by child elements; only certain properties have this effect, mainly text-level properties behave like this. In this case, we set those properties on the `body` element, but they cascaded down to `h1`, `h2`, and our `p`, giving them all the `Arial font` and `line-height` of `1.4`.

I'd like to add in a couple more rules sets to our reset. Let's make some room down at the bottom of the reset. The first one I'd like to add is `clearfix`, as shown in the next piece of code. I'm not going to go into `clearfix` now. I'll explain it in depth in Chapter 3, *Creating a Page Layout with Floats*. This default is very helpful for clearing floats; we're going to need it:

```
/* micro clear fix */
.grouping:before,
.grouping:after {
    content: " ";
    display: table;
}
.grouping:after {
    clear: both;
}
```

The next thing we'll do is set the `max-width` for media elements to ensure responsive media. I'll discuss this more in Chapter 6, *Becoming Responsive*:

```
img, iframe, video, object {
  max-width: 100%;
}
```

Finally, I'd like to un-reset our `strong` and `b` elements and make sure that they *do* have a `font-weight` of `bold`:

```
strong, b {
    font-weight: bold;
}
```

So that's it about the reset. Now, jumping over to our HTML, I want to elaborate on two more pieces of our base layer that aren't in the reset:

```html
<!doctype html>
<html lang="en">
<head>
    <meta charset="UTF-8">
    <meta http-equiv="X-UA-Compatible" content="IE=edge,chrome=1">

<!-- description -->
    <title>Section 2-Ramping Up - Mastering CSS</title>
<!-- stylesheets -->
    <link rel="stylesheet" href="css/style.css">

<!-- stylesheets for older browsers -->
    <!-- ie6/7 micro clearfix -->
    <!--[if lte IE 7]>
        <style>
        .grouping {
            *zoom: 1;
        }
        </style>
    <![endif]-->
    <!--[if IE]>
        <script
src="http://html5shiv.googlecode.com/svn/trunk/html5.js"></script>
    <![endif]-->
</head>
```

First, we have a piece of `clearfix` that handles `IE 7`, as shown in the following code. You don't need to know exactly what this is doing, but you may want to know that it makes `clearfix` work in IE7. If you're not supporting older versions of IE, you can omit that part. Again, we'll look at `clearfix` in detail in `Chapter 3`, *Creating a Page Layout with Floats*:

```html
<!-- stylesheets for older browsers -->
    <!-- ie6/7 micro clearfix -->
    <!--[if lte IE 7]>
        <style>
        .grouping {
            *zoom: 1;
```

```
    }
    </style>
<![endif]-->
<!--[if IE]>
    <script
    src="http://html5shiv.googlecode.com/svn/trunk/
    html5.js"></script>
<![endif]-->
```

If we zoom in to this code, it happens to be an embedded stylesheet. You can see there is an opening and closing `style` tag with a rule set in between:

```
<style>
  .grouping {
    *zoom: 1;
  }
</style>
```

Outside of the embedded stylesheet, the line that precedes the opening `style` tag is what's called an `IE` conditional comment, and it says this: "if lower than or equal to `IE 7`, see the rule below."

```
<!--[if lte IE 7]>
```

Underneath the rule set, we have a `script` pointing to the HTML5 Shiv library, which makes older versions of IE understand the newer HTML5 elements:

```
<!--[if IE]>
    <script
    src="http://html5shiv.googlecode.com/svn/trunk/
    html5.js"></script>
<![endif]-->
```

This is also inside of an IE conditional comment, but it's targeting all versions of IE. Actually, IE 10 and higher don't support IE conditional comments anymore, so this script only supports IE9 and lower versions; however, it makes sure our HTML5 elements are supported in older browsers. Again, if you aren't supporting these older browsers, feel free to omit that as well.

In this section, we dissected our CSS resets and how to get your base layer ready for writing code. Now, let's take a look at the *Chrome DevTools* section.

Chrome DevTools

Most of the CSS we have done so far has been fairly simple. Everything we did worked the first time we tried, and that doesn't always happen. Often, CSS doesn't work and I'm left wondering what I missed. Syntax highlighting in my editor, while helpful, doesn't stop me from overlooking mistakes. Usually, it's a tiny mistake that causes something not to work and it's hard to find the error and fix it. In this section, we'll simply look at how to open up DevTools. Then, we'll modify some CSS in the inspector and finally look at the console to find errors.

How to open developer tools

To open up Chrome's DevTools, all you need to do is right-click or *Ctrl* + click on any part of the page. You'll get a contextual menu, as shown in the following screenshot. When you select the **Inspect Element** option, you get a whole new world of techie goodness:

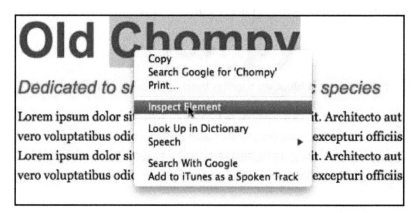

What typically happens is DevTools will occupy the lower half of your screen. As you can see in the following screenshot, on the left-hand side, you have your HTML as rendered by the browser, technically referred to as the DOM. On the right-hand side, you will have all your styles:

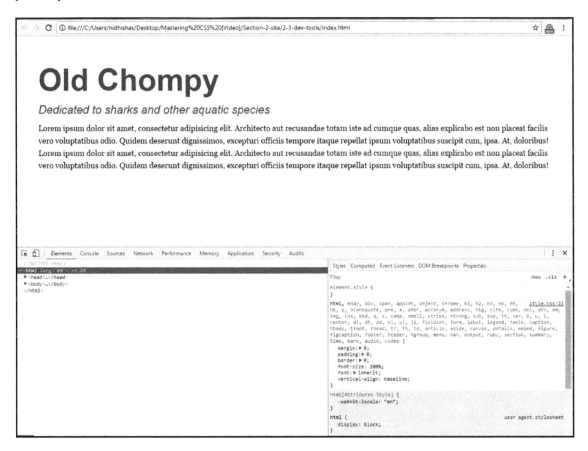

If you hover over something on the left-hand side, it gets highlighted at the top. So, if you hover over h2 or click on it, it gets highlighted, as you can see in the following screenshot:

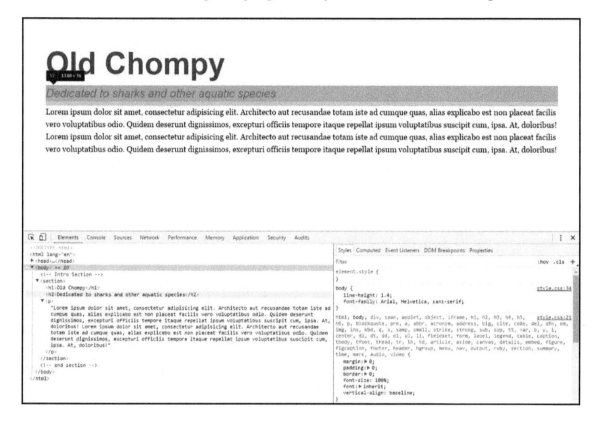

If you hover over `<section>` or click on it, it gets highlighted at the top:

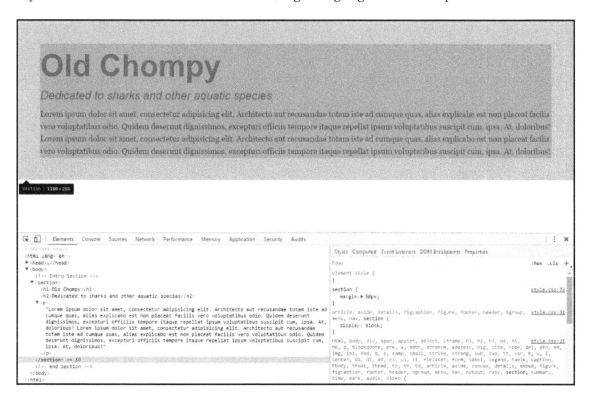

Changing CSS inside the inspector

On the right-hand side of the inspector, you will see all your styles for whatever element you have highlighted in the DOM. You can even click on any of those properties or values and change them. So if you click on 26px, next to font-size, you can increase it to whatever you want. This is updated immediately in the browser, which is very cool:

```
Styles  Computed  Event Listeners  DOM Breakpoints  Properties

Filter                                          :hov  .cls  +

element.style {
}

h2 {                                            style.css:86
    font-size: 26px;
  ✔ font-style: italic;
  ✔ color: ▮#eb2428;
  ✔ margin-bottom: 10px;
}

html, body, div, span, applet, object, iframe, h1, h2, h3,    style.css:21
h4, h5, h6, p, blockquote, pre, a, abbr, acronym, address,
big, cite, code, del, dfn, em, img, ins, kbd, q, s, samp, small, strike,
strong, sub, sup, tt, var, b, u, i, center, dl, dt, dd, ol, ul, li,
fieldset, form, label, legend, table, caption, tbody, tfoot, thead, tr,
th, td, article, aside, canvas, details, embed, figure, figcaption,
footer, header, hgroup, menu, nav, output, ruby, section, summary, time,
mark, audio, video {
    margin: ▶ 0;
    padding: ▶ 0;
    border: ▶ 0;
    font-size: 100%;
    font: ▶ inherit;
```

You can even uncheck certain properties and see that change immediately. So, as you can see in the next screenshot, if you click on the h2 element in the DOM and then uncheck color and margin bottom on the right-hand side, this change to the h2 element takes immediate effect. Simply recheck them to add them back:

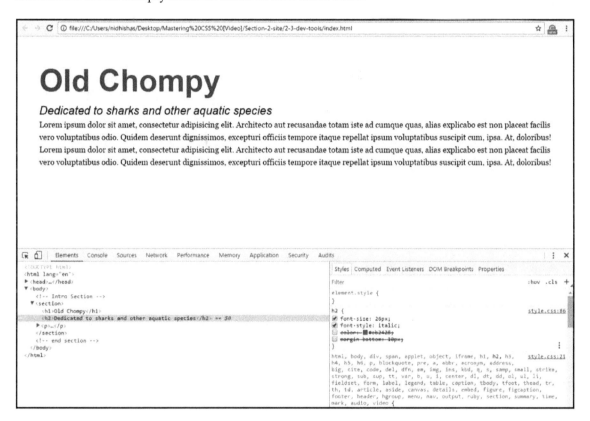

If you click on the last element—in this case, `margin-bottom` and hit *Tab*, it will allow you to type in a new property and value. So add `margin-left` of `-40px` and see what it looks like; this moves this `h2` over `40px` to the left:

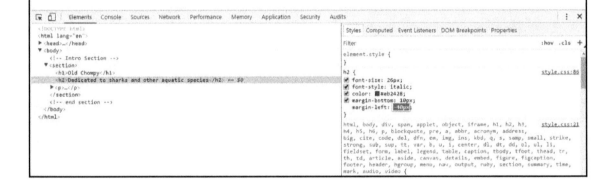

Now these aren't permanent changes. As soon as the browser is refreshed, these styles will disappear; however, you can copy this rule set and paste it into your code if you want to keep these changes we're experimenting with. It even tells us where this rule set is currently located in the style sheet-line 86. If you hover your mouse over that, it will tell you exactly where that file is in your website's folder:

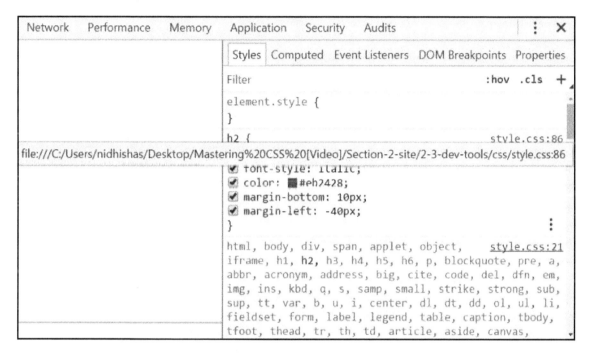

Using the console to find errors

We're just looking at the tip of the iceberg so far when it comes to what you can do with Chrome DevTools. For instance, sometimes adding an image can be tricky. So, let's add the following image tag to the page by typing it into our HTML, above `h2`:

```
<img src="images/sharkey.png" alt="sharky">
```

If we save this and refresh the site, we will see that the image just doesn't show up, so there's something wrong. Refreshing the page, a red error icon with the number one will show up in DevTools. As shown in the following screenshot, there's an error:

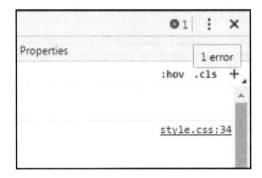

To see what the error is, click on the **Console** tab. You'll see that the sharkey.png file cannot be found:

This is good information. It's telling you it's not a problem related to permissions. It's not a 403; it just can't find the file it's looking for at this location. So one of the things I would do is open up my images folder and make sure that the image is in the folder, and in this case, let's say that it is. There's only one problem, though. The file it's looking for is spelled differently:

It's looking for sharkey, S-H-A-R-K-E-Y, and the file is actually just S-H-A-R-K-Y, so that is easy enough to fix. Now that you know what's wrong, you can just change the name in your HTML:

```
<img src="images/sharky.png" alt="sharky">
```

If you refresh the browser after saving this, this image should show up:

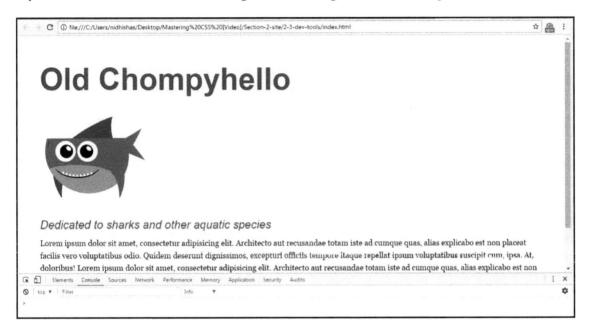

So these two things, the element inspector and the console, can be extremely useful in experimenting with code and troubleshooting code. My biggest suggestion is if things aren't working as you expect them to with your HTML, CSS, and JavaScript, just open up DevTools and take a look under the hood. Chances are that pretty much all day, you'll have DevTools open. I should also add that Firefox, Safari, and IE have DevTools that all do similar tasks and can be just as useful for troubleshooting in those browsers. We've barely scratched the surface of what developer tools can do. Check out my blog post on troubleshooting HTML and CSS with the Chrome DevTools for more information; it is available at `www.richfinelli.com/troubleshooting-html-and-css`.

It explains how to create new selectors and how to access computed values instead of declared values, which is nice when debugging CSS rules and determining which rules take priority. It also walks you through the device emulation mode, among other things:

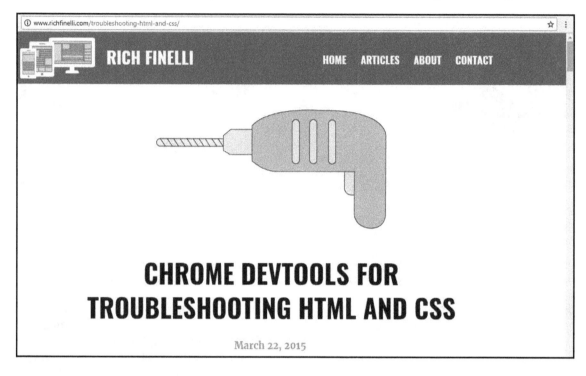

Now you know how to use Chrome DevTools, your ace in the hole for troubleshooting HTML and CSS. Next, you're going to learn how to rename elements, which is where a lot of the power of CSS really takes place.

Renaming elements — classes and IDs

Renaming elements is such a powerful feature of CSS. Let me set this up for you. So far, CSS has been good because we have been able to keep things consistent. All heading 1s are blue with a font size of 20 pixels, for instance, but what if you want your h1 to look different? That's where renaming and classifying elements really becomes useful. In this section, you're going to learn about how to rename and style elements based on classes and IDs. We'll look at how this will pay off on our shark website, first with classes, followed by IDs.

Classes

Look at the `index.html` file. You can see there are several HTML5 `<section>` tags throughout the page: one in the initial section, one in the secondary section, and one in the alternate section, making three all together. One of those is shown below:

```
31  <!-- Intro Section -->
32
33  <section>
34      <h1>Old Chompyhello</h1>
35      <img src="images/sharky.png" alt="sharky">
36      <h2>Dedicated to sharks and other aquatic species</h2>
37      <p>Lorem ipsum dolor sit amet, consectetur adipisicing elit. Architecto aut
        recusandae totam iste ad cumque quas, alias explicabo est non placeat
        facilis vero voluptatibus odio. Quidem deserunt dignissimos, excepturi
        officiis tempore itaque repellat ipsum voluptatibus suscipit cum, ipsa. At,
        doloribus! Lorem ipsum dolor sit amet, consectetur adipisicing elit.
        Architecto aut recusandae totam iste ad cumque quas, alias explicabo est
        non placeat facilis vero voluptatibus odio. Quidem deserunt dignissimos,
        excepturi officiis tempore itaque repellat ipsum voluptatibus suscipit cum,
        ipsa. At, doloribus!</p>
38  </section><!-- end section -->
```

Inside the second `<section>`, there are three `div` tags, each housing an img, h2, p, and an a tag. So there is nothing fancy about this HTML. The last section looks a lot like the first section; it just has h1 and h2 elements and a couple of paragraphs. Here's the dilemma, though: we want h1 at the bottom of the page to be different from the site's main h1 element. The solution is to add a class and a style based on this class. So, down in the alternative section, inside of the h1 element, we're going to add the class attribute. We'll type `class=""` and enter any name or abbreviation we think is fitting:

```
<h1 class="">Feeding Frenzy</h1>
```

I'll tell you right now the hardest job in programming and computer science is naming things. This name should be meaningful enough so that if another person comes across your code and were to pick up from where you left, they won't be completely lost. So, in our case, we'll use `alt-headline`. Classes are case-sensitive, so I recommend you use lowercase and separate words using a dash, which is the common naming convention in CSS. If you use a space, it will be seen as two classes, and that's really not what we want to do:

```
<h1 class="alt-headline">Feeding Frenzy</h1>
```

So we'll save our HTML and hop over to our CSS.

Underneath `h1`, we will add our class name, preceded by a period as our selector. Type `.alt-headline` and add a font size of 40px:

```
h1 {
  font-size: 70px;
  line-height:1.4;
  font-weight: bold;
  color: #0072ae;
}
.alt-headline {
  font-size: 40px;
}
```

Before we save this, we'll make this CSS window smaller so we can see our site adjacent to our code. Scroll down to `h1` on your site and you will see in the preview on the left-hand side that it's currently `70px`:

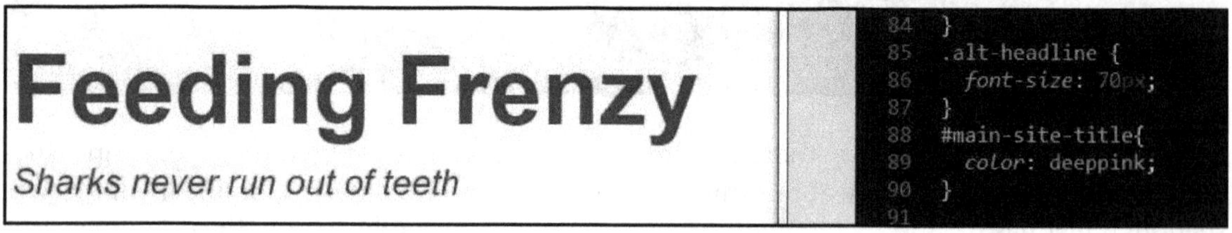

Feeding Frenzy

Sharks never run out of teeth

```
84  }
85  .alt-headline {
86    font-size: 70px;
87  }
88  #main-site-title{
89    color: deeppink;
90  }
91
```

When you save the CSS, `h1` becomes `40px`:

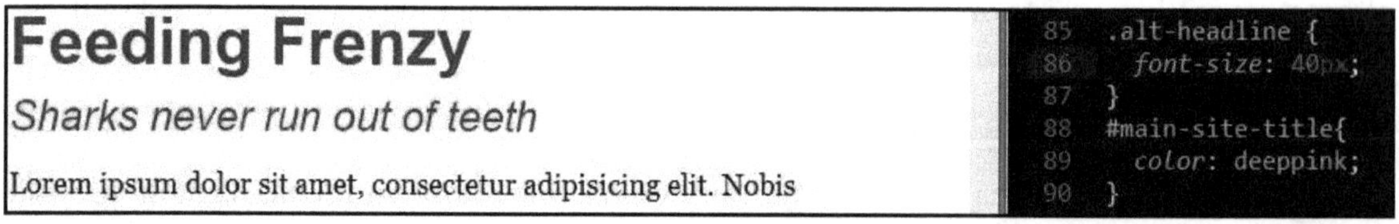

Feeding Frenzy

Sharks never run out of teeth

Lorem ipsum dolor sit amet, consectetur adipisicing elit. Nobis

```
85  .alt-headline {
86    font-size: 40px;
87  }
88  #main-site-title{
89    color: deeppink;
90  }
```

I put this new rule set below the original `h1` rule set, and you might think that because it comes second, it overwrites the one above it. That's actually not what's happening here. Even if I were to switch this rule set to be above `h1`, it would still be `40px`. This is because classes carry more weight than an element when used as a selector:

```
.alt-headline {
  font-size: 40px;
}
h1 {
  font-size: 70px;
  line-height:1.4;
  font-weight: bold;
  color: #0072ae;
}
```

Following is the output of preceding code:

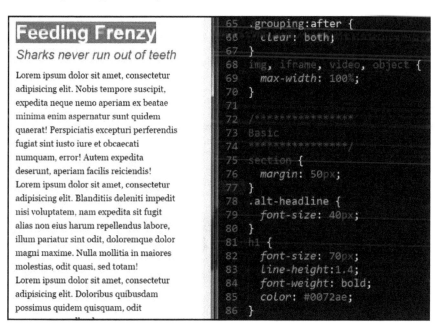

For good measure though, let's keep the `alt headline` rule set below the original `h1` selector.

Classifying multiple elements

Classes are also used for classifying multiple elements. If you want to change the h2 tags in the middle section to all be similar but different to h2 tags elsewhere on the page, using a class will be the perfect option. Let's go into our HTML, add a class to all the div tags in the secondary-section, and call it column-title. Go to the The Octopus, The Crab, and The Whale headings, and use Sublime's nice multiple cursor browser feature to add class="column-title" to each one of them. For example, the The Octopus heading should look like this:

```
<h2 class="column-title">The Octopus</h2>
```

Then, we go to our CSS and add .column-title underneath h2. We'll then add some properties and values. Add font-style as normal; you want to get rid of italic. Our color is blue, #0072ae, and we'll make font-weight bold:

```
.column-title {
  font-style: normal;
  color: #0072ae;
  font-weight: bold;
}
```

Save this, go to the browser, and you'll see that now the h2 tags underneath each image are different to the other h2 tags that you have elsewhere on the site:

The `h2` tags at the bottom and the top of the site are still red and in italic:

Feeding Frenzy
Sharks never run out of teeth

Classes can be very useful for naming and classifying groups of the same element that you want to look the same. Next, let's rename an element using an ID.

IDs

Scroll up to the top of our site, and in our HTML, go to `h1`:

Let's give the first `h1` tag a special ID called `main-site-title`:

```
<h1 id="main-site-title">Old Chompy</h1>
```

With an ID, you can also use whatever name you want inside the quotes as long as it's meaningful. Switch over to the CSS and scroll down to just underneath our `alt-headline` class. This is where we'll add `main-site-title`. The main difference between writing classes and IDs is we start classes with a period and IDs with a number sign or pound sign or a hashtag (whatever you want to call it):

```
#main-site-title
```

In this case, we'll then say the color is different: `deep pink`. Save this and refresh the site to see the effect:

```
#main-site-title{
  color: deeppink;
}
```

Following is the output of preceding code:

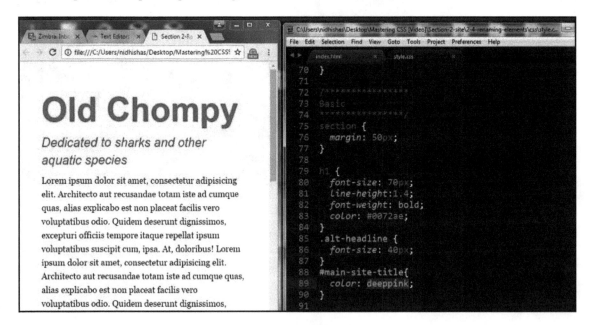

You can see that this changes just the Old Chompy `h1`, the one that has the ID.

Should we use classes or IDs?

Now, you're probably thinking, what's the difference between a class and an ID? Well, the first point to make is an ID has more weight than a class, literally 10 times more weight. Keeping your selectors lightweight is one of the keys to scalable, reusable CSS. What does having more weight really mean? It means it's more specific and an ID will overrule any class. We'll deep dive into specificity rules and weights in Chapter 4, *Creating Buttons with Modular, Reusable CSS Classes, and CSS3*. For now, just know that IDs will overrule classes when targeting the same element. The second point to make is that an ID is unique, and therefore, it can only be used once per page. Given these two points, primarily the first point, as a coding standard, I rarely use IDs for styling because classes are almost always more than sufficient.

Renaming elements with a simple class is so unbelievably powerful and probably the most useful thing in all of CSS. While naming classes, although sometimes tricky, it is important to make names semantic or meaningful. For example, if you're naming your blog post container, it's okay to name it "blog-post-container" because that perfectly describes what it is. IDs, although they have their time and place, aren't as useful as classes. It's best to just use a class in most circumstances to keep your specificity low. In the next section, you'll learn about how we can target elements by their context using descendant selectors.

Descendant selectors

Renaming elements with classes, as you learned in the previous section, is an extremely powerful feature in CSS. However, that's not the only way to target a specific type of element. Descendant selectors will allow you to target elements on a page based on their ancestor elements. This is often necessary because you only want to apply a margin or a new font based on the context of the element. You can use a descendant selector to get that context without putting a class on every element every time you want to target it. I'm going to first explain what parent, sibling, and child elements are as well as what ancestor and descendant elements are. We'll need to be clear about these if we want to use descendant selectors. We'll follow this up by using a practical example of the descendant selector and finishing up by calculating the descendant selector's weight.

Parent, child, and sibling elements

Let's go to our HTML and take a peek at this nicely nested HTML code in the `secondary-section`. So basically, what we have here is a `section` tag and three `div` tags that are inside of that section:

```
<section>
  <div>
    <figure>
      <img src="images/octopus-icon.png" alt="Octopus">
    </figure>
    <h2 class="column-title">The Octopus</h2>
    <p>Lorem ipsum dolor...</p>
    <a href="#" class="button">Tenticals</a>
  </div>
  <div>
    <figure>
      <img src="images/crab-icon.png" alt="Crab">
    </figure>
    <h2 class="column-title">The Crab</h2>
    <p>Lorem ipsum dolor...</p>
    <a href="#" class="button">Crabby</a>
  </div>
  <div>
    <figure>
      <img src="images/whale-icon.png" alt="Whale">
    </figure>
    <h2 class="column-title">The Whale</h2>
    <p>Lorem ipsum dolor...</p>
    <a href="#" class="button">Stuart</a>
  </div>
</section>
```

So <div> is the child element of <section>, while <section> is the parent. In other words, <div> is the descendant of <section>, <section> is the ancestor of <div>. <figure> is also a descendant of <section>, and <img> is a descendant of <section>. Note that <figure>, <h2>, and <p> are on the same level of the HTML so they are siblings, and they are also all descendants of <section>. That's as complicated as it gets; there are no uncles, no aunts, and no third cousins.

Creating descendant selectors

In the previous section, *Renaming elements – classes and IDs*, we added a class to all `<h2>`'s because we knew that `<h2>` tags in the `secondary-section` of our HTML were different than all other `<h2>` tags. So we probably will want to target other elements in this area to be different as well. Here's how we can do that best. Instead of putting the class on the `<h2>` tag, let's put it on the `section` tag and use descendant selectors from there. Let's get rid of `class="column-title"` in all the `<h2>` tags. On the `section` element, let's add a new class, namely `secondary-section`:

```
<section class="secondary-section">
  <div>
    <figure>
      <img src="images/octopus-icon.png" alt="Octopus">
    </figure>
    <h2>The Octopus</h2>
    <p>Lorem ipsum dolor...</p>
    <a href="#" class="button">Tenticals</a>
  </div>
  <div>
    <figure>
      <img src="images/crab-icon.png" alt="Crab">
    </figure>
    <h2>The Crab</h2>
    <p>Lorem ipsum dolor...</p>
    <a href="#" class="button">Crabby</a>
  </div>
  <div>
    <figure>
      <img src="images/whale-icon.png" alt="Whale">
    </figure>
    <h2>The Whale</h2>
    <p>Lorem ipsum dolor...</p>
    <a href="#" class="button">Stuart</a>
  </div>
</section>
```

Save this and you will see the `<h2>` tags lose their blue bold color because in the CSS, we were still targeting the `.column-title` class that no longer exists:

```
44   Secondary Sections
45
46
47   <section class="secondary-section">
48       <div>
49           <figure>
50               <img src="images/octopus-icon.png"
                     alt="Octopus">
51           </figure>
52           <h2>The Octopus</h2>
53           <p>Lorem ipsum dolor sit amet,
             consectetur adipisicing elit. Cumque
             quas amet nulla eveniet ratione,
             facere est assumenda itaque obcaecati
             adipisci. Lorem ipsum dolor sit amet,
             consectetur adipisicing elit. Cumque
             quas amet nulla eveniet ratione,
             facere est assumenda itaque obcaecati
             adipisci. Lorem ipsum dolor sit amet,
             consectetur adipisicing elit. Cumque
             quas amet nulla eveniet ratione,
             facere est assumenda itaque obcaecati
             adipisci. </p>
54           <a href="#" class="button">Tenticals</
             >
55       </div>
```

So now what I'll do is go into the CSS, find the `.column-title` class, update that:

```
.secondary-section h2 {
  font-style: normal;
  color: #eb2428;
  margin-bottom: 10px;
}
```

This is our descendant selector. If we save and refresh, we see that it changes those <h2> tags back to the blue, bold, and non-italic `font-style` that we want:

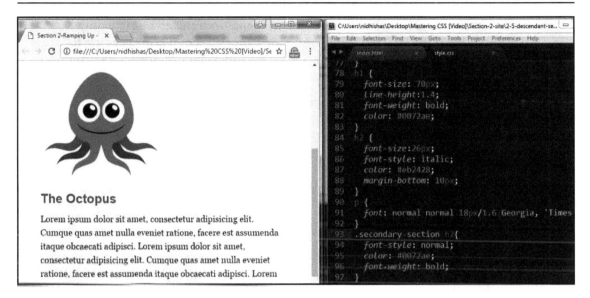

So this `.secondary-section` selector shown in the following CSS is a descendant selector. It's targeting all the h2's that are inside of `secondary-section`:

```
.secondary-section h2 {
  font-style: normal;
  color: #0072ae;
  font-weight: bold;
}
```

If we take a peek back at the HTML, you will see the h2 is indeed inside of `secondary-section`:

```
<section class="secondary-section">
    <div>
        <figure>
            <img src="images/octopus-icon.png" alt="Octopus">
        </figure>
        <h2>The Octopus</h2>
```

Now we can take this a step further. Go into the CSS and underneath our existing `.secondary-section h2` rule set, type `.secondary-section p`. This is going to target our paragraph inside of the `secondary-section`. So add a color of deep pink, save and refresh, and you'll see that now all our paragraphs are pink:

```
.secondary-section p {
  color: deeppink;
}
```

Here's what that looks like:

We can also do this with our `image` tag. If you look back at the HTML, our `image` tag is inside of a `div` tag that's inside of a `figure` tag:

```
<section class="secondary-section">
    <div>
        <figure>
            <img src="images/octopus-icon.png" alt="Octopus">
        </figure>
```

Switching back to our CSS, we can type the selector `.secondary-section div figure img` and then we add a border of `10px`, solid, in this gray color:

```css
.secondary-section div figure img {
  border: 10px solid #333;
}
```

Following is the output of preceding code:

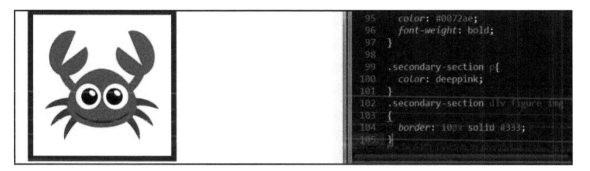

While we can see that works and we have got a gray border round our images on the site, we're being a little more specific than we need to be with our selector. We could just get away with typing `img` without `div` and `figure` and the borders would still be there:

```css
.secondary-section img {
  border: 10px solid #333;
}
```

There's another problem with using a really long selector like this. The following selector carries more weight and could overrule other styles that you may not want it to:

```css
.secondary-section div figure img {
  border: 10px solid #333;
}
```

This is against keeping your code lightweight. Specificity is something I really want to stress; don't overdo it with really long selectors. In fact, as a rule of thumb, try not to go more than three levels deep; there are exceptions to this rule, of course, but try to keep it in mind as you write your CSS. The reason for this is there's an exact science to calculating the weight of your CSS selector, which I'll get into in a later section. I want to at least introduce it now so that we can start getting familiar with it.

Calculating the weight of selectors

A class is worth 10 points, so `.secondary-section` is worth 10 points. A plain old element such as `p` or `div` is worth 1 point. Therefore, the `.secondary-section p` selector is 11 points. The `.secondary-section div figure img` selector is 13 points. Let's create another selector below the one worth 13 points and we have `.secondary-section img`. Then, let's change the `border-color` to `blue`:

```
.secondary-section div figure img {
    border: 10px solid #333;
}
.secondary-section img {
  border: 10px solid blue;
}
```

When we save this, our border is going to remain gray because the point value of our last selector is only 11; it's getting beat out by the previous selector's point value of 13. That's the problem with these long descendant selectors that are longer than they should be, they get weighted heavier:

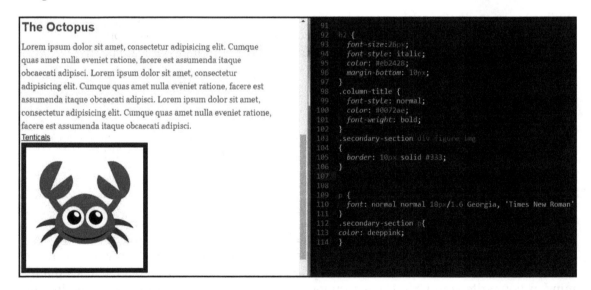

Following is the output of preceding code:

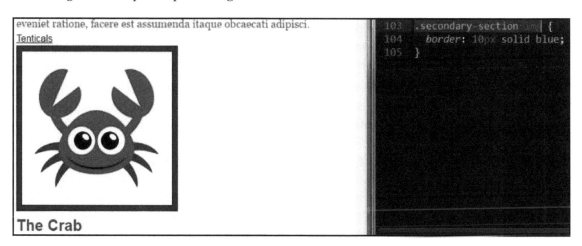

IDs have a point value of 100 points, which is why I advise against using them. They have so much unnecessary weight to them and drive the specificity level through the roof. Assigning point values kind of sounds like keeping score on a video game, but the difference is you want to try and keep your point value as low as possible on this game. If you do that, you will be able to write less complicated CSS.

BEM

One technique for keeping specificity low is avoiding descendant selectors altogether using *BEM*. BEM stands for *Block Element Modifier* and is a naming convention for CSS. The idea is to use a specific naming convention to add a class to every element you are eventually going to style. This way every element has a specificity score of 10, thus every element has the same specificity. There's a lot more to it that just that, and I recommend checking it out at http://getbem.com/ to learn more about it. I tend to use the BEM methodology, but that's not to say descendant selectors need to be completely avoided. I think there's a time and place for them. My suggestion is keep your descendant selectors reasonable and avoid longer descendant selectors with more than 3 levels.

Summary

In this chapter, you learned about the features of a good text editor, discussed CSS resets, explored the troubleshooting power of Chrome's DevTools, and learned how to rename elements with classes. In the final section of this chapter, you learned about descendant selectors.

The next chapter is about creating a multicolumn layer using floats and understanding the solutions to the problems that floats cause.

3
Creating a Page Layout with Floats

In order to create a multicolumn layout supported in all browsers, we are going to use floats. Floats are very simple at first glance but have a few unintuitive quirks to them that can cause some frustration when not completely understood. This may be because the true origination of floats wasn't for layout, it was to achieve the common magazine technique where text flows easily around an image. So in this chapter, we're going to delve into floats. We'll go over the basic usage of floats and follow that up by creating a layout with floats (and curing the headaches caused by floats in later sections)

Float introduction–flowing text around images

Let's start this chapter with an introduction to floats. We'll talk about the original purpose of floats, followed by the basic problem that they cause and how to clear elements that come after floats. In this section, we'll also start work on a new HTML page about shark movies that you can find in the book download package.

The Shark movies page

Here we have a new HTML page about shark movies. If you look at this page, you'll see an image on top of a title, on top of some text, and on top of a link; as you scroll down, you'll see that there are three sections like that for each of the three movies:

The HTML is fairly straightforward. There are three sections, each with a `div` tag with a class of `wrapper`, which is centering the content. Inside the `wrapper` class, there's an anchor tag with an image inside it. Underneath the anchor tag is an `h1` tag containing the title and some paragraph text. This is followed by an anchor tag, which is a link to learn more. Here's a screenshot of the first section:

```
50  <section id="jaws" class="content-block style-1 wave-border">
51      <div class="wrapper">
52          <a href="#" class="figure">
53              <img src="images/jaws.jpg" alt="Jaws movie">
54          </a>
55          <h1>Jaws</h1>
56          <p>Lorem ipsum dolor sit amet, consectetur adipisicing elit. Culpa totam magni repudiandae
             quibusdam corrupti delectus dignissimos officia error fuga recusandae, tempora vel qui minus
             nulla cumque molestiae hic dolores officiis optio deserunt reiciendis id suscipit temporibus,
             iure? Voluptate optio doloremque odit cum blanditiis cumque itaque ipsum doloribus, dolore
             repudiandae numquam perspiciatis omnis maxime ratione molestias quod porro eaque, suscipit
             nemo assumenda! Reprehenderit expedita ea, ipsam recusandae inventore doloribus esse
             accusamus aliquid, saepe blanditiis ipsum dignissimos iste id pariatur ut praesentium dicta
             earum ad cupiditate aliquam. Non, modi, sequi. Incidunt, vel! Reprehenderit expedita ea,
             ipsam recusandae inventore doloribus esse accusamus aliquid, saepe blanditiis ipsum
             dignissimos iste id pariatur ut praesentium dicta earum ad cupiditate aliquam. Non, modi,
             sequi. Incidunt, vel!</p>
57          <a href="">Learn More</a>
58      </div><!-- end of wrapper -->
59  </section>
```

The original purpose of floats

Let's look at the final project, shown in the following figure. We want to float the image to the left and have the headline and text flow around it:

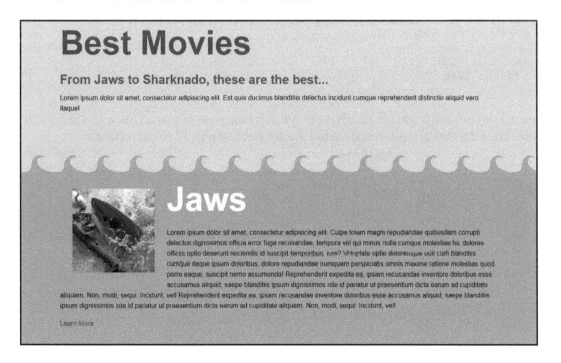

Let's target that image in CSS. Instead of targeting the image in our selector, let's actually target the image's container, which is this anchor tag with a class of `figure`:

```
<a href="#" class="figure">
```

I don't want to just target the `.figure` class as my selector because I may use this class on other image containers and may not want them all to be floated. So, let's use a descendant selector based on its parent. Its parent is up at the top of the section, the `section` tag, which has multiple classes: `content-block`, `style-1`, and `wave-border`:

```
<section id="jaws" class="content-block style-1 wave-border">
```

This is a modular approach that we'll get into more in the next section. The main class we're looking for is `content-block`. The `style-1` and `style-2` classes are only controlling the two different color schemes and `wave-border` adds the repeating background image of the wave to the top of the first section. Finally, in our CSS, our selector is going to be `.content-block .figure`, so we are targeting any element that has a class of `figure` inside an element with a class of `content-block`:

```
.content-block .figure {
    margin: 30px;
}
```

So what we'll type in this rule set, under the `margin` property, is `float: left`:

```
.content-block .figure {
    margin: 30px;
    float: left
}
```

When we refresh the page, we see that everything has gone to plan. This was almost too simple. We achieved almost exactly what we set out to do in all three sections:

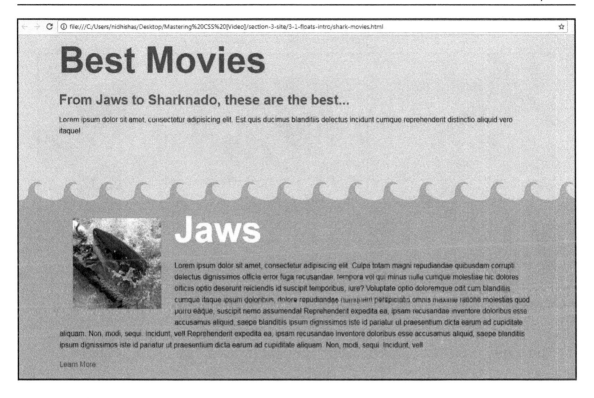

Let's add a background color to `h1` and `p` in our CSS, just to see what's going on here. We'll just give `h1` a background color of `deeppink` and a background color of `green` via `content-block`:

```
.content-block h1 {
  color: #fff;
  background-color: deeppink;
}
.content-block p {
  font-family: Georgia, 'Times New Roman' sans-serif;
  background-color: green;
}
```

Following is the output of preceding code block:

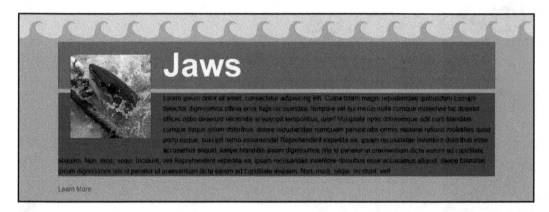

Notice how the backgrounds go behind the image. The text is flowing to the right, but the elements themselves are no longer seeing the floated element, the image, as part of the normal flow. Floated elements themselves change when their display properties are affected. For instance, the anchor tag that was floated, or really the anchor with a class of `figure`, starts acting like a block-level element. It will now respond to width and margin top and bottom; as we've seen, it already responded to the margin bottom. However, it won't necessarily force a new line. Let's float it to the right, and it should have a very similar effect:

```
.content-block .figure {
  margin: 30px;
  float: right;
}
```

Following is the output of preceding code block:

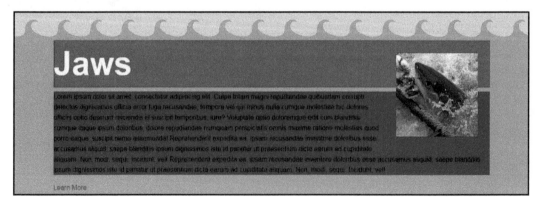

Using the clear property to solve basic problems with floats

We can use the `clear` property to stop elements underneath the floated element from misbehaving. For instance, let's add the `clear` property to the paragraph. We'll add `clear: both`, which clears both left and right floated elements:

```
.content-block p {
  font-family: Georgia, 'Times New Roman' sans-serif;
  background-color: green;
  clear: both;
}
```

Now, when you refresh, you will see the paragraph text seated below the floated element:

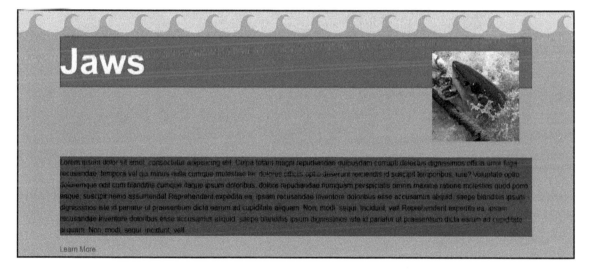

We can do the same thing for `h1` and that will sit below:

```
.content-block .figure {
  margin: 30px;
  float: right;
}
.content-block h1 {
  color: #fff;
  background-color: deeppink;
  clear: right;
}
```

We can also just say `clear: right` because the float in the rule set above it is floated to the right.

After saving the CSS and viewing the site, and you will see it works. The `h1` tag also sits below `.figure`:

However, if you type in `clear: left` to your `h1` rule set, it won't necessarily work because there are no left floated elements here:

```
.content-block h1 {
  color: #fff;
  background-color: deeppink;
  clear: left;
}
```

Following is the output of preceding code block:

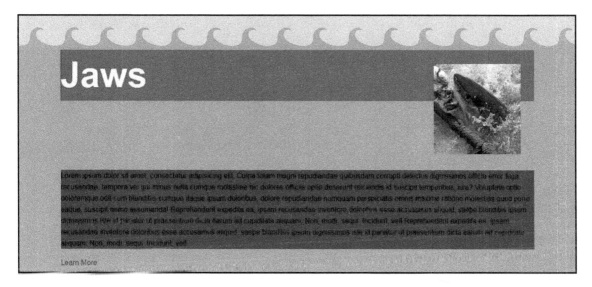

Here, None is the default value of both `float` and `clear`. So, we can say `clear: none` on both of these, and it will go back to how it was before we added the `clear` property:

```
.content-block h1 {
  color: #fff;
  background-color: deeppink;
  clear: none;
}
.content-block p {
  font-family: Georgia, 'Times New Roman' sans-serif;
  background-color: green;
  clear: none;
}
```

Following is the output of preceding code block:

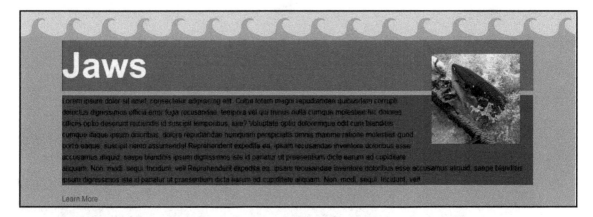

However, since `clear: none` is the default value, you can just take that whole property away from both of those selectors; this will have the same effect on the site. I hardly ever use clear left and clear right; the `both` value seems to be more than adequate most of the time.

In this section, we've seen the traditional use of floating elements and how elements underneath the float flow around the floated element. This can be stopped using the `clear` property. This technique is useful, but honestly, floats are even more useful for building multicolumn layouts. Let's take a look at that now.

Creating a multicolumn layout

Floats were designed to flow text around an image. However, floats are also the most common way of building a multicolumn layout. In this section, we'll look at how to float elements next to each other in order to create a page layout.

So, what we currently have in the HTML in the secondary section are three `div` tags with a class of `column`:

```
40  <!--
41  ========================
42  Secondary Sections
43  ========================
44  -->
45  <section class="secondary-section">
46      <div>
47          <figure>
48              <img src="images/octopus-icon.png" alt="Octopus">
49          </figure>
50          <h2>The Octopus</h2>
51          <p>Lorem ipsum dolor sit amet, consectetur adipisicing elit. Cumque quas amet nulla eveniet ratione, facere est
            assumenda itaque obcaecati adipisci. Lorem ipsum dolor sit amet, consectetur adipisicing elit. Cumque quas amet nulla
            eveniet ratione, facere est assumenda itaque obcaecati adipisci. Lorem ipsum dolor sit amet, consectetur adipisicing
            elit. Cumque quas amet nulla eveniet ratione, facere est assumenda itaque obcaecati adipisci. </p>
52          <a href="#" class="button">Tenticals &raquo;</a>
53      </div>
54      <div>
55          <figure><img src="images/crab-icon.png" alt="Crab"></figure>
56          <h2>The Crab</h2>
57          <p>Lorem ipsum dolor sit amet, consectetur adipisicing elit. Provident quasi aliquam, sapiente quisquam sed, numquam
            illo autem voluptas ut eos. Lorem ipsum dolor sit amet, consectetur adipisicing elit. Cumque quas amet nulla eveniet
            ratione, facere est assumenda itaque obcaecati adipisci. Lorem ipsum dolor sit amet, consectetur adipisicing elit.
            Cumque quas amet nulla eveniet ratione, facere est assumenda itaque obcaecati adipisci.</p>
58          <a href="#" class="button">Crabby &raquo;</a>
59      </div>
60      <div>
61          <figure><img src="images/whale-icon.png" alt="Whale"></figure>
62          <h2>The Whale</h2>
63          <p>Lorem ipsum dolor sit amet, consectetur adipisicing elit. Cumque quas amet nulla eveniet ratione, facere est
            assumenda itaque obcaecati adipisci. Lorem ipsum dolor sit amet, consectetur adipisicing elit. Cumque quas amet nulla
            eveniet ratione, facere est assumenda itaque obcaecati adipisci. Lorem ipsum dolor sit amet, consectetur adipisicing
            elit. Cumque quas amet nulla eveniet ratione, facere est assumenda itaque obcaecati adipisci. </p>
64          <a href="#" class="button">Stuart &raquo;</a>
65      </div>
66  </section>
```

The following screenshot illustrates the final site. This is what we're aiming for. We want three equal columns with a small gutter or margin in between:

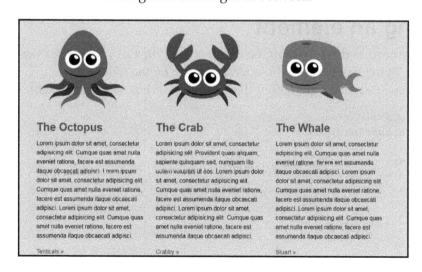

In our current site, columns are stacked on top of one another. Right now, we have simple rows, so we want to fix that using floats. In our final site, we want to have everything centered in the middle of the page, but right now, all of our content goes from one edge of the browser window to pretty much the opposite edge of the browser window:

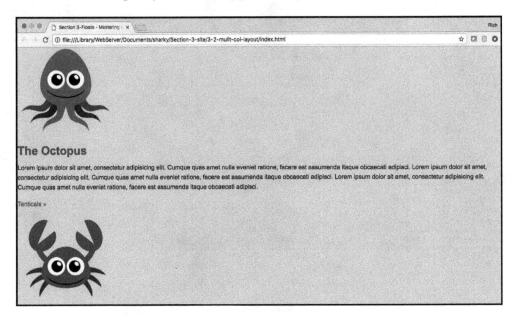

Let's fix this by centering our div tags.

Centering an element

What we really need to do is to wrap the entire content in a div tag; so let's do that. Go into the HTML file. In the line beneath the opening section tag, add <div class="wrapper"> . And right before the closing section tag, close it with </div>:

```
<section class="secondary-section">
    <div class="wrapper">
        <div>...</div>
        <div>...</div>
        <div>...</div>
    </div>
</section>
```

Now, switch over to the CSS file. The `.wrapper` tag is going to be a more reusable class. To center any element, we'll give it a margin, and we'll use the two-value syntax: top and bottom are going to be zero, and left and right are going to be auto. We also have to give it a width of `960px`. Without a width, you really can't center it using this margin technique:

```css
.wrapper {
  margin: 0 auto;
  width: 960px;
}
```

There, we have it; all of the content should now be centered inside this wrapper:

The Whale

Lorem ipsum dolor sit amet, consectetur adipisicing elit. Cumque quas amet nulla eveniet ratione, facere est assumenda itaque obcaecati adipisci. Lorem ipsum dolor sit amet, consectetur adipisicing elit. Cumque quas amet nulla eveniet ratione, facere est assumenda itaque obcaecati adipisci. Lorem ipsum dolor sit amet, consectetur adipisicing elit. Cumque quas amet nulla eveniet ratione, facere est assumenda itaque obcaecati adipisci.

Stuart »

The `wrapper` class, like I said, is nice and reusable. I will use the `wrapper` class anywhere on the site where I want to center a collection of elements.

Floating columns

So, back to the order of our business here: floating the three columns on our home page. To do this, I want to give each `div` tag a class of `column` that we can style. So, in the HTML, let's go to each `div` tag in the secondary section and use the nice multiple cursor feature of Sublime Text to add `class="column"` to all three of them at once:

```html
<section class="secondary-section">
    <div class="wrapper">
        <div class="column">...</div>
        <div class="column">...</div>
        <div class="column">...</div>
    </div>
</section>
```

In my CSS I have made a big comment denoting this section of my CSS for these three columns, I encourage you to as well.

Under this comment, we'll target `.column` and apply `float: left`. The width will be `320px`.

```css
/****************
3 columns
****************/
.column {
  float: left;
  width: 320px;
}
```

Ideally, whenever you float elements, try to add a width. If all three columns are `320px`, that's going to add up to exactly 960 pixels and fit the width of that wrapper perfectly. If we were to use a number that added up to more than 960 pixels, then not all of the three `div` tags would fit in that space. One would wrap to the bottom so they wouldn't have all the three `div` tags on one row. It's important that the width of all the floated `div` tags is never more than the parent `div` tag. So save this and refresh the site:

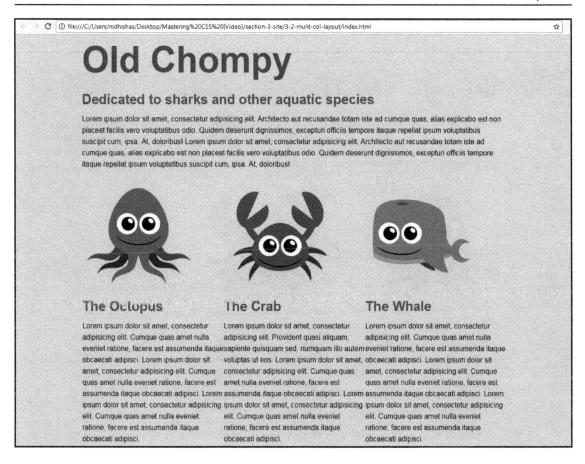

It looks like all the three columns are floated next to each other. That worked out pretty well, except we don't have any margin between columns. So let's go back to our code and let's give it a `margin-left` property of `30px`. Save this and refresh the browser:

```
.column {
  float: left;
  width: 320px;
  margin-left: 30px;
}
```

Following is the output of preceding code block:

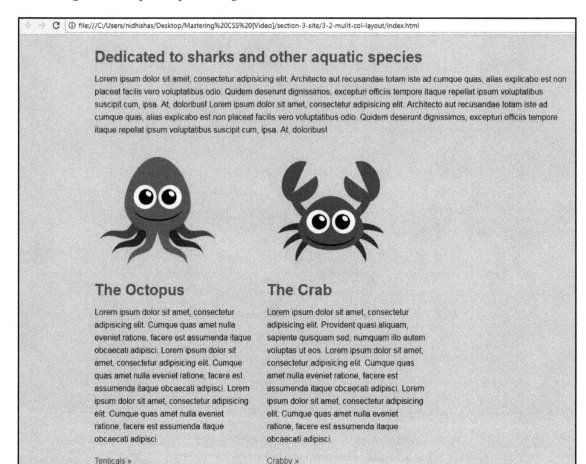

We get a margin of `30px`, but we also get our third column drifted down to the bottom because it can't fit in the width allowed.

Let's fix this by reducing the width of the columns to `300px` each:

```
.column {
  float: left;
  width: 300px;
  margin-left: 30px;
}
```

Now if you look at the browser, you will also see that we don't need a `margin-left` on the first column. We don't need a left margin next to empty space:

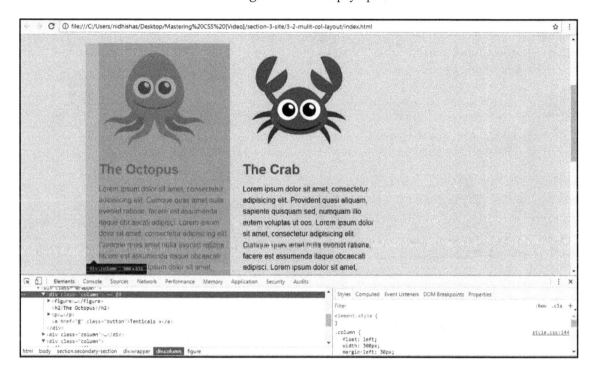

Let's get rid of this margin left on the first column. We can do this by targeting that individual `.column` property using a pseudo class called `first child`.

Targeting .column using a pseudo class

Adding the `.column:first-child` selector will target the first appearance of the column element. We'll add `margin-left` as zero. When we save this, we get three equal columns with a `margin-left` for each of them, except the first:

```
.column:first-child {
  margin-left: 0;
}
```

Following is the output of preceding code block:

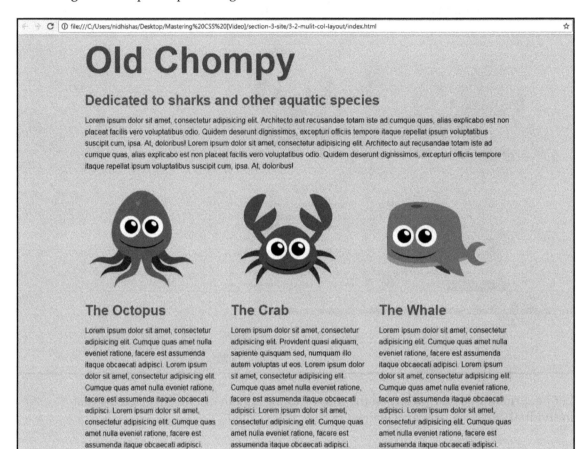

This technique would work just as well with two columns, four columns, or any number of columns.

Collapsed containers

So, everything is great with the columns, except that if you try and scroll the page down, you will see that we are really tight to the bottom.

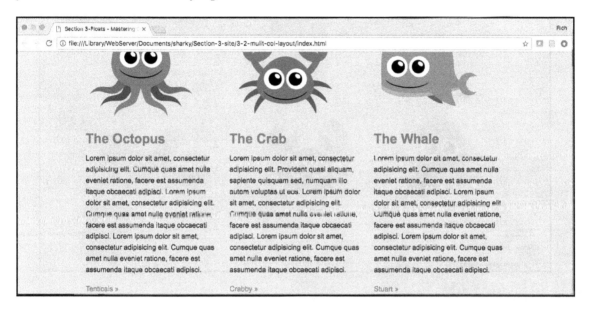

Let's see what happens when we add a `margin-bottom` property to the container that wraps around everything: `secondary-section`. Let's say `margin-bottom: 40px`:

```
/****************
3 columns
****************/
.secondary-section {
  margin-bottom: 40px;
}
```

If we save this, it really does nothing in the browser. The content is still sitting right at the bottom. Let me further illustrate this problem. If I had a background color of green, then you'd expect the entire background to be green:

```
.secondary-section {
  margin-bottom: 40px;
  background-color: green;
}
```

However, if we add the preceding code and save it, the background doesn't become green. So, let's actually inspect this element. Let's inspect secondary-section in the browser using Chrome's DevTools. We will see both margin-bottom and background-color are in the process of getting applied. But we don't see anything in green on the page:

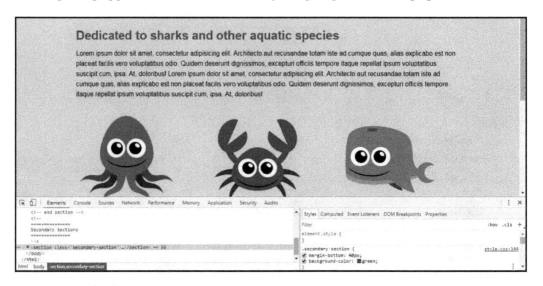

When you put your mouse over the `secondary-section` element, you will see it highlights the space that it occupies in that peachy color on the screen (you'll see it as a different shade of gray in the following screenshot if you're looking at a printed copy):

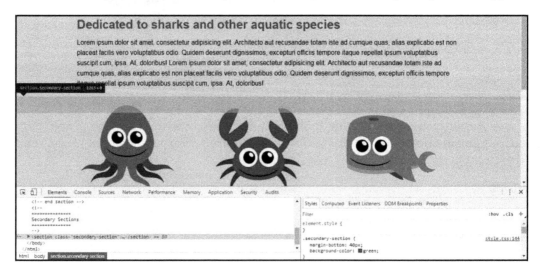

The container has actually collapsed. This is what happens when all the elements inside a parent element are floated: the container collapses, floats are taken outside the normal flow, and the container has no height because of this.

Let's take a look and see what we can do to fix this.

Solving the problems of floats

Okay, so let's look at our problem. You've learned how to change stacked rows into horizontal columns in order to achieve a multicolumn layout, but our containing element around our floated elements has totally collapsed and lost its height because all the elements inside it are floated. As a collapsed element, it doesn't look like it's responding to the `margin-bottom` property or the `background-color` we've assigned to it. So, in this section, we'll look at four separate methods to fix this collapse, and we'll try to understand the best way to deal with it. First, we'll use the `clear` method, followed by the `overflow: hidden` method, followed by the `float` method, and then finally the most preferred method: the `clearfix` hack.

Using the clear method

Let's solve this using the `clear` property. What we'll do at the end of `secondary-section` is add a class of `clear` to a new `div`, using the following code:

```
<div class="clear"></div>
```

Next, we'll go into our CSS, and in the area reserved for global styles, underneath the ruleset targeting the `wrapper` class; this is where we'll create the `clear` selector and add `clear: both`:

```
/***************
Global
***************/
::-moz-selection {
  background-color: #eb2428;
}
::selection {
  background-color: #eb2428;
}
.wrapper {
  margin: 0 auto;
  width: 960px;
}
```

```
.clear {
  clear: both;
}
```

So, if we save this and return to the browser, our background color will be green with a bottom margin of 50px. Everything is working very well:

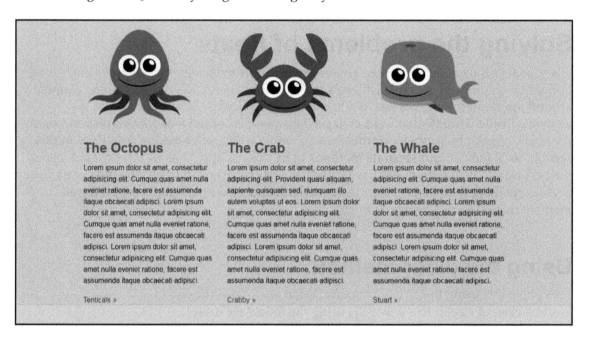

However, we've added extra non-semantic markup to our page. We *may* even get an SEO deduction for this. Let's explore other ways to do this without adding the extra markup. Get rid of that extra markup we just added to our HTML:

```
<div class="clear"></div> <!-- delete this -->
```

Our collapse will return. Now we won't be able to see the green background anymore; that's how we know the collapse is there:

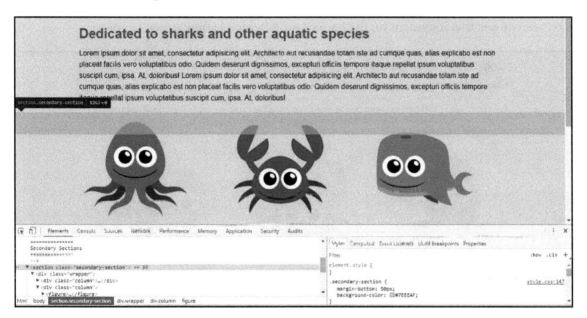

Using overflow property with hidden value

The next method we'll look at is `overflow: hidden`. Go to your CSS and find the `.secondary-section` class. What we can do is add the `overflow` property with the value of `hidden`:

```
.secondary-section {
  margin-bottom: 50px;
  background-color: #7EEEAF;
  overflow: hidden;
}
```

`overflow: hidden` is a true hack. It was never meant for remedying collapsed containers; it was meant for hiding any content image or text that overflowed its container. However, magically, `overflow: hidden` also clears the collapse. If we save our CSS and go to our site, we will see this is evident by the background, which is now green in color:

Dedicated to sharks and other aquatic species

Lorem ipsum dolor sit amet, consectetur adipisicing elit. Architecto aut recusandae totam iste ad cumque quas, alias explicabo est non placeat facilis vero voluptatibus odio. Quidem deserunt dignissimos, excepturi officiis tempore itaque repellat ipsum voluptatibus suscipit cum, ipsa. At, doloribus! Lorem ipsum dolor sit amet, consectetur adipisicing elit. Architecto aut recusandae totam iste ad cumque quas, alias explicabo est non placeat facilis vero voluptatibus odio. Quidem deserunt dignissimos, excepturi officiis tempore itaque repellat ipsum voluptatibus suscipit cum, ipsa. At, doloribus!

The Octopus

Lorem ipsum dolor sit amet, consectetur adipisicing elit. Cumque quas amet nulla eveniet ratione, facere est assumenda itaque obcaecati adipisci. Lorem ipsum dolor sit amet, consectetur adipisicing elit. Cumque quas amet nulla eveniet ratione, facere est assumenda itaque obcaecati adipisci. Lorem ipsum dolor sit amet, consectetur adipisicing elit. Cumque quas amet nulla eveniet ratione, facere est assumenda itaque obcaecati adipisci.

Tenticals »

The Crab

Lorem ipsum dolor sit amet, consectetur adipisicing elit. Provident quasi aliquam, sapiente quisquam sed, numquam illo autem voluptas ut eos. Lorem ipsum dolor sit amet, consectetur adipisicing elit. Cumque quas amet nulla eveniet ratione, facere est assumenda itaque obcaecati adipisci. Lorem ipsum dolor sit amet, consectetur adipisicing elit. Cumque quas amet nulla eveniet ratione, facere est assumenda itaque obcaecati adipisci.

Crabby »

The Whale

Lorem ipsum dolor sit amet, consectetur adipisicing elit. Cumque quas amet nulla eveniet ratione, facere est assumenda itaque obcaecati adipisci. Lorem ipsum dolor sit amet, consectetur adipisicing elit. Cumque quas amet nulla eveniet ratione, facere est assumenda itaque obcaecati adipisci. Lorem ipsum dolor sit amet, consectetur adipisicing elit. Cumque quas amet nulla eveniet ratione, facere est assumenda itaque obcaecati adipisci.

Stuart »

A small problem with `overflow: hidden` is that you may want the content to overflow the container, for instance, a drop-down menu or tooltip. The `overflow: hidden` hack will hide that overflow—no surprises there! It's a solution, but it may not always be ideal. For instance, in our exact scenario, we may want this octopus to kind of creep out of its container. Let's go into Chrome DevTools and give it `margin-top: -50px`. As you can see, now the top of the image is no longer showing and the overflow is hidden:

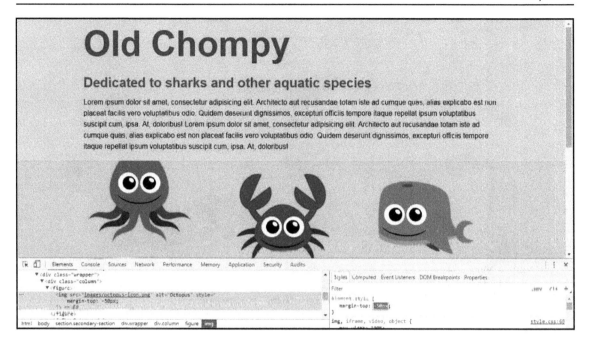

So that's not a good fix for us. Let's delete that `overflow: hidden` declaration from our CSS file and look at the next method: the `float` method.

The float method

We can prevent elements from collapsing by floating the container to the left or to the right. Let's do this; let's add `float: left` or `float: right` to our `secondary-section`. Either will work:

```
.secondary-section {
  margin-bottom: 50px;
  background-color: #7EEEAF;
  float: left;
}
```

Once we save this, we will see that we have the green background, so the collapse is no longer taking place, but the obvious problem is we've floated to the left. We wanted this div to be centered:

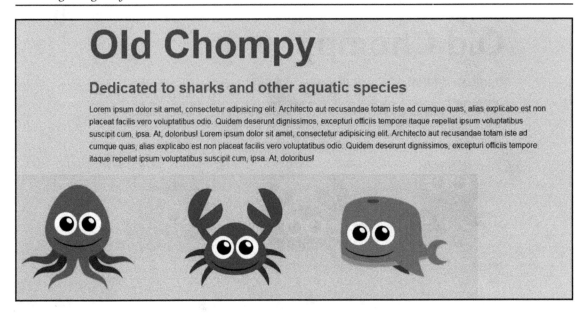

This method has an obvious drawback. There are some circumstances and some situations where it would be a perfect solution, but in this one, there's an obvious problem: we are no longer centered. Remove `float: left` from your CSS and explore my favorite, and I think the best, solution: the **clearfix hack**.

Clearfix hack

If we look at the following CSS, right below our reset, these rulesets make up our **clearfix**:

```
/* clearfix */
.grouping:before,
.grouping:after {
  content: " ";
  display: table;
}
.grouping:after {
  clear: both;
}
```

This code was actually part of our base layer of CSS. Basically, what this does is create a pseudo element before and after any element with a class of `grouping`. This pseudo element has a blank space for content and the display is set to table. Then we have the `after` pseudo element beneath that chunk of code, which has the `clear` property set on it and clears any floats before it.

You might sometimes see `clearfix` as the class name instead of `grouping`. I tend to use `grouping` because I think it makes more sense; you're kind of grouping elements, and that's a little bit more semantic. It doesn't really matter though; `clearfix` and `grouping` both do the same thing.

All right, that's already in the CSS, so there's nothing more we need to do except go to `secondary-section` in the HTML and just add this `grouping` class to it. So we're adding a second class to it:

```
<section class="secondary-section grouping">
```

When we save and refresh, we have our container; the collapse is fixed. In the next screenshot, we see the background color and the bottom margin. We're in pretty good shape here:

The Octopus

Lorem ipsum dolor sit amet, consectetur adipisicing elit. Cumque quas amet nulla eveniet ratione, facere est assumenda itaque obcaecati adipisci. Lorem ipsum dolor sit amet, consectetur adipisicing elit. Cumque quas amet nulla eveniet ratione, facere est assumenda itaque obcaecati adipisci. Lorem ipsum dolor sit amet, consectetur adipisicing elit. Cumque quas amet nulla eveniet ratione, facere est assumenda itaque obcaecati adipisci.

Tenticals »

The Crab

Lorem ipsum dolor sit amet, consectetur adipisicing elit. Provident quasi aliquam, sapiente quisquam sed, numquam illo autem voluptas ut eos. Lorem ipsum dolor sit amet, consectetur adipisicing elit. Cumque quas amet nulla eveniet ratione, facere est assumenda itaque obcaecati adipisci. Lorem ipsum dolor sit amet, consectetur adipisicing elit. Cumque quas amet nulla eveniet ratione, facere est assumenda itaque obcaecati adipisci.

Crabby »

The Whale

Lorem ipsum dolor sit amet, consectetur adipisicing elit. Cumque quas amet nulla eveniet ratione, facere est assumenda itaque obcaecati adipisci. Lorem ipsum dolor sit amet, consectetur adipisicing elit. Cumque quas amet nulla eveniet ratione, facere est assumenda itaque obcaecati adipisci. Lorem ipsum dolor sit amet, consectetur adipisicing elit. Cumque quas amet nulla eveniet ratione, facere est assumenda itaque obcaecati adipisci.

Stuart »

The clearfix will work in IE8 but not IE7 unless you add an IE-specific style sheet. This actually goes in the index. So up in the head of `index.html`, I have this style sheet, shown in the next screenshot, specifically for IE7. What it does is give grouping a zoom of `1`. This triggers something called `hasLayout` in older versions of IE, which clears the collapse:

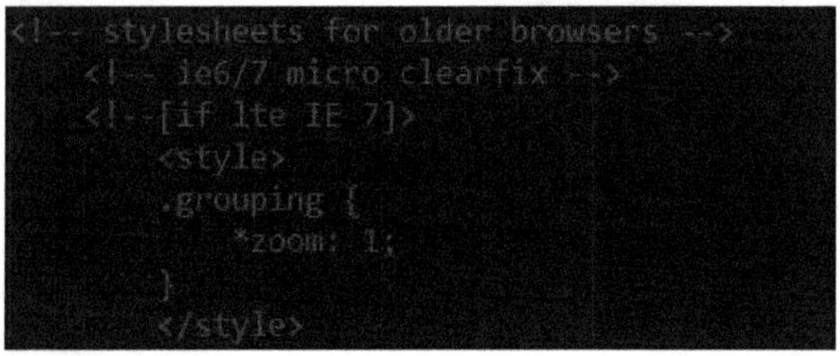

```
<!-- stylesheets for older browsers -->
    <!-- ie6/7 micro clearfix -->
<!--[if lte IE 7]>
    <style>
    .grouping {
        *zoom: 1;
    }
    </style>
```

Don't worry if that doesn't make too much sense to you; it doesn't necessarily have to. However, just know that this allows the clearfix hack to work in older versions of IE. So, all in all, this is very deep browser support, and it's so very easy to use that it's many frontend developers' preferred way of clearing collapsed floats. It's certainly my favorite way of going about it.

In this section, you learned about fixing the collapse of parent elements caused by floats using:

1. An empty clear div.
2. The `overflow: hidden`.
3. By floating the parent element. All three of these worked but had minor to major flaws.
4. The clearfix hack with very deep support, ease of use, and semantic style tends to win as the best method. I use it on every project. It can easily solve one of the biggest problems with floats: collapse. Another thing I like about the clearfix hack is that it is a very modular approach to CSS. Just add the `clearfix` class anywhere to your markup and you've gotten rid of collapsed containers.

Summary

In this chapter, we went over the traditional use of floating elements: flowing text around images. We then looked at using floats to build a multi-column layout. Finally, we learned how to tackle the problems that come with using floats. We found that the clearfix hack is the best method for fixing collapsed floats. In the next chapter, we're going to expand on modular CSS as we create modern buttons using a modular approach.

4

Creating Buttons with Modular, Reusable CSS Classes, and CSS3

Having CSS that is modular and reusable makes it organized and concise, thereby avoiding situations where you may feel like pulling your hair out. Wouldn't it be awesome to just add the class of `.button` to an anchor element, no matter where that anchor element is in your markup, and have it transform into a button? CSS is "reusable" if you're able to use its classes anywhere and don't need these classes to be qualified by parent elements as long descendant selectors. The term "modular" refers to the ability to add variations to the button by adding another class to it so that one element can have two classes that could come together to form something very different.

A good example of how to write modular and reusable CSS is this: creating buttons. However, this concept should be applied everywhere, across all components of your website. We have a lot to go over in this chapter. We will cover modular CSS and multiple classes in the first two sections, before we switch gears and talk about how selectors can overrule each other in the specificity rules section. We'll then get into CSS3 pretty heavily with transitions, transforms, and gradients, and we'll go through every step of creating and styling a big call-to-action button.

Creating buttons with modular CSS

In this section, we'll create buttons with modular CSS classes. We'll find out what exactly modular CSS is and why it's useful. First, let's look at the final site we're going to create and explore the different button types we'll use.

Different button types

At the very top, we have our enormous **Go Premium** call-to-action button:

Scrolling down a bit on the home page and we'll find these "ghost" buttons with a nice hover state:

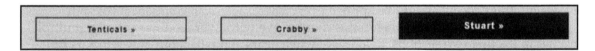

On the movies page, we have that same standard button. It just has a different color and is positioned a little differently. This appears in all three movie sections:

Jaws

Lorem ipsum dolor sit amet, consectetur adipisicing elit. Culpa totam magni repudiandae quibusdam corrupti delectus dignissimos officia error fuga recusandae, tempora vel qui minus nulla cumque molestiae hic dolores officiis optio deserunt reiciendis id suscipit temporibus, iure? Voluptate optio doloremque odit cum blanditiis cumque itaque ipsum doloribus, dolore repudiandae numquam perspiciatis omnis maxime ratione molestias quod porro eaque, suscipit nemo assumenda! Reprehenderit expedita ea, ipsam recusandae inventore doloribus esse accusamus aliquid, saepe blanditiis ipsum dignissimos iste id pariatur ut praesentium dicta earum ad cupiditate aliquam. Non, modi, sequi. Incidunt, vel! Reprehenderit expedita ea, ipsam recusandae inventore doloribus esse accusamus aliquid, saepe blanditiis ipsum dignissimos iste id pariatur ut praesentium dicta earum ad cupiditate aliquam. Non, modi, sequi. Incidunt, vel!

Learn More

So, in this section, we're going to build these standard buttons at the bottom of each of all three columns:

The Octopus

Lorem ipsum dolor sit amet, consectetur adipisicing elit. Cumque quas amet nulla eveniet ratione, facere est assumenda itaque obcaecati adipisci. Lorem ipsum dolor sit amet, consectetur adipisicing elit. Cumque quas amet nulla eveniet ratione, facere est assumenda itaque obcaecati adipisci. Lorem ipsum dolor sit amet, consectetur adipisicing elit. Cumque quas amet nulla eveniet ratione, facere est assumenda itaque obcaecati adipisci.

Tenticals »

The Crab

Lorem ipsum dolor sit amet, consectetur adipisicing elit. Provident quasi aliquam, sapiente quisquam sed, numquam illo autem voluptas ut eos. Lorem ipsum dolor sit amet, consectetur adipisicing elit. Cumque quas amet nulla eveniet ratione, facere est assumenda itaque obcaecati adipisci. Lorem ipsum dolor sit amet, consectetur adipisicing elit. Cumque quas amet nulla eveniet ratione, facere est assumenda itaque obcaecati adipisci.

Crabby »

The Whale

Lorem ipsum dolor sit amet, consectetur adipisicing elit. Cumque quas amet nulla eveniet ratione, facere est assumenda itaque obcaecati adipisci. Lorem ipsum dolor sit amet, consectetur adipisicing elit. Cumque quas amet nulla eveniet ratione, facere est assumenda itaque obcaecati adipisci. Lorem ipsum dolor sit amet, consectetur adipisicing elit. Cumque quas amet nulla eveniet ratione, facere est assumenda itaque obcaecati adipisci.

Stuart »

Building standard buttons

Our starting point has us a long way to go, but it should be pretty easy:

Old Chompy

Dedicated to sharks and other aquatic species

Lorem ipsum dolor sit amet, consectetur adipisicing elit. Architecto aut recusandae totam iste ad cumque quas, alias explicabo est non placeat facilis vero voluptatibus odio. Quidem deserunt dignissimos, excepturi officiis tempore itaque repellat ipsum voluptatibus suscipit cum, ipsa. At, doloribus! Lorem ipsum dolor sit amet, consectetur adipisicing elit. Architecto aut recusandae totam iste ad cumque quas, alias explicabo est non placeat facilis vero voluptatibus odio. Quidem deserunt dignissimos, excepturi officiis tempore itaque repellat ipsum voluptatibus suscipit cum, ipsa. At, doloribus!

The Octopus

Lorem ipsum dolor sit amet, consectetur adipisicing elit. Cumque quas amet nulla eveniet ratione, facere est assumenda itaque obcaecati adipisci. Lorem ipsum dolor sit amet, consectetur adipisicing elit. Cumque quas amet nulla eveniet ratione, facere est assumenda itaque obcaecati adipisci. Lorem ipsum dolor sit amet, consectetur adipisicing elit. Cumque quas amet nulla eveniet ratione, facere est assumenda itaque obcaecati adipisci.

Tenticals »

The Crab

Lorem ipsum dolor sit amet, consectetur adipisicing elit. Provident quasi aliquam, sapiente quisquam sed, numquam illo autem voluptas ut eos. Lorem ipsum dolor sit amet, consectetur adipisicing elit. Cumque quas amet nulla eveniet ratione, facere est assumenda itaque obcaecati adipisci. Lorem ipsum dolor sit amet, consectetur adipisicing elit. Cumque quas amet nulla eveniet ratione, facere est assumenda itaque obcaecati adipisci.

Crabby »

The Whale

Lorem ipsum dolor sit amet, consectetur adipisicing elit. Cumque quas amet nulla eveniet ratione, facere est assumenda itaque obcaecati adipisci. Lorem ipsum dolor sit amet, consectetur adipisicing elit. Cumque quas amet nulla eveniet ratione, facere est assumenda itaque obcaecati adipisci. Lorem ipsum dolor sit amet, consectetur adipisicing elit. Cumque quas amet nulla eveniet ratione, facere est assumenda itaque obcaecati adipisci.

Stuart »

Let's jump into the HTML of our secondary section:

```html
<!--
=================
Secondary Sections
=================
-->
<section class="secondary-section grouping">
    <div class="wrapper">
        <div class="column">
            <figure>
                <img src="images/octopus-icon.png" alt="Octopus">
            </figure>
            <h2>The Octopus</h2>
            <p>Lorem ipsum dolor sit amet, consectetur adipisicing elit. Cumque quas amet nulla eveniet
            ratione, facere est assumenda itaque obcaecati adipisci. Lorem ipsum dolor sit amet,
            consectetur adipisicing elit. Cumque quas amet nulla eveniet ratione, facere est assumenda
            itaque obcaecati adipisci. Lorem ipsum dolor sit amet, consectetur adipisicing elit. Cumque
            quas amet nulla eveniet ratione, facere est assumenda itaque obcaecati adipisci. </p>
            <a href="#">Tenticals &raquo;</a>
        </div>
        <div class="column">
            <figure><img src="images/crab-icon.png" alt="Crab"></figure>
            <h2>The Crab</h2>
            <p>Lorem ipsum dolor sit amet, consectetur adipisicing elit. Provident quasi aliquam, sapiente
            quisquam sed, numquam illo autem voluptas ut eos. Lorem ipsum dolor sit amet, consectetur
            adipisicing elit. Cumque quas amet nulla eveniet ratione, facere est assumenda itaque
            obcaecati adipisci. Lorem ipsum dolor sit amet, consectetur adipisicing elit. Cumque quas amet
            nulla eveniet ratione, facere est assumenda itaque obcaecati adipisci.</p>
            <a href="#">Crabby &raquo;</a>
        </div>
        <div class="column">
            <figure><img src="images/whale-icon.png" alt="Whale"></figure>
            <h2>The Whale</h2>
            <p>Lorem ipsum dolor sit amet, consectetur adipisicing elit. Cumque quas amet nulla eveniet
            ratione, facere est assumenda itaque obcaecati adipisci. Lorem ipsum dolor sit amet,
            consectetur adipisicing elit. Cumque quas amet nulla eveniet ratione, facere est assumenda
            itaque obcaecati adipisci. Lorem ipsum dolor sit amet, consectetur adipisicing elit. Cumque
            quas amet nulla eveniet ratione, facere est assumenda itaque obcaecati adipisci. </p>
            <a href="#">Stuart &raquo;</a>
        </div>
    </div><!-- end wrapper -->
</section>
```

I'll add the class of `button` to all three anchor elements at the bottom of each column.

```html
<a href="#" class="button">Tenticals &raquo;</a>
```

Now, jumping down to the bottom of our CSS, let's add a huge comment for our new section and name "Buttons".

```css
/****************
Buttons
****************/
```

This is where all our button styles will go.

What we want to do is create the `.button` selector. All the stylistic properties that are shared across buttons will go here. We won't put any positioning properties in the button selector because buttons could be positioned anywhere:

```
/ * * * * * * * * * * * * * * * *
Buttons
* * * * * * * * * * * * * * * */
.button {
}
```

Let's start by adding a border. We'll go with two pixels solid and a dark gray color. We'll apply the same color to the text:

```
.button {
    border: 2px solid #333;
    color: #333;
}
```

After saving and refreshing the browser it starts to ever so slightly resemble a button:

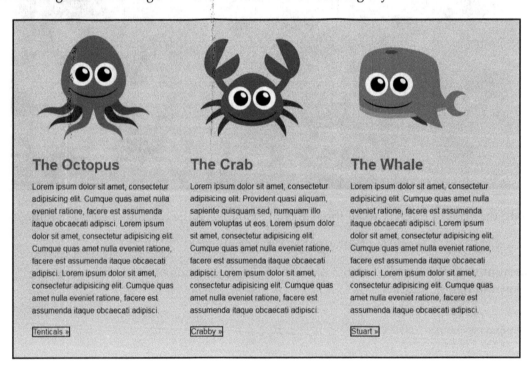

We now need to add some padding. Let's go back to our CSS and use the two-value padding shorthand: `10px` for the top and bottom, and `0px` for the left and right. This is because we're going to end up centering the text. Let's also change the display property to `block` because these are inline elements and we want them to behave like block-level elements:

```
.button{
    border: 2px solid #333;
    color: #333;
    padding: 10px 0;
    display: block;
}
```

Save this, refresh the browser, and see the effect:

The Octopus

Lorem ipsum dolor sit amet, consectetur adipisicing elit. Cumque quas amet nulla eveniet ratione, facere est assumenda itaque obcaecati adipisci. Lorem ipsum dolor sit amet, consectetur adipisicing elit. Cumque quas amet nulla eveniet ratione, facere est assumenda itaque obcaecati adipisci. Lorem ipsum dolor sit amet, consectetur adipisicing elit. Cumque quas amet nulla eveniet ratione, facere est assumenda itaque obcaecati adipisci.

Tenticals »

The Crab

Lorem ipsum dolor sit amet, consectetur adipisicing elit. Provident quasi aliquam, sapiente quisquam sed, numquam illo autem voluptas ut eos. Lorem ipsum dolor sit amet, consectetur adipisicing elit. Cumque quas amet nulla eveniet ratione, facere est assumenda itaque obcaecati adipisci. Lorem ipsum dolor sit amet, consectetur adipisicing elit. Cumque quas amet nulla eveniet ratione, facere est assumenda itaque obcaecati adipisci.

Crabby »

The Whale

Lorem ipsum dolor sit amet, consectetur adipisicing elit. Cumque quas amet nulla eveniet ratione, facere est assumenda itaque obcaecati adipisci. Lorem ipsum dolor sit amet, consectetur adipisicing elit. Cumque quas amet nulla eveniet ratione, facere est assumenda itaque obcaecati adipisci. Lorem ipsum dolor sit amet, consectetur adipisicing elit. Cumque quas amet nulla eveniet ratione, facere est assumenda itaque obcaecati adipisci.

Stuart »

As you can see, we now have to add some text-level properties. First, let's add a font family. We'll go with the typical `sans-serif` stack: `Arial, Helvetica, sans-serif`. Then, use the `text-align` property to align the text in the center of the element. We'll also set the `font-weight` to `bold`, then use another property called `letter-spacing` and add a value of `1.5px`. If you're not familiar with the `letter-spacing` property, it does pretty much what you think it does—it creates a horizontal space between each letter:

```
/***************
Buttons
***************/
.button{
  border: 2px solid #333;
  color: #333;
  padding: 10px 0;
  display: block;
  font-family: Arial, Helvetica, sans-serif;
  text-align: center;
  font-weight: bold;
  letter-spacing: 1.5px;
}
```

Once we save this and refresh the site, we will have our button elements. There's no hover state yet; we'll get into that in another section:

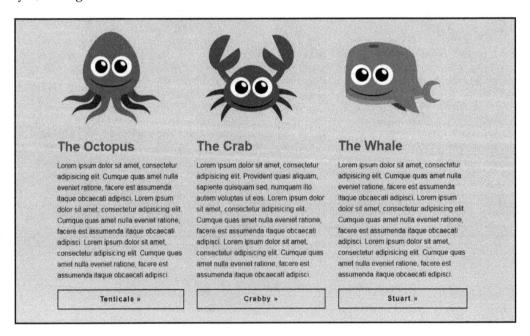

If you go over to the movies page now, you will see the **Learn More** links there, which need to be buttons as well:

So let's jump over to that markup in the `shark-movies.html` file, and do the same thing. Add the class of `button` to each anchor tag at the bottom of each movie section:

```
<a href="" class="button">Learn More</a>
```

Save this and refresh, and you'll get a button instantly:

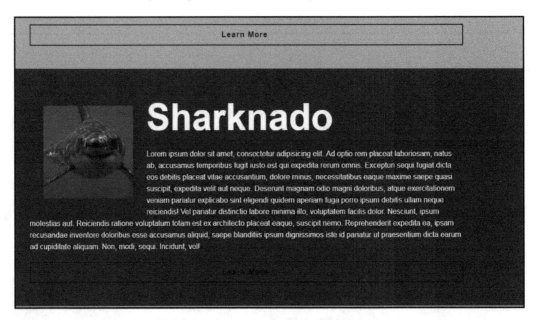

It sort of works; we have a button, but not entirely. They look like buttons but they are of the wrong color, too wide, and not positioned to the right. Also, the text doesn't contrast well with the background, especially in darker sections. So there is some fixing we have to do, essentially because these buttons are different to the ones on the home page, which were full-width buttons.

Let's go ahead and fix those buttons now and look at how we can get even more modular and add multiple classes in order to vary the buttons.

Multiple classes

To recap, so far you've learned how to create a class that can be reused anywhere on our web page in order to create a button. However, buttons tend to vary across a website. You may have, for instance, buttons like: Okay, Close, Cancel, Submit, and Add to cart. All of which have different meanings so are all colored or styled slightly differently. In some scenarios, as in the case of our movies and index pages, the buttons just end up varying based on the page that they're on because of the layout differences between the pages. In this section, we'll get even more modular and learn how to use multiple classes in order to change the appearance of our buttons. We'll look at a few examples of how multiple classes can provide us some affordances in regard to styling our buttons throughout the site.

The following screenshot illustrates the final site. We're shooting for buttons that look like the **Learn More** button. They're floated to the right, they're white, they have a white border, and their width is narrower:

The following is where we stand with regard to our site at the moment. Our buttons are dark gray in color and have full width, they're just not what we're looking for here:

Changing the width of the buttons

First, let's address the width issue by creating a new class called `button-narrow`. So in our CSS, where our button section is, below the `.button` rule set we created in the last section, create a new class called `.button-narrow`. Very simply, the width is going to be 25%:

```
/****************
Buttons
****************/
.button {
    border: 2px solid #333;
    color: #333;
    padding: 10px 0;
    display: block;
    font-family: Arial, Helvetica, sans-serif;
    text-align: center;
    font-weight: bold;
    letter-spacing: 1.5px;
}
.button-narrow {
    width: 25%;
}
```

Save this. Next, go to the `shark-movies.html` file. Go to each of the three anchor tags with a class of button. I'll just show the Learn More button here, but the code changes are the same for all of them:

```
<a href="" class="button ">Learn More</a>
```

Let's add our new `button-narrow` class to these elements:

```
<a href="" class="button button-narrow">Learn More</a>
```

Save this, go to the browser, and you will see that the buttons are now much smaller in all three sections:

Let's take this a step further and create another class called `button-alt`, which will control the border and font colors.

Changing the border and font colors of the buttons

Let's add the `button-alt` class as well to each of the 3 **Learn More** buttons.

```
<a href="" class="button button-narrow button-alt">Learn More</a>
```

Now go to the CSS and type `.button-alt` as our new selector beneath our `.button-narrow` selector. I chose `button-alt` as the class because this is an alternative button color. Then, specify `color` as white and the `border-color` as white:

```
.button-alt {
  color: #fff;
  border-color: #fff;
}
```

Save this, go to the site, and you will now see that we're almost there:

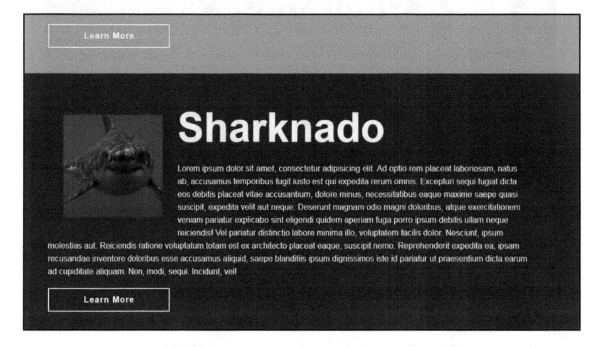

Positioning the button

The final thing is the position of the button. It is currently on the left-hand side and it needs to sit on the right. Naturally, we could create a class called `button-right` that floats the buttons to the right. However, floating elements to the left or right is very common, even outside of buttons. It is preferable to keep the class names more generic, such as float right and float left. This way, we can float anything to the right or left. In my case, before the `Buttons` section in the CSS, I have my global styles:

```
/************
Global
************/
::-moz-selection {
  background-color: #eb2428;
}
::selection {
  background-color: #eb2428;
}

.wrapper {
  width:960px;
  margin: 0 auto;
}
body {
  background-color: #dcdcdc;
  font-family: Arial, Helvetica, sans-serif;
  font-weight: 100;
  font-size: 16px;
}
a {
  text-decoration: none;
  color: #eb2428;
}
h1 {
  font-weight: 700;
  font-size: 30px;
  color: #0072ae;
  margin-bottom: 10px;
}
h2 {
  font-size: 30px;
  margin-bottom: 10px;
  color: #eb2428;
  font-weight: 700;
}
p {
  line-height: 1.6;
  margin-bottom: 20px;
}
```

Right below this global list, I'm going to copy my standard library of modular styles:

```css
p {
  line-height: 1.6;
  margin-bottom: 20px;
}
/*******************
Modular Styles
*******************/
.float-left {
  float: left;
}
.float-right {
  float: right;
}
.clear {
  clear: both;
}
.bold {
  font-weight: bold;
}
.hidden,
.hide {
  display: none;
}
.relative {
  position: relative;
}
.absolute {
  position: absolute;
}
.block {
  display: block;
}
.inline-block {
  display: inline-block;
}
.text-centered {
  text-align: center;
}
```

This is part of the base boilerplate I've built over the years, and it has classes such as `float-left`, `float-right`, `clear`, `bold`, `hidden`, and some other common modular classes. You can see the full list in the download package. These can be reused throughout the site. Now, in the `shark-movies.html` file, let's simply add the `float-right` class to our three anchor tags:

```html
<a href="" class="button button-narrow button-alt float-right">Learn
More</a>
```

Save this and refresh the shark movie site. You'll now see the buttons floated to the right:

I should also point out that our container that surrounds each of these sections is not going to collapse. Let's go into DevTools to see why. The section highlighted in the following screenshot with a class of `content-block` has not collapsed because I added the clearfix `grouping` class to it:

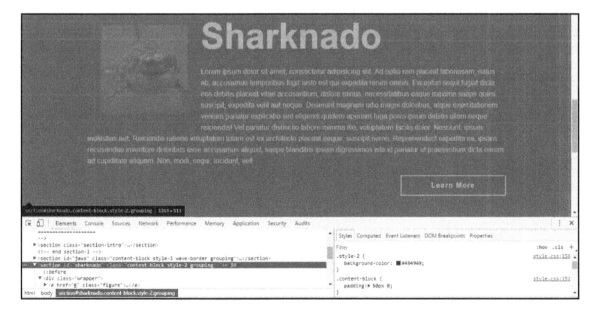

If I were to take this out and delete `grouping` from that line, you will see how the collapse would take effect. Because we have this `grouping` class, we make sure this section doesn't collapse:

So, in conclusion, we followed a very modular and reusable approach to build our button and created a few modular button-related classes that can be used to vary the style of the button. There are other ways we could have done this. I could have used a descendant selector to style the buttons based on their parent. That way, all the buttons inside of content-block would always be floated to the right and be white instead of dark gray. This would have been a decent alternative if it would have provided other areas, besides content blocks, the same alternative button styles, which is highly likely. Next, let's talk about why a modular, reusable, and light approach to CSS is necessary. We'll do this by talking about the rules of specificity.

Specificity rules

We're beginning to understand how a modular approach to CSS allows us to use classes as little chunks of CSS that can be used anywhere on the web page to style any element. This makes writing CSS very convenient. However, it only works if the CSS is kept lightweight. As you'll learn in this section, every CSS selector can be weighed on a scale, and the heaviest selector wins the style battle between two competing selectors. So, I'll start by explaining the weights of different selectors and how they can overrule one another. Then, we'll talk a bit about how the universal selector and the !important declaration fit into the weights of the selectors.

The weights of different selectors

All selectors are assigned a weight, and the heaviest selector takes precedence when conflicting CSS rules exist. It's natural when architecting a website that you have general styles that get overridden with more specific styles in different circumstances. In the global area at the top of the style sheet, a very broad style has been set for all paragraph elements:

```
p {
  font-size: 16px;
  line-height: 1.6;
  margin-bottom: 20px;
}
```

The font size is 16px. There is a line-height property of 1.6 and 20px of margin-bottom. Naturally, I might want to overwrite either line-height or margin-bottom under varying circumstances. Let's try and override that with a new rule set with a selector of .content-block p:

```
p {
  font-size: 16px;
  line-height: 1.6;
  margin-bottom: 20px;
}
.content-block p {

}
```

This is a descendant selector. Now let's add a `line-height` of `1.8` and `margin-bottom` of `40px`:

```
.content-block p {
  line-height: 1.8;
  margin-bottom: 40px
}
```

Switch over to the website to view the original setup. This descendant selector should target any content or paragraph text in the main text area:

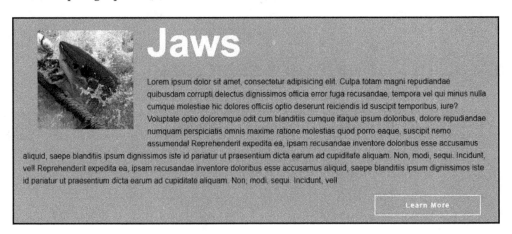

When we save our CSS and refresh the site, we get more line height and margin bottom, as you can see in the following screenshot:

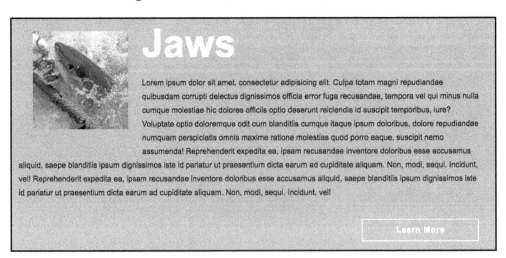

So how much does each selector weigh? Well, you can think of inline styles as worth 1,000 points, IDs as worth 100 points, classes as worth 10 points, and elements as worth one point each. In the example we have been looking at, the single p element selector is worth just 1 point, whereas .content-block p, which was a class and an element, is worth 11 points:

Specificity Weight	
Points	**Type**
1000	Inline Style
100	ID
10	Class (or pseudo class)
1	Element

This point system figures out which selector is going to win. In this case, the selectors were both targeting the paragraph element; however, because .content-block p is worth 11 points, it's going to trump the rule set above it which, as an element selector, is only worth one point:

```
p {
   font-size: 16px;
   line-height: 1.6;
   margin-bottom: 20px;
}
.content-block p {
   line-height: 1.8;
   margin-bottom: 40px
}
```

IDs are worth 100 points, which is 10 times as much as a class. In our shark-movies.html file, you can see that the first section of Jaws has the jaws ID:

```
<section id="jaws" class="content-block style-1 wave-border grouping">
```

Now let's switch back to our style sheet and create a new rule set, like so:

```
#jaws p {
   line-height: 3;
}
```

When we refresh the browser, you will see that line-height of 3 does take effect:

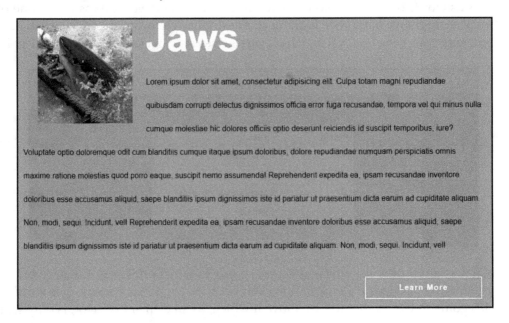

Our selector that uses an ID that's worth 101 points overrides the selector that has a class and an element worth just 11 points as well as the selector that's just an element worth just 1 point. The weight of the ID, in my case means I tend to stay away from them for styling purposes when I can. IDs are also less versatile than classes; they can only be used once on a page. I really try to avoid using them altogether because they're not very reusable.

Another thing to avoid is inline styles, which we can think of as worth a whopping 1,000 points. Inline styling will beat everything, including selectors with an ID. Let's target the paragraph again to demonstrate this. We'll jump right into the shark-movies.html file and actually add an inline style. Beneath the h1 selector inside the jaws section, we have our paragraph, so let's add our inline style to it. We'll type style="line-height: 1":

```
<p style="line-height: 1">
```

When we save this, we'll return to our site and refresh the browser. Once we do this, we'll see that `line-height` is using that inline style because it's worth more. It's heavier than all the other selectors we have in our style sheet:

So what beats inline styles? There is one ace up your sleeves: the `!important` declaration.

The !important declaration

Let's see how the `!important` declaration works. We go back to this element selector in the CSS that's just a paragraph:

```
p {
    font-size: 16px;
    line-height: 1.6;
    margin-bottom: 20px;
}
```

We can go inside of the `line-height` value itself, then add `!important` to the end of that line. The line height will go up to `1.6`:

```
p {
    font-size: 16px;
    line-height: 1.6 !important;
    margin-bottom: 20px;
}
```

Following is the output of preceding code:

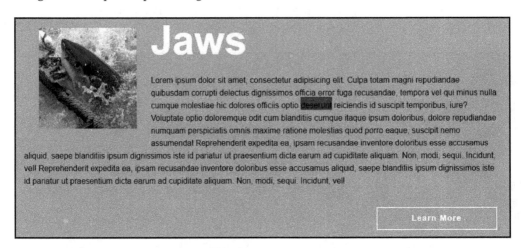

Let's inspect this paragraph to make sure that it's actually using the !important declaration. As you can see in Chrome's DevTools, the inline style of 1 is being crossed out; we can see the ID worth 101 points with an element is also being crossed out:

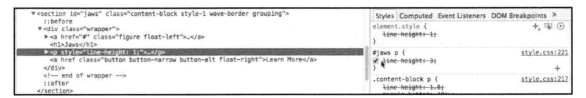

If we scroll down the styles a little more, we see our class plus the element that is being crossed out too:

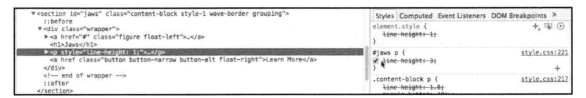

Scroll down a bit more and you'll see that indeed it is using `line-height` from our element selector with the `!important` declaration:

```
Styles | Computed  Event Listeners  DOM Breakpoints  »
    line-height: 1.8;
    margin-bottom: 40px;
}

p {                                          style.css:211
☑ font-size: 16px;
☑   line-height: 1.6 !important;
☑   margin-bottom: 20px;
}                                                     +

html, body, div, span, applet, object,     style.css:10
```

Adding the `!important` declaration can actually be thought of as being worth 10,000 points, beating all the classes, IDs, and inline styles of that one property. Like you want to stay away from inline styles and IDs, you also want to stay away from using the `!important` declaration unless you have to for a really good reason. There is one other selector that is worth less than a point: the universal selector.

The universal selector

The universal selector is just an asterisk. It's worth zero points, so it only works when no other selector is in contention. Take out the `!important` declaration in our CSS. Above our other rule sets, let's add a * as a selector and add a `font-size` of 9px and `line-height` of .5:

```
* {
  font-size: 9px;
  line-height: .5;
}
```

Technically, this star should apply to every element unless something more specific is defined. Anything beats the * selector. Now when you go to the site, you will see that once you take the !important declaration out, you fall back to your inline style's line-height property:

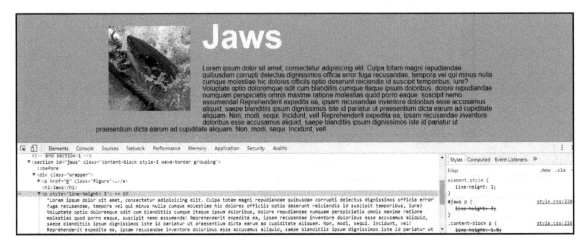

In DevTools, we can see the universal selector is eventually getting crossed out. It's not being applied to this paragraph text or really anything. It's not being applied too much on the page:

```
* {                                          style.css:223
    font-size: 9px;
    line-height: .5;
}
```

Because its weight is worth so little, a lot of the times what you'll see is the universal selector being used as a primitive reset. You could add the properties and values of margin: 0 and padding: 0 to the universal selector and something like that at the top of your style sheet. This would really reset the margin and padding down to zero for every single element:

```
* {
    margin: 0;
    padding: 0;
}
```

Let's revisit our chart showing the weights of different selectors. You've learned that you can think of `!important` as being worth 10,000 points and the universal selector as being worth zero points:

Points	Type
10000	!Important
1000	Inline Style
100	ID
10	Class (or pseudo class)
1	Element
0	Universal Selector (*)

Specificity Weight

Reality of the point system

In reality though, the point system I'm describing is not completely truthful. Let's say you have this selector of 11 elements: `div div p p p p p p p p p { ... }`. Using the system I already described, this is worth 11 points. And I described a class selector as being worth 10 points. However, the long element selector will never beat one single class: `.i-beat-any-number-of-elements`. So technically, elements are worth 0,0,0,1 and classes are worth 0,0,1,0, ID's are worth 0,1,0,0, and inline styles are worth 1,0,0,0. But! Pause for emphasis. You'd be having a pretty bad experience if you ever created a selector consisting of more than 10 elements. That would be a very bad idea, and I recommend that you try not to go more that 3 or 4 at the very most. So, instead of thinking of elements as worth 0,0,0,1 and classes as worth 0,0,1,0, we can think in the terms I described previously where classes are worth 10 points and elements are worth 1 point, and so on.

Also, it is important to remember that authoring CSS at any reasonable scale is easier when you keep your selectors lightweight because you can then easily create modular, reusable classes in the form of a button. A big part of creating a modern website is overriding styles when you have to; you don't want to make this difficult. I strongly urge you to stick to classes and element selectors and be very conservative with your use of the `!important` declaration; steer clear of inline styles and IDs altogether.

Transitions

Understanding CSS specificity and how selectors overrule each other can alleviate a lot of frustration when using CSS. Now that we've got a better understanding of this, let's get back to our project and finish styling the buttons we have been working on. A button is incomplete unless it has a slick hover state with a smooth transition. We'll start this section by creating a hover state using the pseudo selector :hover. Then, we'll smooth it out with a transition before finally discussing when vendor prefixes are necessary.

Creating a hover state

At the moment, the buttons on our site are ghost buttons. They have no background color, a dark gray border, or dark gray text, as you can see in the following screenshot:

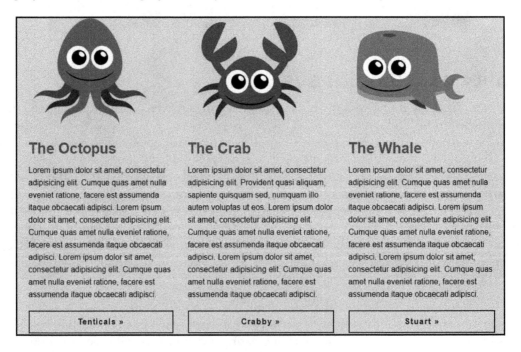

We want to create a button that will have a dark gray background color and will show text in white when hovered. So let's knock this out using the :hover pseudo class. Under the first existing .button rule set, add a new selector called .button:hover. Add background-color: #333 and add the color of the text as white:

```
/***************
Buttons
***************/
.button {
 border: 2px solid #333;
 color: #333;
 padding: 10px 0;
 display: block;
 font-family: Arial, Helvetica, sans-serif;
 text-align: center;
 font-weight: bold;
 letter-spacing: 1.5px;
}
.button:hover {
  background-color: #333;
  color: #fff;
}
```

Notice how I'm not using the full six characters of the hex code. If all six characters are the same, it's alright if you use only three characters. Now if we save this and refresh, we will have our hover state when we hover the mouse over a button:

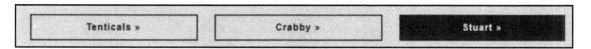

The hover state's transition is very abrupt though; it's happening immediately. So the next step is to use the CSS3 transition property to smooth out the state change from no hover to hover.

Using the transition property

We can choose which properties to transition, the duration of the transition, and the timing function of the transition. All three properties can be listed out separately as transition-property, transition-duration, and transition-timing-function; however, using the shorthand seems to be the easiest way. So we'll type in transition as a new property in the .button rule set and use .25s, or a quarter of a second. And we'll specify all for which properties we'll be transitioning. We'll use a linear timing function:

```
.button {
  border: 2px solid #333;
  color: #333;
  padding: 10px 0;
  display: block;
  text-align: center;
  font-weight: bold;
  letter-spacing: 1.5px;
  font-family: Arial, Helvetica, sans-serif;
  transition: .25s all linear;
}
```

Now when we view this in the browser and as you move your mouse over each button, it is a much more gradual change:

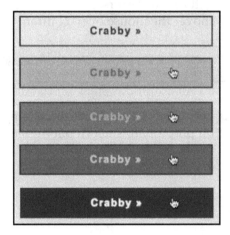

It takes 0.25 seconds to transition from dark gray to white text and the same thing for the background color and border. A quarter of a second seems to be just right, but you can experiment with a faster transition or a slower one. You could change it to one-tenth of a second and that would be good too, very fast, almost immediate. You could change it to one second, which would be ten times slower and probably way too slow. I find that 0.2 to 0.3 seconds tend to be that "Goldilocks-zone" for transitioning.

The next value we added after `0.25s` was `all`:

```
transition: .25s all linear;
```

This can be set to a certain property you want to transition or to all the properties. So, if you want to, you could set this to just `color`:

```
transition: .25s color linear;
```

The only thing that would transition would be the text color. If you try this, you'll see how the button's background color of dark gray transitions immediately, but the text color transitions over 0.25 seconds:

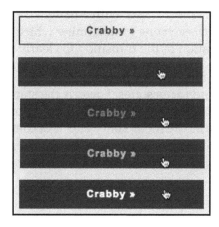

If we wanted to, what we could add a comma separate list of properties to transition. In this case, I'm transitioning both `color` and `background-color`. One reason this is nice is if you need to transition more than one property, but not every property.

```
transition: .25s color linear, .25s background-color linear;
```

Because of this, both the background color and the text color will transition at the same speed. We accomplished this much more efficiently using the `all` keyword to transition both the text color and the background color. However, in some cases, it might be useful to keep properties' transition at a different speed than the other. Let's change the `background-color` to have a timing-function of 1.25 seconds:

```
transition: .25s color linear, 1.25s background-color linear;
```

The color transition would now be faster than the background color transition. This is not super useful in our immediate situation, so let's change it back to the way we had it earlier:

```
transition: .25s all linear;
```

In our case, the timing function is set to `linear`. We can also use `ease`, `ease-in`, `ease-out`, and `ease-in-out`:

```
transition: .25s all ease-in-out;
```

For short transitions like the one we're using, the linear method or the default will work just fine; any of them will work just fine. It's actually quite difficult to tell the difference between `ease`, `ease-in`, `ease-in-out`, and `linear` with a really fast transition like this. I recommend experimenting with each one to determine which one suits your needs best. You may need to alter the duration of the transition to clearly see the effect.

Okay, so the transition adds a nice little experience layer to our buttons when hovered. We can also transition the active and focus states. Focus is the state when your user tabs to the button using their *Tab* key instead of hovering their mouse pointer over the button. I like to make all hover states the same as the focus state. This is accomplished easily by adding the selector using a comma. So just like we have `.button:hover`, we can do `.button:focus`:

```
.button:focus,
.button:hover {
  background-color: #333;
  color: #fff;
}
```

If you add this, the focus state will also be triggered. When you hit the *Tab* key and the *Shift + Tab* key to move from button to button, their hover states will also be their focus states. That's nice and good for accessibility reasons.

Vendor prefixes

As mentioned earlier, transitions are a CSS3 property. All modern (major) browsers support them: Chrome, Firefox, Safari, Internet Explorer, and Edge. Older browsers, such as IE9 and below, don't support them. They still get the hover state, but it will be abrupt without any transition. This isn't a problem as transitions typically aren't a core feature of your website, but more of an added experience level. Still, they are CSS3, and we can get a little more mileage out of them by including the vendor prefixed versions. Traditionally, the `-webkit-` prefix was used for Safari and Chrome; `-moz-` was used for Firefox and `-o-` for Opera. However, Firefox and Opera also now use `-webkit-`, so technically you don't need `-moz-` and `-o-` as much as you used to need them; however, for older versions of these browsers, you can still include them:

```
-webkit-transition: .25s all ease-in-out;
-moz-transition: .25s all ease-in-out;
-o-transition: .25s all ease-in-out;
transition: .25s all ease-in-out;
```

Or you can get by with half the CSS and still have 99% of all users see your transition just with the `-webkit-` vendor prefix:

```
-webkit-transition: .25s all ease-in-out;
transition: .25s all ease-in-out;
```

Transitions are a great feature of CSS3, and they add an extra layer of nice-ness to the user experience. So far, we've created a hover state for our ghost buttons and used the transition effect to smooth out the state change. We then added vendor prefixes to support older browsers. Next, we'll look at another feature of CSS3: transforms.

Transforms

Like transitions, transforms are a feature of CSS3. They have a little more support though as all major browsers, including IE9 and up, provide support. Transforms allow you to do several things, including rotate, scale, and translate. We'll look at a few practical examples in this section. First, we'll apply a scale to our button, then we'll do a translation, followed by a unique use of the rotate value.

Applying a scale to our button

Let's jump right in where we left off with our button in the CSS. Underneath the transitions, let's add a transform. We'll add `transform: scale(.9, .9)`, like so:

```
-o-transition: .25s all ease-in-out;
transition: .25s all ease-in-out;
transform: scale(.9,.9);
```

Notice that by using a value of `.9` for both the width and height, we're actually making our buttons smaller, nine-tenths of their original size:

Let's add the `scale` property again to the buttons' hover/focus state to get even neater interaction:

```
.button:focus,
.button:hover {
  background-color: #333;
  color: #fff;
  transform: scale(1.1, 1.1);
}
```

The scale value is a css function that takes a width and height respectively. 1.1 being 1.1x the original size.

When you save and refresh, you will see that the button actually gets much bigger as you hover over it. It's a nice smooth transition because we already have the transition property applied:

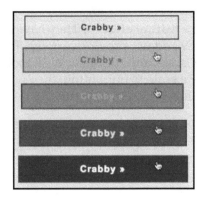

Using the translate function

Let's go one step further and also use the `translate` function. This will be added to the same line, or declaration, as the `transform: scale` code that we just wrote. The `translate` function can move the element to the left, right, top, or bottom. As you can see in the following line of code, the first value is for left and right movements. But we're not going to move it to left or right, so we'll use `0`. The second value is for the top and bottom movement. I'm actually going to push it up by `-5px`. If I were to use a positive value, that would push it down:

```
transform: scale(1.1,1.1) translate(0, -5px);
```

Now when we refresh and hover over a button, we will see it does nudge up slightly, five pixels to be exact:

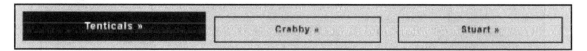

Notice that I separated the two functions with a space. The syntax is very important here:

```
transform: scale(1.1,1.1) translate(0, -5px);
```

You might naturally reach to add a comma there, but if I were to actually add a comma between the two functions, `scale` and `translate`, we would get no interaction at all as far as the `transform` goes because this syntax is incorrect:

```
transform: scale(1.1,1.1), translate(0, -5px); /* don't use a comma to
separate transforms :-( */
```

Using the rotate value

There is another transform function that I'd like to go over, but if we add anymore flair to these buttons they will be far too distracting. Instead, let's add a very interesting hover effect to the movie images on the movie page. The images next to each movie title are actually external links to the movie:

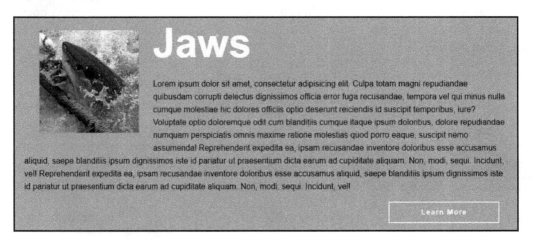

However, I want a visual interaction to take place upon hover, which really indicates that this is a hyperlink, or at least letting the user know there is some type of action that can be performed. Let's use `transform: rotate()` to make this happen.

This is what we're aiming for in our final site. A white frame with an image inside of it, and the hover effect is a rotate inside of this white frame:

As you can see in the following figure, when you hover over it, the image rotates and gets scaled slightly larger than normal - and - even though the image is scaling larger, it doesn't overflow it's parent container:

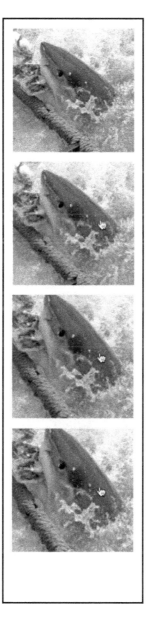

We need to have an element that wraps around our image in order to accomplish this. We do have this—an anchor tag with the class of `figure` that is the parent of each image. This is where we'll add this thick white border. We're going to need to add `overflow: hidden` to the `a` tag because when we scale the image more and rotate it, the overflow hidden prevents it from popping out of its container.

Let's get to work. The `.content-block` `.figure` selector already exists, so let's add the white border to it first. I'm going to wait to add the `overflow: hidden` until a little bit later. First, let's make the `border` property 10px, `solid`, and `white`:

```
.content-block .figure {
  float: left;
  margin: 30px;
  border: 10px solid #fff;
}
```

Before we refresh our current site, this is what it looks like:

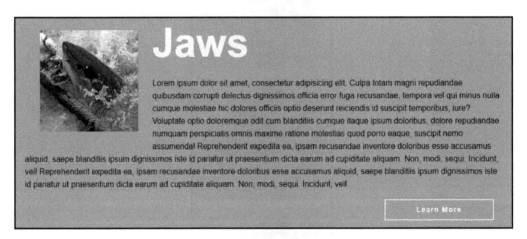

When we refresh the browser, we get the white border:

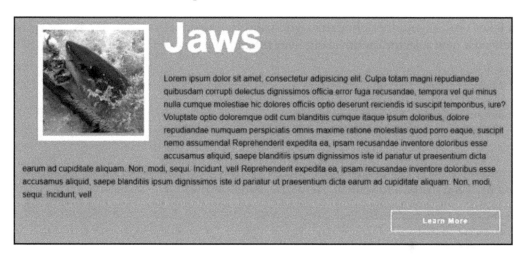

As you can see, we get a gap between the bottom of the image and the border. We can rectify this in two ways. We can set the container such that it has the exact height of the image; we can do this using the `height` property, which isn't the best solution. Alternatively, we can float the image to the left. To do this, we can use the `float` property as it's easy enough and a stronger solution. However, we want to target the image itself that's inside of `.content-block` `.figure`. So let's do that and float it left.

```
.content-block .figure img {
  float: left;
}
```

When we refresh the browser now, we will see this gets rid of that gap between the image and the border:

We're going to add `rotate` and `scale` to the image as well. The `rotate` function is a little different than `scale` and `transition` as it doesn't take two parameters inside the function. It just takes one: the number of degrees you want to rotate. In our case, this is `15deg`. So we'll create a new selector for hovering over the image:

```
.content-block .figure img {
  float: left;
}
.content-block .figure img:hover {
  transform: rotate(15deg);
}
```

Next, add the scale: `1.25` horizontally and `1.25` vertically, remembering to *not* add a comma between the two functions. Here's the code for this:

```
.content-block .figure img {
  float: left;
}
.content-block .figure img:hover {
  transform: rotate(15deg) scale(1.25, 1.25);
}
```

Save all this, go to the site, and now when you hover, the image pops right out of its container:

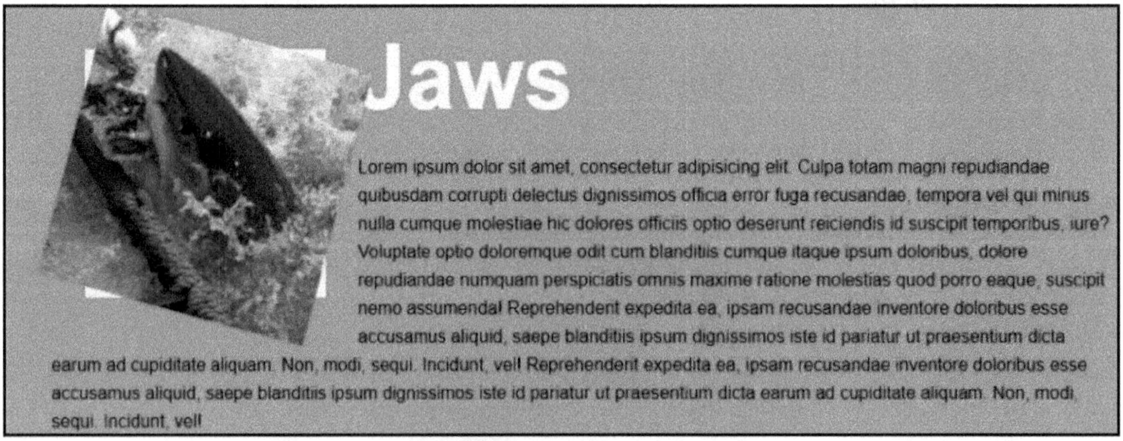

Let's add the `overflow:hidden` to the `parent` `.figure` selector. This is exactly what `overflow:hidden` is for:

```
.content-block .figure {
  float: left;
  margin: 30px;
  border: 10px solid #fff;
  overflow: hidden;
}
.content-block .figure img {
  float: left;
}
.content-block .figure img:hover {
  transform: rotate(15deg) scale(1.25, 1.25);
}
```

When we go to the site now, we see that it works fine. We get the rotate and we get the scale a little bit larger and more contained inside of its container with no overflow:

The change from the default state to hover is still way too abrupt though. Let's add a `transition` property in order to make it a lot smoother. We want to add the transition to the non-hover state of the image. Let's add a transition of a quarter second:

```
.content-block .figure img {
  float: left;
  transition: .25s all ease-in-out;
}
```

Now we have a smooth transition from the default state to the hover state:

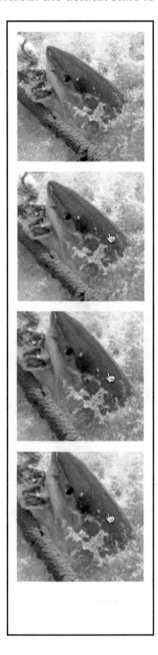

Adding vendor prefixes and :focus states

The last thing we have to do is add vendor prefixes to our `transform` and `transition` properties. Like with transition, I'm going to add the `-webkit-` prefixed version of the declaration in order to support older versions of Chrome, Safari, Firefox, and Opera. And also I'm going to add in the `-ms-` prefixed version to support Internet Explorer 9.

```
.content-block .figure img {
  float: left;
  -webkit-transition: .25s all ease-in-out;
  transition: .25s all ease-in-out;
}
.content-block .figure img:hover {
  -webkit-transform: rotate(15deg) scale(1.25, 1.25);
  -ms-transform: rotate(15deg) scale(1.25, 1.25);
  transform: rotate(15deg) scale(1.25, 1.25);
}
```

Maybe it's worth emphasizing that with the `transform` property, I added the `-ms-` vendor prefix. It just so happens that IE9 will support transforms if you provide it with the `-ms-` prefix:

```
-ms-transform: rotate(15deg) scale(1.25, 1.25);
```

However, I didn't do this with transitions because adding the `-ms-` vendor prefix wouldn't make any difference as IE9 just wasn't built with transition support.

Let's also add the `:focus` state to make it more web accessible:

```
.content-block .figure img {
  float: left;
  -webkit-transition: .25s all ease-in-out;
  transition: .25s all ease-in-out;
}
.content-block .figure img:hover,
.content-block .figure img:focus {
  -webkit-transform: rotate(15deg) scale(1.25, 1.25);
  -ms-transform: rotate(15deg) scale(1.25, 1.25);
  transform: rotate(15deg) scale(1.25, 1.25);
}
```

Okay, that wraps up our brief look at transitions and transforms. We took our experience layer to another level by adding the different types of transforms coupled with transitions to smooth out transformations. There are other transforms available that we didn't go over, such as `skew`, `translate x`, `translate y`, `scale x`, `scale y`, and so on. There are also 3D transformations that really take it to another level that are totally worth exploring as browser support has gotten much better. Next, we'll continue on our style train by styling the main call-to-action button on our site.

Styling the call-to-action button

We've really come a long way in this chapter with regard to styling buttons. Now it's time to add one more. In the final site, we also have a call-to-action button on the home page that needs to be built. In this section, let's walk through each step of styling the call-to-action button. First, we'll add the HTML, then position it properly and add the appropriate CSS; finally, we'll add a nice hover effect to it.

Here's our current site:

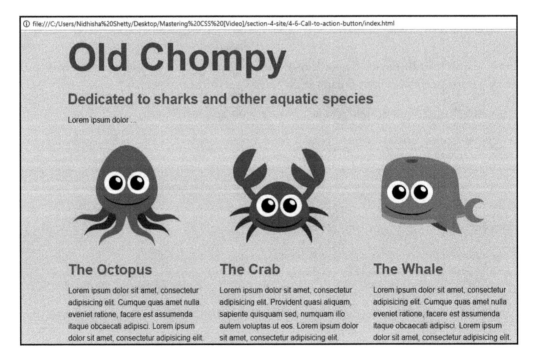

The following is the final site that we're aiming for, and the **Go Premium** call-to-action button is what we'll be creating:

Adding the HTML

Let's add the markup t0 our `index.html` file. In the `Intro Section` use an anchor tag for the button with the text `Go Premium`:

```
<!--
===============
Intro Section
===============
-->
<section>
  <div class="wrapper">
    <h1>Old Chompy</h1>
    <h2>Dedicated to sharks and other aquatic species</h2>
    <p>Lorem ipsum dolor ...</p>
    <a href="#">Go Premium</a>
  </div><!-- end wrapper -->
</section><!-- end section -->
```

Right underneath this, add a `p` tag with the reasons why you need to click on this soon-to-be gigantic call-to-action button. This paragraph tag will also have an anchor in it to learn more about our fictional premium offerings:

```
<!--
===============
Intro Section
===============
-->
<section>
  <div class="wrapper">
    <h1>Old Chompy</h1>
    <h2>Dedicated to sharks and other aquatic species</h2>
    <p>Lorem ipsum dolor ...</p>
    <a href="#">Go Premium</a>
    <p>So many awesome features when you go premium. <a href="#">Learn more
&raquo; </a></p>
  </div><!-- end wrapper -->
</section><!-- end section -->
```

Now we're really creating a two-column layout in this top section. We need to float the left chunk of the content to the left and the **Go Premium** section of content to the right. The best way to do this is to wrap both in a `div` tag with a unique class name, add widths to each, and float both of them. So start by adding the markup:

```
<section>
    <div class="wrapper">
        <div class="intro-content">
            <h1>Old Chompy</h1>
            <h2>Dedicated to sharks and other aquatic species</h2>
            <p>Lorem ipsum dolor ...</p>
        </div><!-- end of intro-content -->
        <div class="go-premium">
            <a href="#">Go Premium</a>
            <p>So many awesome features when you go premium. <a
href="#">Learn more &raquo;</a></p>
        </div><!-- end of go-premium -->
    </div><!-- end wrapper -->
</section><!-- end section -->
```

When we apply this and have a look at our site, we see the call-to-action button lives where we'd expect it to, directly under the intro content because we haven't added the layout-specific CSS yet:

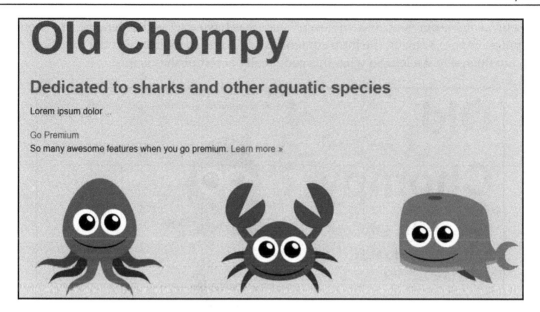

Let's dive into the CSS and change this.

Positioning using CSS

Positioning should be nothing new for us here. Just create a `Go Premium` section in our CSS with the following rule sets:

```
/****************
Go Premium
****************/
.intro-content {
  width: 360px;
  margin-right: 60px;
  float: left;
}
.go-premium {
  width: 300px;
  float: left;
}
```

Both our `.intro-content` and `.go-premium` areas have a set width defined. We should also put `margin-right` on the intro content to add some space between the two. Both of them are floated to the left. So what this code really accomplishes is this:

We get our introductory content on the left-hand side and our `Go Premium` content on the right. We have a few problems here, though. The go premium stuff is way too high on the page and then below that, our content is encroaching and flowing to the right of the intro content. That's the problem we face with the float not clearing.

A top margin should fix our first problem, so add `margin-top` of `125px` to the `.go-premium` selector:

```
.go-premium {
  width: 360px;
  float: left;
  margin-top: 125px;
}
```

Following is the output of preceding code:

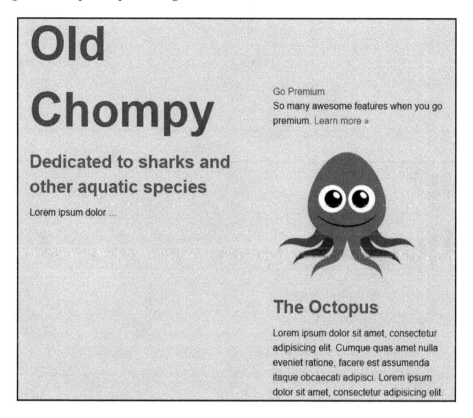

Our second problem is that the content is actually flowing around the floated element and kind of creeping up on our **Go Premium** button. We can solve this using the clearfix hack class on the container that wraps the entire top section. Look at the intro section in our `index.html` file. That entire top section, both the intro content and go premium, is wrapped inside of a wrapper:

```
<section>
    <div class="wrapper">
        <div class="intro-content">
            <h1>Old Chompy</h1>
            <h2>Dedicated to sharks and other aquatic species</h2>
            <p>Lorem ipsum dolor ...</p>
        </div><!-- intro-content -->
        <div class="go-premium">
            <a href="#">Go Premium</a>
            <p>So many awesome features when you go premium. <a
            href="#">Learn more
```

```
            &raquo;</a></p>
        </div><!-- end of go-premium -->
    </div><!-- end wrapper -->
</section><!-- end section -->
```

Let's add the clearfix hack to this wrapper, using our `grouping` class, which will fix the problem on our site:

```
<div class="wrapper grouping">
```

Following is the output of preceding code:

Styling the button

Let's go ahead and style the button. For styling purposes, let's add a class of `call-to-action` to our go premium anchor tag:

```
<a class="call-to-action" href="#">Go Premium</a>
```

Looking quickly at the final site, this is what we were aiming for with our **Go Premium** button. There's a white border, white text, blue gradient, and plenty of padding around it:

The hover state removes the gradient and changes the text color and border color to blue:

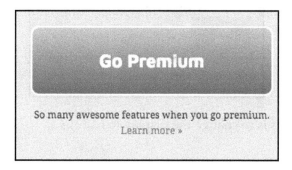

Note that we won't be able to use this exact web font pictured above. We'll use a solid blue background instead of the gradient for now as we'll come back to it in the next section and add the gradient as well as return to the font later in this book.

In the CSS, underneath the `.go-premium` rule set, add a `.call-to-action` selector and a 2px solid white border. We'll also make the text color white and make the background color blue. Add padding of `25px` to the top and bottom and zero to the left and right positions because we're going to end up centering the text:

```
/****************
Go Premium
****************/
.intro-content {
  width: 360px;
  margin-right: 60px;
  float: left;
}
.go-premium {
  width: 300px;
  float: left;
}
.call-to-action {
  border: 2px solid #fff;
  color: #fff;
  background-color: #0072ae;
  padding: 25px 0;
}
```

Now our button is kind of funky looking because the anchor is an inline element, and its padding is not pushing down against the text below it. That's just how inline elements roll:

The easiest way to fix this is to change the display to `block`:

```
.call-to-action {
  border: 2px solid #fff;
  color: #fff;
  background-color: #0072ae;
  padding: 25px 0;
  display: block;
}
```

Following is the output of preceding code:

We need to align the text to the center and add rounded corners now. Add these like so:

```
.call-to-action {
  border: 2px solid #fff;
  color: #fff;
  background-color: #0072ae;
  padding: 25px 0;
  display: block;
  text-align: center;
  border-radius: 10px;
}
```

We don't need to add vendor prefixes to the border radius anymore, as this CSS3 property specification is more mature than the transform and transition properties that both require vendor prefixes. Refresh the browser and you will see our button is starting to look pretty good:

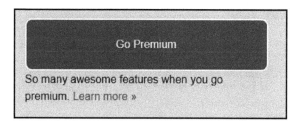

Now we can increase the font size and font weight:

```
font-size: 22px;
font-weight: bold;
```

Following is the output of preceding code:

Our button is looking awesome. Let's add the hover styles. Add a :hover and :focus selector to the CSS. We need to change the color of the border and the text from white to blue; border-color will take care of this. Using the background property with the keyword of none will get rid of the background color:

```
.call-to-action {
  border: 2px solid #fff;
  color: #fff;
  background-color: #0072ae;
  padding: 25px 0;
  display: block;
  text-align: center;
  border-radius: 10px;
}
.call-to-action:hover,
.call-to-action:focus {
  border-color: #0072ae;
  color: #0072ae;
  background: none;
}
```

If we now go to our site and hover over or focus our button, we will see a different treatment on our call-to-action button:

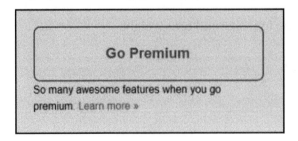

Lastly, let's add in a transition to make the state change more subtle. Add `transition: all .25s ease-in-out` with vendor prefixes to the non-hover state of the button in our CSS:

```
.call-to-action {
  border: 2px solid #fff;
  color: #fff;
  background-color: #0072ae;
  padding: 25px 0;
  display: block;
  text-align: center;
  border-radius: 10px;
  font-size: 22px;
  font-weight: bold;
  -webkit-transition: all .25s ease-in-out;
  transition: all .25s ease-in-out;
}
```

With the transition added, we have a fully styled call-to-action button (minus the correct web font and the gradient).

We've now positioned our call-to-action area and styled the button itself to look extra awesome. Next, let's finish the call-to-action button and learn a little more about CSS gradients.

Gradients

Our big ol' call-to-action button is almost complete. We just need to add a gradient, which, like transforms, transitions, and border-radius, is a feature in CSS3.

Using the ultimate CSS gradient generator

Since the gradient specification and syntax is somewhat lengthy and isn't consistent between browsers, the easiest way to use it is through an app that will create the CSS output for us. Normally, I shy away from things such as these, as I prefer to write my own code, but I will make an exception for gradients. The ultimate CSS gradient generator seems to work very well for me. The site is `www.colorzilla.com/gradient-editor/`. The gradient that we're shooting for is fairly simple. It goes from light blue at the top to darker blue at the bottom:

Let's go to `www.colorzilla.com/gradient-editor/`. The tool defaults to something like this. At the top right, there is even a preview:

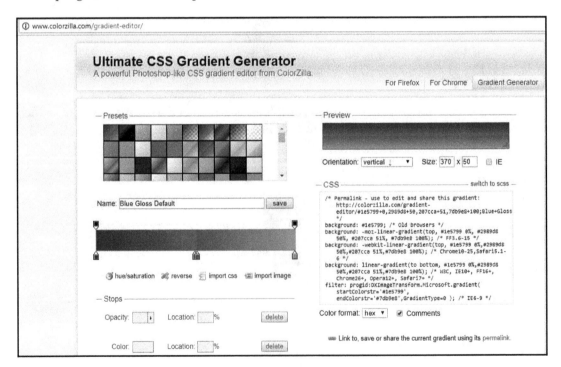

There are four color stops by default and all we need are two. So click on the two stops in the middle of the gradient bar and delete both of them. Clicking on a color stop reveals a new set of controls, including a delete button:

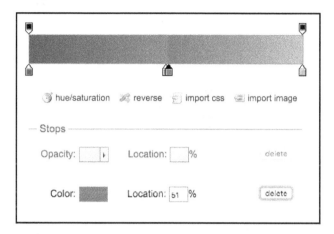

Our gradient bar should look as follows:

Now double-click on the first stop. Your screen should look like this:

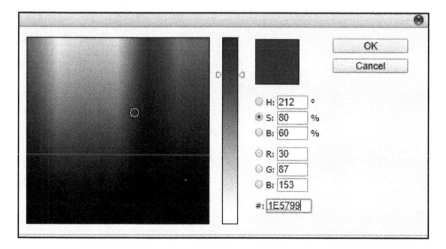

Now we type in the color that we're going to use, which is 33D3FF, and hit **OK**. It's a nice Photoshop-like interface all around:

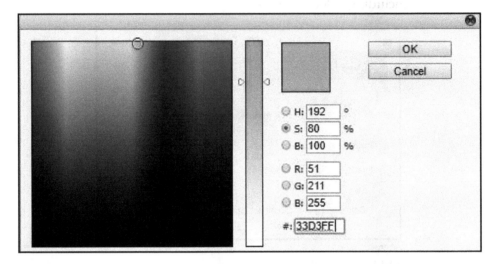

Now, double-click on the second color stop and add the 00718e color:

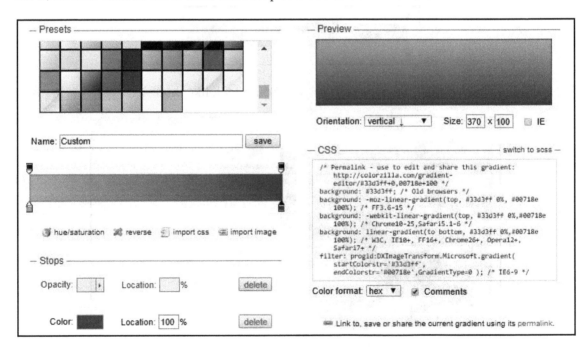

This color and gradient look like what we've been aiming for. But we can move the Color stop up and down the gradient bar a little bit to change the gradient. I'm going to drag it about a third of the way over:

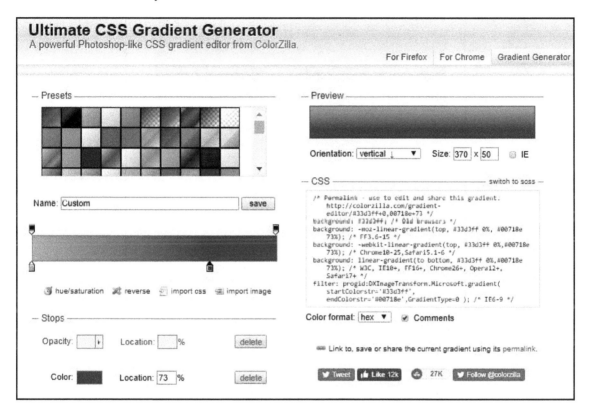

We can also adjust the height of the preview display to look more like the height of our actual call-to-action button by changing the size to 370 x 100:

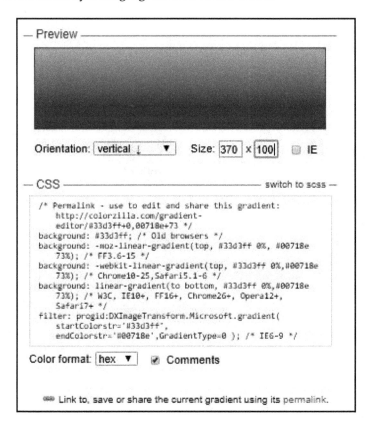

The CSS output is right underneath the preview bar. We can just copy it by clicking on copy. Switch over to our CSS file and paste it inside of our call-to-action selector:

```css
.call-to-action {
  border: 2px solid #fff;
  color: #fff;
  background-color: #0072ae;
  padding: 25px 0;
  display: block;
  text-align: center;
  border-radius: 10px;
  font-size: 22px;
  font-weight: bold;
  -webkit-transition: all .25s ease-in-out;
  transition: all .25s ease-in-out;
  /* Permalink - use to edit and share this gradient:
```

```
http://colorzilla.com/gradient-editor/#33d3ff+0,00718e+73 */
background: #33d3ff; /* Old browsers */
background: -moz-linear-gradient(top, #33d3ff 0%, #00718e 73%);
/* FF3.6-15 */
background: -webkit-gradient(top, #33d3ff 0%,#00718e 73%);
/* Chrome10-25,Safari5.1-6 */
background: -webkit-linear-gradient(to bottom, #33d3ff 0%,#00718e 73%);
/* W3C, IE10+, FF16+, Chrome26+, Opera12+, Safari7+ */
background: -o-linear-gradient(top, #33d3ff 0%, #0071ae 72%);
/* Opera 11.10+ */
background: -ms-linear-gradient(top, #33d3ff 0%, #0071ae 72%);
/* IE10+ */
background: linear-gradient(to bottom, #33d3ff 0%, #0071ae 72%);
/* W3C */
filter:
progid:DXImageTransform.Microsoft.gradient(startColorstr='#33d3ff',
endColorstr='#00718e',GradientType=0 );
/* IE6-9 */
}
```

The CSS output of the ultimate gradient generator

The ultimate gradient generator created eight different properties. Wow! The first is just the background color for older browsers that don't support the gradient's syntax:

```
background: #33d3ff; /* Old browsers */
```

We actually want to change that to #0072AE because that's our official branded color for this site. So add that and delete the background-color: #0072AE property mentioned earlier in the declaration:

```
.call-to-action {
  border: 2px solid #fff;
  color: #fff;
  padding: 25px 0;
  display: block;
  text-align: center;
  border-radius: 10px;
  font-size: 22px;
  font-weight: bold;
  -webkit-transition: all .25s ease-in-out;
  transition: all .25s ease-in-out;
  /* Permalink - use to edit and share this gradient:
  http://colorzilla.com/gradient-editor/#33d3ff+0,00718e+73 */
  background: #0072ae; /* Old browsers */
  background: -moz-linear-gradient(top, #33d3ff 0%, #00718e 73%);
```

```
  /* FF3.6-15 */
  background: -webkit-gradient(top, #33d3ff 0%,#00718e 73%);
  /* Chrome10-25,Safari5.1-6 */
  background: -webkit-linear-gradient(to bottom, #33d3ff 0%,#00718e 73%);
  /* W3C, IE10+, FF16+, Chrome26+, Opera12+, Safari7+ */
  background: -o-linear-gradient(top, #33d3ff 0%, #0071ae 72%);
  /* Opera 11.10+ */
  background: -ms-linear-gradient(top, #33d3ff 0%, #0071ae 72%);
  /* IE10+ */
  background: linear-gradient(to bottom, #33d3ff 0%, #0071ae 72%);
  /* W3C */
  filter:
progid:DXImageTransform.Microsoft.gradient(startColorstr='#33d3ff',
endColorstr='#00718e',GradientType=0 );
  /* IE6-9 */
  }
```

This is a ton of generated CSS. If we take a closer look at some of these, I wonder how many folks out there are using Firefox 3-15, given that the current version is 55? And likewise for Chrome 10-25 when the current version is 60?

```
background: -moz-linear-gradient(top, #33d3ff 0%, #00718e 73%);
/* FF3.6-15 */
background: -webkit-gradient(top, #33d3ff 0%,#00718e 73%);
/* Chrome10-25,Safari5.1-6 */
```

Also, both Chrome and Firefox are evergreen browsers, meaning they automatically update themselves silently without prompting the user.

So, I need a second opinion on all these prefixed versions. Let's see what "Autoprefixer CSS Online" says about this, https://autoprefixer.github.io/. Autoprefixer bills itself as a tool for managing vendor prefixes. It adds missing prefixes and deletes obsolete ones... based on current data on the popularity of browsers and support for vendor prefixes by those browsers.

I'll type in the non-prefixed declaration on the left-side of the Autoprefixer tool and it will spit out what vendor prefixes are needed based on the browser popularity criteria I provide. I want my gradients to show up in all browsers with greater than .1% of market share.

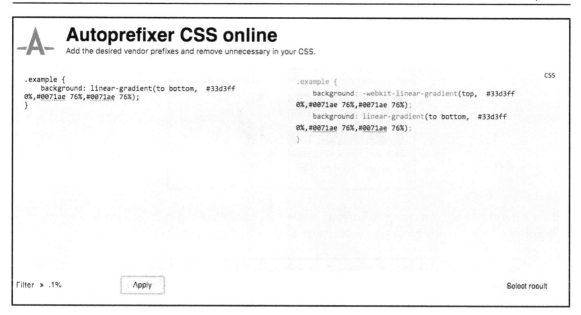

All that leaves is the `-webkit-` vendor prefix and the non-prefixed or W3C standard version:

```
background: -webkit-linear-gradient(top, #33d3ff 0%,#0071ae 76%,#0071ae 76%);
background: linear-gradient(to bottom, #33d3ff 0%,#0071ae 76%,#0071ae 76%);
}
```

So let's update our rule set:

```
.call-to-action {
  border: 2px solid #fff;
  color: #fff;
  padding: 25px 0;
  display: block;
  text-align: center;
  border-radius: 10px;
  font-size: 22px;
  font-weight: bold;
  -webkit-transition: all .25s ease-in-out;
  transition: all .25s ease-in-out;
  background: -webkit-linear-gradient(top, #33d3ff 0%,#0071ae
  76%,#0071ae 76%);
  background: linear-gradient(to bottom, #33d3ff 0%,#0071ae 76%,#0071ae
  76%); }
}
```

I don't know about you, but I feel really good about what we just did!

We'll save this and go to our button. Before a browser refresh, you can see it's a solid color:

When we refresh, we get our gradient, as shown in the following figure. This is very good. It is going to work in all browsers with more than .1% market share.

And just to be very clear, I didn't say 1% market share. I said .1% market share.

In this section, we successfully styled the call-to-action button and applied the gradient using a program that handles the hard stuff for us, allowing us to work that much faster.

Summary

In this chapter, you learned how to create buttons with modular CSS and use multiple classes to change the appearance of our buttons. You also discovered how CSS specificity works and how selectors can overrule each other. You now know how to keep your CSS lightweight and manageable. Finally, you learned how to use transitions, hover states, transforms, and gradients to style our buttons.

In the next chapter, we'll move on to creating our primary navigation tool. By doing this, you'll learn about CSS positioning, CSS3 pseudo classes, CSS3 animations, and how you can create a drop-down menu purely in CSS. This was a lot of fun!

5
Creating the Main Navigation and Drop-Down Menu

In this chapter, we'll build all of the functionality and presentation for the site's primary navigation. This chapter is pretty deep, as building our main nav involves pseudo classes; static, absolute, relative, and fixed positioning; and CSS animations.

Starting the navigation

In this section, we'll begin by creating the cleanest HTML possible and then plug in the basic CSS to get it started. The following is what our final site should look like; this is what we're aiming for:

We have a typical horizontal navigation bar. Some of the items have a drop-down menu. We also have a shark logo on the left-hand side of the nav bar, which is overhanging nicely.

The semantic HTML for building a menu

Let's jump right in and type the HTML we need. We'll start with this nice, big HTML comment. As you may have noticed, I like these big guys. This is because it's easier to locate parts of the code I need quickly:

```
<!--
===============
Nav
===============
-->
```

We'll wrap everything in the HTML5 `nav` element and apply the `grouping` class because we'll be floating everything in there. A clearfix will eventually be necessary so that the container doesn't collapse:

```
<!--
===============
Nav
===============
-->
<nav class="grouping">

</nav>
```

Now let's add a `figure` element that will wrap our shark image:

```
<nav class="grouping">
    <figure>
        <img src="images/sharky.png" alt="sharky">
    </figure>
</nav>
```

Next, we'll start an unordered list with the `primary-nav` class. Long ago, it was determined that it is very semantic to use a list for navigation because it's essentially a list of links:

```
<nav class="grouping">
    <figure>
        <img src="images/sharky.png" alt="sharky">
    </figure>
    <ul class="primary-nav">
    </ul>
</nav>
```

We'll start with four list items. We'll put an anchor tag inside each one of them:

```
<nav class="grouping">
    <figure>
        <img src="images/sharky.png" alt="sharky">
    </figure>
    <ul class="primary-nav">
      <li><a href="#"></a></li>
      <li><a href="#"></a></li>
      <li><a href="#"></a></li>
      <li><a href="#"></a></li>
    </ul>
</nav>
```

When we apply this to our site, we'll end up with a shark image and four links, all stacked vertically:

We need to lay out these four links horizontally, like blocks. We'll do this with floats and a few other properties.

Using CSS to style the navigation

In our CSS, first we'll find the big block comment for the navigation:

```
/***************
nav
***************/
```

We'll then target the `primary-nav.` class. Let's use a special type of descendant selector that only targets the first level of list items:

```
.primary-nav > li
```

This is important. We're doing this because later we'll nest another unordered list within these list items to get a drop-down menu. Let's say we create the same selector without the greater than symbol:

```
.primary-nav li
```

This targets any and every `li` tag inside of `primary-nav`--children, grandchildren, great-grandchildren, and so on. If you only want to target immediate children, use this selector; it is known as the child combinator:

```
.primary-nav > li
```

The greater than sign between the elements ensures we are only targeting direct children. Let's also float those list items to the left, then refresh the browser:

```
.primary-nav > li {
   float: left;
}
```

Following is the output of preceding code:

That's a start; there's a lot more to do.

Let's use the same type of child combinator to target only direct children anchors of a direct children list item of `.primary-nav`:

```
.primary-nav > li {
  float: left;
}
.primary-nav > li > a {

}
```

So we're going to add padding of `25px` to the top and `0` to the left and right. We'll also add a width; each one will be `150px` wide, and we'll give each one a `border-left` of 1 pixel solid and color them gray:

```
.primary-nav > li > a {
  padding: 25px 0;
  width: 150px;
  border-left: 1px solid #ada791;
}
```

We see that it's now starting to loosely resemble our final nav:

We'll now drop this whole ruleset in our CSS, under the primary nav selectors:

```css
.primary-nav > li > a {
  padding: 25px 0;
  width: 150px;
  border-left: 1px solid #ada791;
}
nav li a{
  font-family: Arial, Helvetica, sans-serif;
  color: #766e65;
  text-transform: uppercase;
  font-size: 15px;
  text-align: center;
  -webkit-transition: 0.15s background-color linear;
  transition: 0.15s background-color linear;
}
```

This is a more familiar descendant selector for some of the styles that we'll apply to the main navigation items - as well as - the drop-down navigation items. This is a nice **DRY (Don't Repeat Yourself)** approach, so we don't have to re-write this code later for the drop-down menu. Let's examine this ruleset more closely. Basically, we're setting `font-family` to `Arial`:

```css
font-family: Arial, Helvetica, sans-serif;
```

We have this text color:

```css
color: #766e65;
```

We're using `text-transform: uppercase`. This is going to make sure that we could type lowercase letters for the navigation items in the HTML, and it would transform each one of those letters into uppercase characters. This way, if we decide later that the regular case is better than all uppercase, then all we would need to do is change it in one place, instead of updating the entire HTML:

```css
text-transform: uppercase;
```

Next, we have a font size:

```css
font-size: 15px;
```

We also align the text to the center:

```css
text-align: center;
```

We add a transition as well, as discussed in the previous chapter. This is to transition the background color in:

```
-webkit-transition: 0.15s background-color linear;
transition: 0.15s background-color linear;
```

This is what we get when we save the changes and refresh the browser:

We have some problems. One problem is that our anchor tags are inline elements, so what's happening is they're not actually behaving like block-level elements. Therefore, one of the things we can do is float them to the left as well. For this, add a `float: left` property to the `.primary-nav > li > a` ruleset:

```
.primary-nav > li > a {
  float: left;
  padding: 25px 0;
  width: 150px;
  border-left: 1px solid #ada791;
}
```

Following is the output of preceding code:

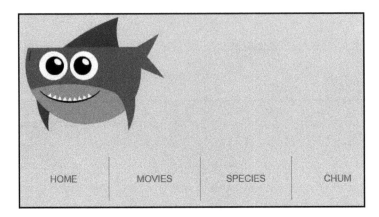

This looks a lot better.

Now let's target the focus and hover states. Underneath our last ruleset, we'll add another ruleset:

```
nav li a:focus,
nav li a:hover,
nav li a.active {
   background-color: #eb2428;
   color: #fff;
}
```

This is going to target not only the focus and hover states, but also the class of active. This isn't a "state" necessarily, as you would think of a focus or hover state. This is a class that we're going to apply to elements to signify that you're on that page. It's going to be the same as the hover state. Moving on, we apply the color red to the background and the color white to the text. Now, when we refresh it, we get the hover and focus states, which is good:

The only thing we have to do now is figure out the position of the nav bar and push the whole thing to the right, because right now it's sitting underneath our image. So let's float the entire nav bar to the right. Let's do that:

```
.primary-nav {
  float: right;
}
```

Following is the output of preceding code:

As you can see, this works out fairly well. We have the entire nav sitting below the shark. We could fix this by floating the shark to the left, but a few nice features can be achieved if we use absolute positioning, which is what we'll get to a little later in this chapter.

Finally though, let's tidy up this nav just a little bit more by adding a white background and restricting our image to just 160px of width.

```
/****************
nav
****************/
nav {
  background-color: #fff;
}
nav img {
  width: 160px;
}
```

Here's the site without the white background and our shark is quite large:

When we refresh the site, though, we will have the white background we want and a smaller shark:

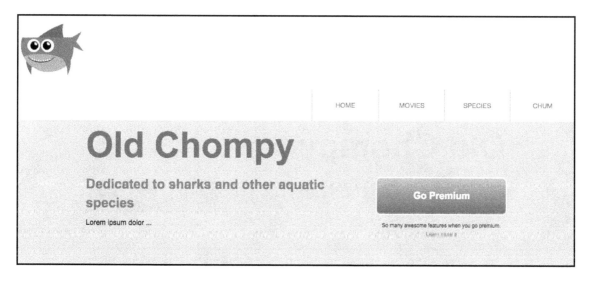

Okay, we've built the HTML and most of the CSS for the first layer of the nav. Next, you'll learn how pseudo - classes can help with certain issues in our navigation.

Using pseudo classes

You have already learned how to add classes to elements to apply special styles to them. You are always required to go into the HTML to add the class. Sometimes this can be a problem. For instance, when the content is generated dynamically through a content management system, you may not be able to edit any element because it may not exist in a static HTML file. Enter pseudo classes. Pseudo classes allow you to target elements based on their position in the HTML, and based on other qualities. In this section, we'll look at the `first-child` pseudo class that can help us style our navigation. We'll then look at several other pseudo classes, for example, `last-child` and `nth-child`.

Ultimately, I don't want the home menu, which is the first menu, to have `border-left` because it's the first element. So, I want to get rid of it:

The first child

In order to target the first element in our CSS, we'll add `first-child` after the anchor element. So we'll copy this selector and paste it underneath itself:

```
.primary-nav > li > a {
  float: left;
  padding: 25px 0;
  width: 150px;
  border-left: 1px solid #ada791;
}
```

We'll then add `:first-child` to the selector, delete the properties, and add `border-left` with the value set as `none`:

```
.primary-nav > li > a:first-child {
  border-left: none;
}
```

Save this, go to the site, and refresh the page:

The result isn't what we might have expected. We actually removed the left border from every item in our navigation. This is because, firstly, all the anchors are children inside of their immediate parent, li. So we should actually go about this differently.

Taking a quick look at nav in our HTML. The anchor is the first element that's inside of li; there is no second element. So, if we want to target the first element inside of ul, it wouldn't be the anchor, but the list item, which is <li>:

```
<nav class="grouping">
    <figure>
        <img src="images/sharky.png" alt="sharky">
    </figure>
    <ul class="primary-nav">
        <li><a href="#">Home</a></li>
        <li><a href="#">Movies</a></li>
        <li><a href="#">Species</a></li>
        <li><a href="#">Chum</a></li>
    </ul>
</nav>
```

In our CSS, we're going to actually move the pseudo class from here:

```
.primary-nav > li > a:first-child {
```

We'll remove it from the a and attach it to the li, as demonstrated here:

```
.primary-nav > li:first-child > a {
```

We now have our `border-left` property on all of the nav elements, except for the first one:

One thing about `first-child` is that it has to be the first element that appears inside of the parent. So even though we targeted `li` specifically as the first child of the primary nav, if we had something else inside of `ul` before the first `li` tag, then our selector wouldn't have worked. Let's take a look at this. Let's add an `h2` as a child of the `ul` element:

```
<nav class="grouping">
    <figure>
        <img src="images/sharky.png" alt="sharky">
    </figure>
    <ul class="primary-nav">
        <h2>not valid html</h2>
        <li><a href="#">Home</a></li>
        <li><a href="#">Movies</a></li>
        <li><a href="#">Species</a></li>
        <li><a href="#">Chum</a></li>
    </ul>
</nav>
```

This is not valid HTML, but for fun, note that we get our left-hand side border back on the first `li` tag:

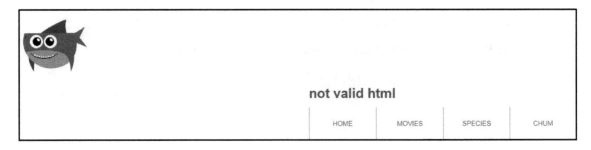

That's because it's no longer the first child. The `h2` is now the first child. This is a common mistake when working with the `first-child` pseudo class.

The last child

Now let's look at the `last-child` pseudo class. Let's create a new selector:

```
.primary-nav > li:last-child > a {
}
```

We'll make the example a little more obvious by setting the background color as bright pink and the color of the text as white:

```
.primary-nav > li:last-child > a {
  background-color: deeppink
  color: #fff;
}
```

Now our last child gets those properties applied to it:

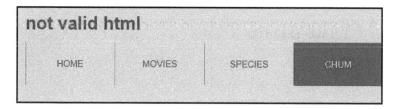

I prefer `first-child` because it has deeper support going back to IE7, whereas `last-child` support starts at IE9.

nth-child pseudo class

The `nth-child` class allows us to pick any occurrence of an element within its parent. Let's get into the CSS and change `last-child` to `nth-child(2)`:

```
.primary-nav > li:nth-child(2) > a {
  background-color: deeppink;
  color: #fff;
}
```

Save the code and refresh the site:

So, on our site, the pink color should actually be applied to h2 and **HOME** because the h2 is the first element inside the ul and **HOME** is the second.

If you are a JavaScript person, nth-child is not zero indexed, so the first one is not zero: The first one is one.

With this in mind, let's set nth-child to 1: which is essentially the same as using first-child:

```
.primary-nav > li:nth-child(1) > a {
  background-color: deeppink;
  color: #fff;
}
```

Let's get rid of this h2 tag from our HTML real quick:

```
<nav class="grouping">
    <figure>
        <img src="images/sharky.png" alt="sharky">
    </figure>
    <ul class="primary-nav">
        <!--<h2>not valid html</h2>-->
        <li><a href="#">Home</a></li>
        <li><a href="#">Movies</a></li>
        <li><a href="#">Species</a></li>
        <li><a href="#">Chum</a></li>
    </ul>
</nav>
```

We now see that the pink color stays on the first nav item:

You can also use the keywords `odd` and `even`. So if I were to throw `even` or `odd` in there, you'll get the numbers two and four with those properties applied:

```
.primary-nav > li:nth-child(even) > a {
  background-color: deeppink;
  color: #fff;
}
```

Refresh the site and you will get the following result:

This is an excellent technique for zebra striping a table or a list for added readability.

nth-of-type pseudo class

There is also `nth-of-type`. Add `nth-of-type(2)` to the `primary-nav` selector in our CSS:

```
.primary-nav > li:nth-of-type(2) > a {
  background-color: deeppink;
  color: #fff;
}
```

The difference between `nth-of-type` and `nth-child` is that `nth-of-type` is pre-qualified to only look for an element that it's attached to. For example, in our case we've attached `nth-of-type` to an `li`, so it only matches `li` tags:

```
.primary-nav > li:nth-of-type(2) > a {
  background-color: deeppink;
  color: #fff;
}
```

Let's see this in action. Let's add back our h2 tag:

```
<nav class="grouping">
    <figure>
        <img src="images/sharky.png" alt="sharky">
    </figure>
    <ul class="primary-nav">
        <h2>not valid html</h2>
        <li><a href="#">Home</a></li>
        <li><a href="#">Movies</a></li>
        <li><a href="#">Species</a></li>
        <li><a href="#">Chum</a></li>
    </ul>
</nav>
```

It's not going to refer to just any child inside of the ul. We now see that the second li tag has those properties applied:

So nth-of-type is more precise than nth-child. Browser support for nth-child and nth-of-type starts at IE9 and later versions, as well as other major browsers.

In this section, we've learned about a few pseudo classes that allow you to target elements based on their order in the HTML. However, these aren't the first pseudo classes we've used so far. I'm mainly referring to state-based pseudo classes, such as hover and focus, which we've been using plenty up to this point. In the next section, we'll switch gears and discuss CSS positioning to further advance our navigation.

Absolute positioning

In this section, we're going to start working on the different CSS positioning properties, as well as their complementary offset properties. First, we'll absolutely position the shark logo and follow that up by using fixed positioning for the entire navigation bar.

Absolutely positioning the shark

We've got our menu in place, but the shark clearly sits on top of the nav. We need it to be aligned horizontally, more or less. We need to fix the shark so it overhangs the nav bar as well. We'll also want the entire nav to remain stuck to the top of the browser window:

So let's go to our CSS and add `position: absolute` to the `nav figure` selector. Create a new selector underneath the `nav` ruleset. We'll call it `nav figure` and give it a `position` property with the value of `absolute`:

```
/****************
nav
***************/
nav {
  background-color: #fff;
}
nav figure{
  position: absolute;
}
nav img {
  width: 160px;
}
```

Right away, that looks a lot better:

Let's talk about what we've just done. All elements, by default, have a `static` position. Static elements adhere to the *normal flow*, meaning block-level elements simply are stacked on top of each other as long as they're not floated. Changing `position` to `absolute` takes it out of the normal flow. Its block qualities disappear and other elements aren't affected by it at all. It can be thought of as something that exists on another plane or level. Once positioned absolutely, you can start using offset properties, such as `top`, `right`, `bottom`, and `left`.

Let's do that. Add two more properties to the `nav figure` element, namely `top` and `left`:

```
nav figure{
   position: absolute;
   top: -50px;
   left: 50px;
}
```

These are going to function a lot like `margin-top` and `margin-left`. If you view the results, you should see that the shark is `50px` from the left and `-50px` from the top:

So what happens when we switch the `top` property with `bottom` and the `left` property with `right`:

```
nav figure{
   position: absolute;
   bottom: : -50px;
   right: 50px;
}
```

It actually moves the shark all the way to the bottom and the right of the page!

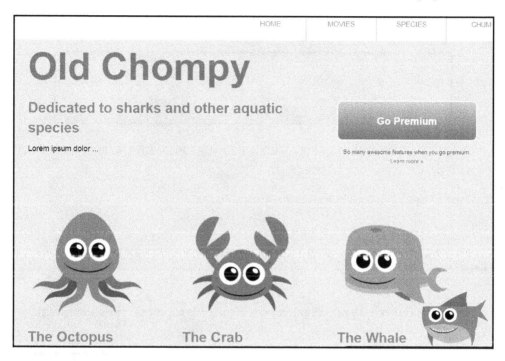

This image makes it a lot clearer how offset properties work combined with absolute positioning. The offset properties are based on the browser viewport now, but typically we don't want to do this; instead, we want to base the absolute position off of its parent element by setting the parent element to position: relative.

The parent element of the image is the nav selector, so let's set that to relative:

```
nav {
  background-color: #fff;
  position: relative;
}
nav figure{
  position: absolute;
  bottom:  50px;
  right: 50px;
}
```

You can see that even now we're `50px` from the right because the nav extends all the way to the right edge, and we're `-50px` from the bottom of the nav because the shark is extending below the nav bar there:

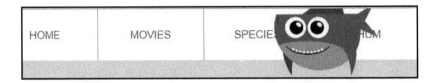

The `position: relative` declaration establishes itself as a coordinate system for children elements with `position: absolute`.

Let's move the shark back to where it is supposed to be:

```
nav figure{
  position: absolute;
  top: -20px;
  left: 50px;
}
```

The shark overlaps our nav bar nicely. It's now sitting on top of our headline, which is kind of funny, but we'll come back to this in a moment:

First, let's make the entire nav bar stick to the top by adding `position: fixed`.

Using fixed positioning for the nav bar

Let's change the nav bar's `position` property from `absolute` to `fixed` and take a look at the result:

```
nav {
  background-color: #fff;
  position: fixed;
}
```

Following is the output of the preceding code:

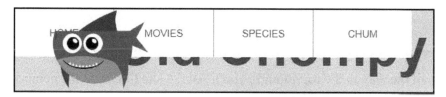

The `fixed` value, such as `relative`, still acts like a coordinate system for any absolutely positioned child or descendant elements, but it also has some superpowers. *Right now, those superpowers are totally breaking our nav.* Here's the issue: `position: relative` still keeps its block-element qualities, while `position: fixed` loses a lot of those block qualities when it's removed from the *normal flow*, and the nav now looks kind of funny: it's not stretching to the full width of the browser window. Let's fix this with some offset properties.

We can actually stretch the nav by saying `left: 0` and `right: 0`. Let's also add `top: 0` to make sure there's no doubt it'll be positioned at the very top:

```
nav {
  background-color: #fff;
  position: fixed;
  left: 0;
  right: 0;
  top: 0;
}
```

That looks better. And, because the nav's position is set to fixed, as we scroll down the page everything inside the nav is stuck to the top and everything else moves underneath it:

If you scroll all the way to the top though, you'll see the site title now sits behind the nav. This is because the nav is no longer part of the normal flow:

Let's fix this by adding `margin-top` to `intro-content` and our `go-premium` button. We'll go to our `go-premium` ruleset and add a value of `150px` to `margin-top`:

```
.go-premium {
    width: 300px;
    float: left;
    margin-top: 150px;
}
```

We'll also go to our `intro-content` ruleset and add a `margin-top` of `125px`:

```
.intro-content {
    width: 600px;
    margin-right: 60px;
    float: left;
    margin-top: 125px;
}
```

Now it looks very good:

So you've learned about relative, absolute, and fixed positioning. You also learned that the default position of every element is static. `relative` position creates a coordinate system for children. `absolute` position allows you to move an element into its own universe and position it aggressively, based on the closest relatively positioned parent element. `fixed` position will make the element sticky based on the browser's viewport, and not based on any relatively positioned elements. Both `absolute` and `fixed` elements will serve as coordinate systems, relative to other child elements. In the next section, we'll look at building the drop-down menu, where we'll again use absolute positioning.

Building the drop-down menu

Let's create a pure CSS drop-down menu! We'll start by adding the markup and follow it up by adding the CSS.

Creating the basic HTML list

Typically, when building a component such as a drop-down menu that's usually hidden from view, I build it as if it were not hidden. Then, once it's complete and fully styled, I create the drop-down behavior. That's what we'll do here as well. So let's create the HTML within our existing `index.html` document. We'll go to the unordered list of our nav bar, as shown here:

```
<nav class="grouping">
    <figure>
        <img src="images/sharky.png" alt="Shark">
    </figure>
```

```
        <ul class="primary-nav grouping">
            <li><a href="#">Home</a></li>
            <li><a href="shark-movies.html">Movies</a></li>
            <li><a href="#">Species</a></li>
            <li><a href="#">Chum</a></li>
        </ul>
    </nav>
```

It's best practice to build menus inside of an unordered list, where each menu item is an anchor inside of a list item. For drop-down menus, we'll need to nest another `ul` tag inside of the `li` with the dropdown. We'll nest it here:

```
<li><a href="shark-movies.html">Movies</a></li>
```

But first, we'll add a special class called `has-submenu` to any nav item that will have a dropdown:

```
<li class="has-submenu"><a href="shark-movies.html">Movies</a></li>
```

This way, with the `has-submenu` class, we can target these `li` tags and their descendants specifically in the CSS. Inside of this movies `li` tag, we'll create a new `ul` with `li` tags, and inside these `li` tags, we'll put in an anchor tag. Here's the markup for the dropdown menu:

```
<nav class="grouping">
    <figure>
        <img src="images/sharky.png" alt="Shark">
    </figure>
    <ul class="primary-nav grouping">
        <li><a href="#">Home</a></li>
      <li class="has-submenu"><a href="shark-movies.html">Movies</a>
            <ul>
                <li><a href="#">Jaws</a></li>
                <li><a href="#">Sharknado</a></li>
                <li><a href="#">Open Water</a></li>
            </ul>
        </li>
        <li><a href="#">Species</a></li>
        <li><a href="#">Chum</a></li>
    </ul>
</nav>
```

There are three submenus in the dropdown:

We just need to style this to make it look like our final menu.

Styling the dropdown

We need to style the dropdown appropriately to fit with our existing menu. This is the effect we're going to aim for:

I want to separate the drop-down menu's styling from the main nav's styling. We'll do this by creating this big `Drop Down Menu` comment we have here underneath the main nav:

```
/***************
Drop Down Menu
***************/
```

The dropdown can have its own little section here. So let's start by targeting only the `ul` inside of `has-sub menu`. In order to have the submenu placed outside of the white nav bar, let's position it absolutely and `70px` from the `top`:

```
/ ***************
Drop Down Menu
*************** /
.has-submenu ul{
  position: absolute;
  top: 70px;
}
```

This gives us the following effect:

Now all we need to do is style the drop-down menu so it looks like it's supposed to. Note how, on our site, none of the `li` tags are floated to the left like our main nav. This is because, as you'll remember, we used a type of descendant selector that only targeted direct children `li` of `primary-nav`. We don't need to cancel out those styles from before. Lets' go back though and see what would happen if we didn't do that by changing those selectors.

Here is where are child combinator selectors are:

```
.primary-nav > li {
  float: left;
}
.primary-nav > li > a {
  float: left;
  padding: 25px 0;
  width: 150px;
  border-left: 1px solid #ada791;
}
```

For a quick test, let's remove the greater than symbols from both selectors:

```
.primary-nav li {
  float: left;
}
.primary-nav li a {
  float: left;
  padding: 25px 0;
  width: 150px;
  border-left: 1px solid #ada791;
}
```

Here's what that looks like:

Note that all of the styles that we have in the top menu are repeated in the submenu. That's kind of what we want to avoid, because we don't want to write additional CSS that cancels out the whole menu floating left and having borders where we don't need them. So let's add those greater than signs back to our .primary-nav selectors:

```
.primary-nav > li {
  float: left;
}
.primary-nav > li > a {
  float: left;
  padding: 25px 0;
  width: 150px;
  border-left: 1px solid #ada791;
}
```

Alright, let's add the white background and the borders to .has-submenu. Where changing the background-color and adding borders on the bottom, left, and right. We don't want a border at the top, so instead of using the border shorthand, we will be using border-bottom, border-left, and border-right:

```
/ * * * * * * * * * * * * * * * *
Drop Down Menu
* * * * * * * * * * * * * * * * /
.has-submenu ul {
  position: absolute;
  top: 70px;
  background-color: #fff;
```

```
    border-bottom: 1px solid #ada791;
    border-left: 1px solid #ada791;
    border-right: 1px solid #ada791;
}
```

Now its starting to resemble a drop-down menu:

One of the obvious problems is the width. We need to give it a `width` of `150px` to match the width of its parent element. Also, let's add `border-radius` to the `bottom-left` and `bottom-right` corners:

```
/***************
Drop Down Menu
***************/
.has-submenu ul{
    position: absolute;
    top: 70px;
    background-color: #fff;
    border-bottom: 1px solid #ada791;
    border-left: 1px solid #ada791;
    border-right: 1px solid #ada791;
    width: 150px;
    border-radius: 0 0 15px 15px
}
```

Note the shorthand for `border-radius`. It's very similar to the margin and padding shorthand. The first value is for the top-left corner, then it goes clockwise from there. So the second value is for the top-right corner, the third is for bottom-right, and the fourth for bottom-left.

Now we have the `width` and `border-radius` we need:

One weird thing is that it looks like the text of our nav items isn't centrally aligned. The text of the anchor elements is aligned in the center. You can see this if you inspect this element by right-clicking on the `a` tags text and selecting "inspect":

The problem is that `li` tags take the full width, whereas `a` tags are inline elements and only take up as much width as they need. Let's add a new selector: `.has-submenu a` with `display: block` and `padding` of `20px` for the top and bottom:

```css
.has-submenu a{
    display: block;
    padding: 20px 0;
}
```

The dropdown looks much better:

Our hover states carry over from our main nav, which is good. The only problem is that our last hover state--**Open Water**--is hiding the rounded corners:

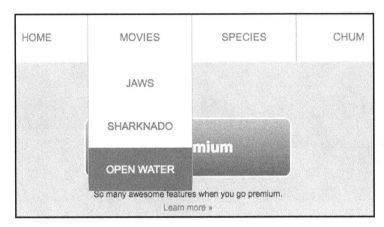

Fixing the hover state

There are two ways in which we can fix the rounded corners getting lost when we hover over the **Open Water** submenu item. The first is using the last-child pseudo class, which you learned about a couple of sections earlier, to target the a selector and the last li selector of the submenu. This should work just fine, but if we want to get even deeper browser support, we need to use a different technique that uses overflow: hidden on the ul element—the parent. I tend to like the overflow: hidden approach here because it's minimal and has deeper browser support:

```
/***************
Drop Down Menu
***************/
.has-submenu ul{
  position: absolute;
  top: 70px;
  background-color: #fff;
  border-bottom: 1px solid #ada791;
  border-left: 1px solid #ada791;
  border-right: 1px solid #ada791;
  width: 150px;
  border-radius: 0 0 15px 15px;
  overflow: hidden;
}
```

If we look at the browser now, the problem is fixed:

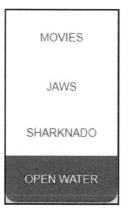

Now we're left with the static menu. It's always open. We need to create a drop-down behavior to appear when you hover your mouse over the **MOVIES** navigation item. One way to do this is to hide the drop-down menu by default and then show it using the `hover` and `focus` pseudo classes.

Hide the drop-down menu by default using `display:  none`. Let's start by hiding the entire `ul` tag using `display:  none`:

```
/***************
Drop Down Menu
***************/
.has-submenu ul{
  position: absolute;
  top: 70px;
  background-color: #fff;
  border-bottom: 1px solid #ada791;
  border-left: 1px solid #ada791;
  border-right: 1px solid #ada791;
  width: 150px;
  border-radius: 0 0 15px 15px;
  overflow: hidden;
  display: none;
}
```

We can target `ul` only when `has-submenu` is hovered by creating a new selector, `.has-submenu:hover ul`:

```
/***************
Drop Down Menu
***************/
```

```
.has-submenu ul{
  position: absolute;
  top: 70px;
  background-color: #fff;
  border-bottom: 1px solid #ada791;
  border-left: 1px solid #ada791;
  border-right: 1px solid #ada791;
  width: 150px;
  border-radius: 0 0 15px 15px;
  display: none;
}
.has-submenu a {
  display: block;
  padding: 20px 0;
}
.has-submenu:hover ul {
  display: block;
}
```

As per this ruleset, whenever you hover over the **Movies** menu, the `ul` element that sits inside of it is going to be displayed. Then, because we added `display: none` to the previous selector—the nonhover state, by default, that `ul` tag, which is a drop-down menu, won't be displayed. There is no submenu available by default now:

Now when we hover over the **Movies** menu, the submenu appears:

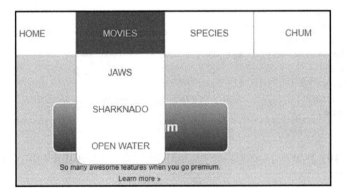

One thing I should also mention is that `display: none` has accessibility issues, as screen readers are unable to announce content with `display: none`.

There is an alternative as well: use an **off-screen hidden technique**, which involves a little extra work, but is well worth it.

Hiding the drop-down menu using the off-screen hidden technique

The basic idea is to absolutely position an element far, far away from the visible screen so that it isn't visible, but screen readers can still announce it. There's a lot more to learn about accessibility. I recommend that you start by checking out the article at `https://css-tricks.com/places-its-tempting-to-use-display-none-but-dont/` for more information, at least on how to use off-screen hidden techniques, and then go from there with regard to accessibility:

Web accessibility is a topic with so much depth that it deserves a book of its own. So I cannot do it thorough justice here. Although, instead of using `display: none` to hide our drop-down menu, we can replace it with something similar to the following to make it more accessible:

```
.accessibly-hidden {
  position: absolute;
  top: -9999px;
  left: -9999px;
}
```

This will *hide* the content from sighted users, but still announce the content for screen reader users.

We have put the drop-down menu to bed without much of a fuss. It worked out perfectly. Your first attempt at creating a drop-down menu may not always go this smoothly, but using these tips, you can avoid some of the problems you might encounter when creating it.

My two biggest tips are the following:

- Build the drop-down menu initially as if it will always be visible, then hide it after you have styled it up and it looks good.
- Since the recommended approach is to use an unordered list inside an unordered list, it's worth carefully setting up your rules sets to avoid confusion. For instance, one ruleset for styles that apply to both the parent `ul` and the child `ul` (that is, `ul li`); another ruleset that only applies to the parent `ul` and `li` selector using the child combinator (that is, `ul > li`); and finally, a ruleset that applies only to the child `ul` (that is, `.has-submenu ul`). This way, you won't have to create a bunch of potentially confusing override styles for the child `ul` later.

The next piece of the navigation requires us to actually create the drop-down effect; we will use a CSS animation to achieve this.

CSS animations (part 1)

Our main navigation is now coming together, and our drop-down functionality is almost complete. One of the last finishing touches required for the dropdown is the CSS animation, to allow the drop-down menu to animate downward smoothly. Animations are a lot of fun, and modern browsers, including Chrome, Firefox, Opera, and browsers starting with IE10, support them. IE9 will still show a drop-down menu, but it will simply appear/disappear. An animation is very similar to a transition, but instead of simply animating a state change, we can animate static elements and use different animation properties and key frames to control the animation. We'll get more into this later. So here's what we're going to do in this section: We'll define the `animation-name`, `animation-duration`, and `animation-timing-function` inside the selector of the element we want to animate. After that, we'll go ahead and define the key frames of what we're going to animate.

Defining the animation name, duration, and timing function

Let's recall our dropdown menu's CSS:

```
/****************
Drop Down Menu
****************/
.has-submenu ul{
  position: absolute;
  top: 70px;
  background-color: #fff;
  border-bottom: 1px solid #ada791;
  border-left: 1px solid #ada791;
  border-right: 1px solid #ada791;
  width: 150px;
  border-radius: 0 0 15px 15px;
  overflow: hidden;
  display: none;
}
.has-submenu a {
  display: block;
  padding: 20px 0;
}
.has-submenu:hover ul {
  display: block;
}
```

Let's target the `hover` state of `has-submenu` as follows:

```
.has-submenu:hover ul {
  display: block;
}
```

For now, we'll use use the nonprefixed/W3C standard property names and go back and add the needed prefixes at the end. So, to do an animation, we use `animation-name` and use `slideDown` as the animation name:

```
.has-submenu:hover ul {
  display: block;
  animation-name: slideDown;
}
```

I can name this animation anything I want, provided I don't use any spaces. Like class names, I can't begin it with a number either. Also, the keyword **none** can't be used as an animation name as it is reserved as a special keyword for removing the animation. Next, we're going to specify the animation duration in seconds, and the animation's timing function:

```
.has-submenu:hover ul {
  display: block;
  animation-name:slideDown;
  animation-duration: .25s;
  animation-timing-function: ease;
}
```

For the `timing-function` I've used `ease`, but you can also specify `linear`, `ease-in`, `ease-out`, and `ease-in-out` functions, which are the same timing functions we used for `transitions`. This code by itself doesn't do anything. We have to specify what happens when we animate using `@keyframes`. So below the last ruleset, we'll add a `@keyframes` *at-rule* with our animation name that we came up with previously `slideDown`:

```
@keyframes slideDown {
}
```

Inside curly braces, we'll specify the `from` and `to` time offsets:

```
@keyframes slideDown {
    from {}
    to {}
}
```

What ever's inside the `from` curly braces will be the starting point, and what ever's inside the `to` curly braces will be the end point of the animation. We could put several properties inside of the animation; let's start with the `translateY` transform function with negative 100 percent:

```
@keyframes slideDown {
    from {transform: translateY(-100%);}
    to {}
}
```

This is going to move the unordered list up by negative 100 percent to make it the starting point. The percentage being the height of the element. `50%` would move it down half the elements height, whereas `100%` would move it down the full height of the element. So `-100%` is going to push it up vertically the entire height of the element. The `translateY` function is new to us here. It's a lot like `translate`, except that it's only for vertical translations. The `translateX` function can do horizontal translations. Inside the `to` curly braces, we'll set `translateY` to `0%`:

```
@keyframes slideDown {
    from {transform: translateY(-100%);}
    to {transform: translateY(0%);}
}
```

We can now see the menu animating downward:

Setting additional keyframes

So far, our animation could just as easily have been done with a `transition`, as nothing new has really been introduced. But the power of animation comes where we can set additional keyframes. Let's change `from` and `to` in our CSS to `0%` and `100%`, respectively, like so:

```
@keyframes slideDown {
  0% {transform: translateY(-100%);}
  100% {transform: translateY(0%);}
}
```

Instead of adding just a start and an end, we can add any number of stops between these two points. Let's add a new keyframe, say `90%`, with a `translateY` of `10%`:

```
@keyframes slideDown {
  0% {transform: translateY(-100%);}
  90% {transform: translateY(10%);}
  100% {transform: translateY(0%);}
}
```

We're translating the position of the dropdown going from -100% to 10% during the first 90% of that 0.25 seconds. Then, in the last 10% of the 0.25 seconds, the vertical movement goes from 10% to 0%. This gives the animation a little bit of a hop, or bounce, at the end:

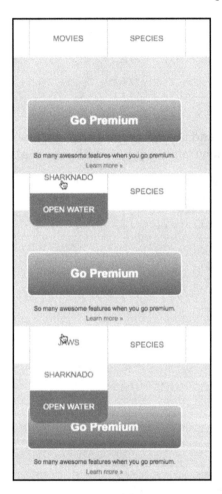

Not only can we add multiple keyframes, but also multiple properties per keyframe. So let's add opacity to our animation. Let's say we start with the keyframes being invisible and end at an opacity of 1, which is fully visible. We won't animate opacity at 90% keyframe:

```
@keyframes slideDown {
  0% {transform: translateY(-100%);opacity: 0;}
  90% {transform: translateY(10%);}
  100% {transform: translateY(0%);opacity: 1;}
}
```

The menu now animates downward and fades in:

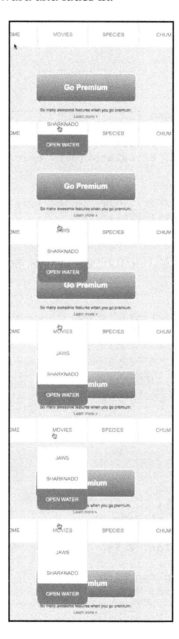

Vendor prefixes

To wrap up our drop-down animation, let's get maximum browser support by adding in the necessary vendor prefixes:

```
/****************
Drop Down Menu
****************/
@-webkit-keyframes slideDown {
  0% {-webkit-transform: translateY(-100%); opacity: 0; }
  90% {-webkit-transform: translateY(10%);}
  100% {-webkit-transform: translateY(0%); opacity: 1; }
}
@keyframes slideDown {
  0% {transform: translateY(-100%); opacity: 0; }
  90% {transform: translateY(10%);}
  100% {transform: translateY(0%); opacity: 1; }
}
.has-submenu ul{
  position: absolute;
  top: 70px;
  background-color: #fff;
  border-bottom: 1px solid #ada791;
  border-left: 1px solid #ada791;
  border-right: 1px solid #ada791;
  width: 150px;
  border-radius: 0 0 15px 15px;
  overflow: hidden;
  display: none;
}
.has-submenu a {
  display: block;
  padding: 20px 0;
}
.has-submenu:hover ul {
  display: block;
  -webkit-animation-name: slideDown;
  animation-name: slideDown;
  -webkit-animation-duration: 2.5s;
  animation-duration: 2.5s;
  -webkit-animation-timing-function: ease;
  animation-timing-function: ease;
}
```

Both @keyframes animation need the -webkit- vendor prefix, as well as the transform, animation-name, animation-duration, and animation-timing-function property.

As we come to the end of this section, we have our drop-down menu animation in place. CSS animations are supported in IE10 and later, so older versions of IE and other older browsers won't show the animation, but they will still have access to the menu and all of its content. In our case, since it's just an extra touch to the overall experience, it's not a serious issue if older browsers miss out on this; they can still get all of the core content they need. In the next section, we'll continue with CSS animations by experimenting with our shark logo to create a far more robust animation.

CSS animations (part 2)

Our main navigation dropdown's sliding motion is complete. Now let's deep dive into CSS animations by experimenting with our shark logo and exploring other animation properties, such as delay, iteration-count, fill-mode, as well as, animation—which is the shorthand.

Animation delay, iteration-count, and fill-mode

Let's add an animation for the shark image to get a different perspective of what animations can do, and have it occur every time the page loads. We'll name it crazyShark:

```
nav figure {
  position: absolute;
  top: -20px;
  left: 50px;
  animation-name: crazyShark;
  animation-duration: .25s;
  animation-timing-function: ease;
}
@-webkit-keyframes crazyShark {

}
nav img {
  width: 160px;
}
```

Let's add a bunch of @keyframes that are translating and simultaneously rotating the shark image:

```
@keyframes crazyShark {
    0% {transform: translate(90%, 70%);}
    33% {transform: translate(40%, 20%) rotate(90deg);}
    66% {transform: translate(10%);}
    100% {transform: translate(0%) rotate(0deg);}
}
```

Now, let's go to our animation properties and change the duration from 0.25 seconds to 1 second:

```
animation-duration: 1s;
```

The shark is really moving around, hence our animation is named crazyShark:

Note that the `translate` syntax I'm using is slightly different than what we've used previously. The two values separated by a comma are for *x* and *y* coordinates, respectively, whereas one single value can be used when the *x* and *y* coordinates are the same:

```
/*translate shorthands for translateX and translateY*/

transform: translate(40%, 20%);
/*2 values (x first, y second) when both values are different*/

transform: translate(10%);
/*1 value is used when x and y coordinates are the same*/
```

There are several other animation properties, two of which are `animation-delay` and `animation-iteration-count`. I find both of these useful:

```
nav figure {
    position: absolute;
    top: -20px;
    left: 50px;
    animation-name: crazyShark;
    animation-duration: 1s;
    animation-timing-function: ease;
    animation-delay: 2s;
    animation-iteration-count: 2;
}
```

Now, we'll have a 2 second delay before the animation starts, *which I won't try to illustrate in book format*. Then it should animate fully through twice:

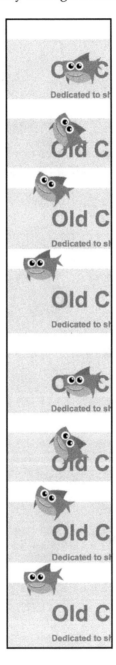

We could also endlessly repeat the animation if we wanted to; we could just add the `infinite` keyword instead of a number, and the shark would keep on going forever. *I'm definitely not going to try to illustrate this in book format either!* Let's get rid of the `animation-delay` and `animation-iteration-count`:

```
nav figure {
    position: absolute;
    top: -20px;
    left: 50px;
    animation-name: crazyShark;
    animation-duration: 1s;
    animation-timing-function: ease;
}
```

animation-fill-mode

The animation-fill-mode property tells the element being animated what to do with itself before the animation starts and after the animation completes. Using `animation-fill-mode` fills the space before and/or after the animation. We don't need an `animation-fill-mode` property yet. That's because the shark animation starts on page load and then lands the shark in its static position—we're saying no translate and no rotate:

```
100% {transform: translate(0%) rotate(0deg);}
```

However, what if we end the animation with *x* at 10 percent, *y* at 70 percent, and a rotation at 10 degrees?

```
100% {transform: translate(10%, 70%) rotate(10deg);}
```

If you apply this and go to the site, you'll notice that the shark seems to end the animation near the first heading and then jumps back to its native position. This is illustrated by the following two screenshots:

The shark at the very end of its animation:

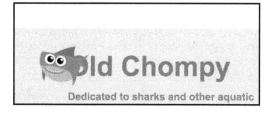

The shark teleports to its static position following the animation:

We could use `animation-fill-mode: forwards` to fix this:

```
nav figure {
  position: absolute;
  top: -20px;
  left: 50px;
  animation-name: crazyShark;
  animation-duration: 1s;
  animation-timing-function: ease;
  animation-delay: 2s;
  animation-iteration-count: 2;
  animation-fill-mode: forwards;
}
```

Now, after the animation concludes, the shark will stay put in that position without jumping back to its native position:

That's neat!

The `animation-fill-mode` property with a value of `backwards` will make sure that the element being animated is *filled* to its starting position even before the animation starts. The `both` keyword is a way to fill both the starting and ending position.

Let's reduce our ruleset down to just these three animation properties:

```
animation-name: crazyShark;
animation-duration: 1s;
animation-timing-function: ease;
```

Let's also touch up and tone back this entire animation. This way, our crazy shark will become a little less crazy, *but still crazy enough*:

```
@keyframes crazyShark {
   0% {transform: translate(90%, 70%);opacity: 0;}
   33% {transform: translate(40%, 20%) rotate(90deg);}
   66% {transform: translate(10%, 50%);}
   100% {transform: translate(0%) rotate(0deg);opacity: 1;}
}
```

We'll have to add the vendor prefixes for each animation property. But, before we do this, let's make our coding lives easier using the animation property shorthand that combines all of the animation properties into one line.

Using the animation shorthand

Take these declarations in our `nav figure` ruleset:

```
animation-name: crazyShark;
animation-duration: 1s;
animation-timing-function: ease;
```

Remove `-name` from `animation-name` and the bottom two declarations; so we are left with this:

```
animation: crazyShark;
```

Now, we'll add `1s` and `ease`:

```
animation: crazyShark 1s ease;
```

Here's what we should end up with now:

```
nav figure {
  position: absolute;
  top: -20px;
  left: 50px;
  animation: crazyShark 1s ease;
}
```

Also, you can dump all the different animation properties into one shorthand. It doesn't really matter what order you put them in as long as `animation-duration` comes before `animation-delay`. The following is one possible way to use all the animation properties that we've talked about inside one convenient shorthand:

```
animation: [name] [duration] [timing-function] [delay] [fill-mode]
[iteration-count];
```

Now that we have the shorthand in place, it's going to make it a little easier to add in the vendor prefixed version.

Vendor prefixes

Let's add the `-webkit-` prefixed version of the `animation` property:

```
nav figure {
  position: absolute;
  top: -20px;
  left: 50px;
  -webkit-animation: crazyShark 1s ease;
  animation: crazyShark 1s ease;
}
```

We will do the same for `@keyframes`:

```
@-webkit-keyframes crazyShark {
  0% {-webkit-transform: translate(90%, 70%);opacity: 0;}
  33% {-webkit-transform: translate(40%, 20%);}
  66% {-webkit-transform: translate(10%, 50%);}
  100% {-webkit-transform: translate(0%);opacity: 1;}
}
@keyframes crazyShark {
  0% {transform: translate(90%, 70%);opacity: 0;}
  33% {transform: translate(40%, 20%);}
  66% {transform: translate(10%, 50%);}
  100% {transform: translate(0%);opacity: 1;}
}
```

Notice that I've prefixed the `@keyframes` with `@-webkit-keyframes`, as well as, the `transform` with `-webkit-transform`.

Additional info on animations

For more information on CSS animations, I recommend checking out my article, `CSS animations aren't that tough.`, at `richfinelli.com/css-animations-arent-that-tough`:

In conclusion, we've explored other animation properties, such as `animation-delay`, `animation-iteration-count`, and `animation-fill-mode`, on our way to creating a fancy, over-the-top animation. We also simplified all these properties into a single, convenient shorthand. We also added the `-webkit-` prefixed version of each property for greater browser support. In the next and final section of this chapter, we'll add `box-shadow` to our entire nav, as well as fix a bug with our drop-down menu, namely `z-index`.

Finalizing the navigation

We're almost done with our main navigation but still have a couple small things left to do. First, we'll fix a `z-index` issue, which I'll elaborate on more in a moment. Then we need to add `box-shadow` to the bottom of our nav bar to complete the design.

Fixing the Z index issue

First, we're going to fix a bug using the `z-index` property. When you hover over the **MOVIES** navigation item, a dropdown appears. You will notice a couple of things:

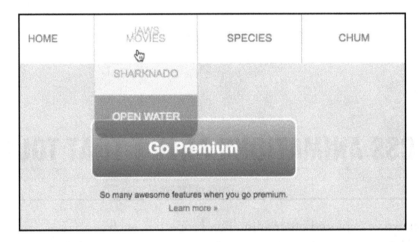

First, one of the nav items in the dropdown items gets highlighted—when it really shouldn't. Second, the nav is actually animating on top of the **MOVIES** navigation item.

We can slow down the animation speed to `2.5s` to get an easier look at this issue:

```
.has-submenu:hover ul {
  display: block;
  -webkit-animation: slideDown 2.5s ease;
  animation: slideDown 2.5s ease;
}
```

This can make it easier to see that the dropdown menu is dropping down on top of the **MOVIES** menu item.

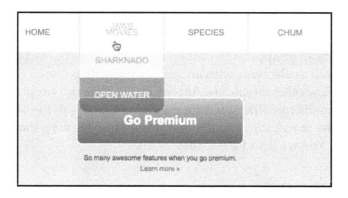

That's our problem, and that's why we're ending up with one of the dropdown menu items highlighted.

Here we are in our CSS file:

```
/***************
Drop Down Menu
***************/
.has-submenu ul{
  position: absolute;
  top: 70px;
  background-color: #fff;
  border-bottom: 1px solid #ada791;
  border-left: 1px solid #ada791;
  border-right: 1px solid #ada791;
  width: 150px;
  border-radius: 0 0 15px 15px;
  overflow: hidden;
  display: none;
}
.has-submenu a {
  display: block;
  padding: 20px 0;
  position: relative;
}
.has-submenu:hover ul {
  display: block;
  -webkit-animation: slideDown 2.5s ease;
  animation: slideDown 2.5s ease;
}
```

This bug, so to speak, can be fixed with a new property called `z-index`. The `z-index` property sets the stacking order of elements that overlap. Our drop-down menu appears at the top because it comes after the anchor tag's main nav item for movies. Naturally, absolutely positioned elements will appear on top of elements that do not have a `position` property set. This is why the dropdown appears on top of the main nav. The value of `z-index` is a number. It can be applied to elements that are set to `relative`, `absolute`, or `fixed` positions as well as elements with an `opacity` less than one or with a `transform` applied, as well as a few other situations. As long as we have our drop-down menu—that is, a `z-index` less than its container—we are good to go. Going to the `.has-submenu a` selector, let's apply the `position:relative` declaration. This way, the element is going to accept the `z-index`. And we'll add a `z-index` of `10`:

```
.has-submenu a {
  display: block;
  padding: 20px 0;
  position: relative;
  z-index: 10;
}
```

On a `.has-submenu ul`, we don't need to apply `position:relative` because it's already set to `position: absolute`; it will accept `z-index` of 5, which is less than 10. So we should, in theory, have our bug fixed:

```
.has-submenu ul{
  position: absolute;
  z-index: 5;
  top: 70px;
```

Save this and take a look at our site. At full speed, none of the menu items get highlighted when you hover over the navigation item and the drop-down appears behind the main nav. Now just to be sure, slow down the animation again. You should see it appear behind the **MOVIES** menu, which is great:

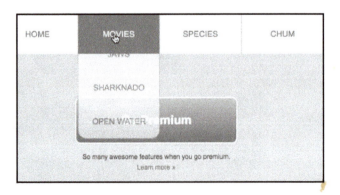

Let's also change the `animation-duration` back to `.5s`:

```
.has-submenu:hover ul {
  display: block;
  -webkit-animation: slideDown .5s ease;
  animation: slideDown .5s ease;
}
```

Adding box-shadow

Let's talk about the `box-shadow` property. On our final site, you can see we have this shadow below the main nav:

Let's move back to our CSS and find our `nav` selectors. `box-shadow` is a CSS3 property:

```
nav {
  background-color: #fff;
  position: fixed;
  left: 0;
  right: 0;
  top: 0;
  z-index:1;
  box-shadow: 0 8px;
}
```

We're targeting the `nav` element and using the nonprefixed version, which is supported in all major browsers, starting with IE9 and above. We don't have to go back and any vendor prefixes because the specification has matured enough, as all the browsers now support the nonprefixed version. The first two values we add are *x* and *y*. We set the *x* value at `0` and the *y* value at `8px`; this is going to make the `box-shadow` property emanate downward:

```
box-shadow: 0 8px;
```

If I use a negative value, that would have the submenu emanate from the top of the nav. We want it to emanate from the bottom of the nav.

The next value is blur. We'll set it to 15px:

```
box-shadow: 0 8px 15px;
```

If I were to leave the blur value at 0, we would get a hard, 8-pixel border. The blur is what makes it look more like a shadow than a border.

The final value we're going to use is a color. We'll use a new color value, called rgba, which is a CSS3 color value. We'll then add 0, 0, 0. This means the red, green, and blue colors are all going to be zero, meaning their output will be black. The a variable refers to the alpha channel, and we'll set it to .1:

```
box-shadow: 0 8px 15px rgba(0, 0, 0, .1);
```

So if you go to the site and check and uncheck **box-shadow** in DevTools, you will see the effect the box-shadow property has. Here is what it looks like without this property:

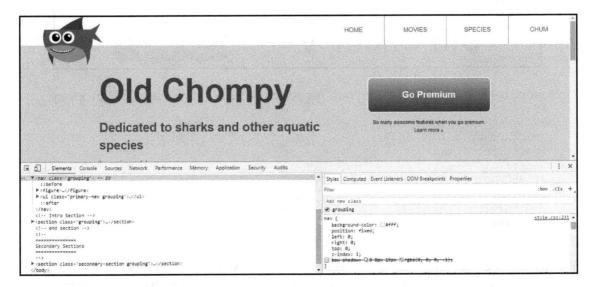

This figure shows our site with box-shadow applied:

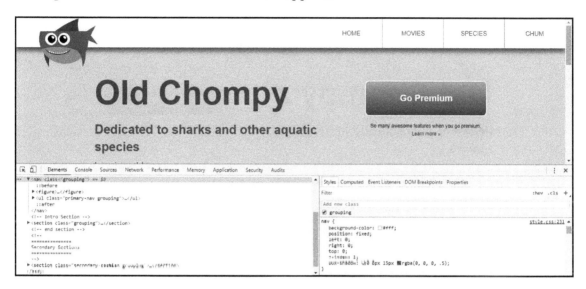

Sometimes with these CSS properties, it's nice to visit the DevTools. Let's see what they look like if we change their values. We can see what box-shadow looks like with more or less blur. In the following screenshot, we see what it looks like with the value increased from 15px to 26px—you can see that the blur fades away:

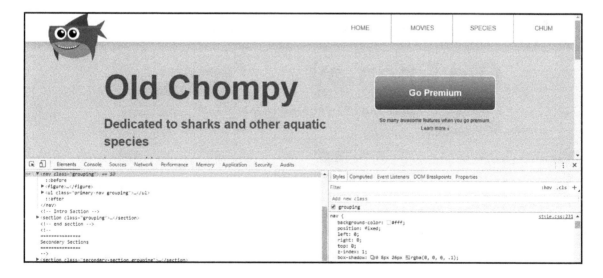

With less blur, say `0px`, it turns into hardened shadow:

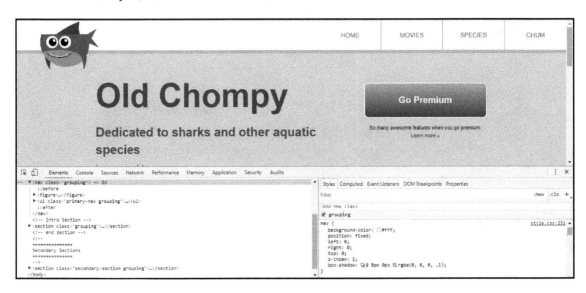

I think that about `15px` was just right. You can also see what it looks like with greater opacity—rather a greater alpha channel. If we change the alpha channel from `.1` to `.5`, the box-shadow gets a lot darker:

I think `.1` is about right. This has turned out well.

Summary

This was an extensive chapter; we covered a lot. We built and styled our menu. You learned about pseudo classes and how we can use them to target elements based on their position in the HTML. We familiarized ourselves with positioning properties, using `absolute` positioning for our shark icon. We built a dropdown for our menu and added animations to it. We explored animation properties, such as `animation delay`, `iteration count`, and `fill-mode`, and applied them to our shark icon. We finished off by finalizing the nav, fixing the `z-index` issue, and completing our design using the `box-shadow` property. In the next chapter, we'll look at one of my favorite subjects, responsive web design, as we get this site ready for varying device sizes.

6

Becoming Responsive

Up to this point, we've built almost everything with a fixed size. Our layout had a fixed width, our images had fixed widths, and our menu had a fixed width as well. But this is not going to deliver a favorable experience when using phones, tablets, and a multitude of other device sizes that are out there. Luckily, responsive web design is here to transform our static website into a fluid, device-friendly website.

The book that started it all - *Responsive Web Design*, by *Ethan Marcotte, 2011*. He outlined three main technical pillars of responsive web design:

- Fluid grids,
- Flexible images, and
- Media queries.

We'll discuss these three fundamental CSS foundations of responsive web design, followed by how to build accommodations for primary navigation at smaller screen sizes, and finally, the `viewport` meta tag.

Fluid grids

In this section, we'll discuss the first of the three main components of responsive web design, the fluid grid, or a percentage-based layout. We'll look at converting a fixed width layout into a fluid grid, and to do this, you'll need to learn the formula for converting pixels into percentages.

Converting pixels to percentages

Right now, we have a fixed width layout, as shown in the following screenshot:

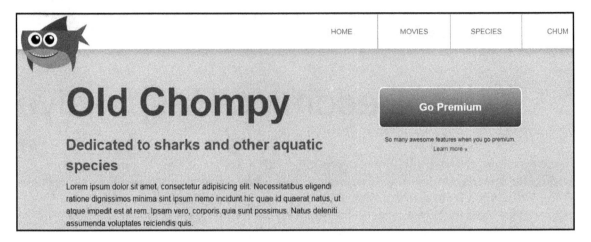

If you shrink the browser, you can see how it breaks down into smaller sizes, as shown in the following screenshot:

Creating a fluid grid is the first step in fixing this. The goal is to convert all our pixel-based widths, as well as left and right margins and left and right padding, into percentages. We're going to ignore our main navigation for now, but we'll circle back to it in a later section. We'll start with the `div` tag, which is the `wrapper` class, that I have used to wrap a lot of the content. Let's change the property `width` to `max-width`. This indicates that this element can be smaller than `960px` wide, but it can't be any wider than that. Let's also set the width to `90%`:

```
.wrapper {
  width:960px;
  width: 90%;
  margin: 0 auto;
}
```

So, as per this code, we're making the width 90 percent of its parent element, which has no width. Therefore, it will be 90 percent of the browser window. This will give it a 5 percent gutter on either side with widths narrower than `960px`. Let's look at the site in the browser. You can refresh the browser and make it smaller again. The following screenshot shows that it doesn't have a dramatic effect and looks pretty bad:

We want to create these elements inside `wrapper` percentages as well. Since we're starting with fixed pixel widths, we to convert all pixels into percentages.

Calculating percentage widths

According to *Responsive Web Design*, by *Ethan Marcotte*, there is a formula for converting pixel-based layouts to percentage-based layouts: *target / context = result*. The *target* is the desired width of an element. The *context* is typically the width of its parent element. The *result* is the percentage we can plug into our CSS.

If we look at our HTML inside the `intro-content` section, we can see the `wrapper` class and the two `div` tags inside of it, namely `intro-content` and `go-premium`, as shown in the following code snippet:

```
<section class="grouping">
    <div class="wrapper">
        <div class="intro-content">
            <h1>Old Chompy</h1>
            <h2>Dedicated to sharks and other aquatic species</h2>
            <p>Lorem ipsum dolor sit amet...</p>
        </div><!-- end intro-content -->
        <div class="go-premium">
            <a href="#" class="call-to-action">Go Premium</a>
            <p class="reasons">So many awesome features...
                <a href="#">Learn more &raquo;</a>
            </p>
        </div><!-- end go-premium -->
    </div><!-- end wrapper -->
</section><!-- end section -->
```

Back to our CSS, our first element is `intro-content`, which is the section that appears inside of the wrapper, as shown in the following code snippet:

```
.intro-content {
  width: 600px;
  margin-right: 60px;
  float: left;
}
```

The target here is 600 pixels and the context is 960 pixels. So our calculation would be 600 divided by 960, which equals 0.625. We'll plug this in as our width, add a percentage as our unit of measure, and move the decimal point over two places so that it comes out to 62.5%:

```
.intro-content {
  width: 62.5%; /* 600/960 */
  margin-right: 60px;
  float: left;
}
```

As you can see, my comment at the end of the declaration tells me that the element was originally 600 pixels wide, and the parent element was originally 960 pixels wide.

The `margin-right` property needs to be a percentage too. The formula remains the same—*target* divided by *context* equals *result*. Our target is 60 pixels, and our context is still 960 pixels—the parent element, which is the `wrapper` class. 60 divided by 960 comes out 0.0625. We convert this into a percentage by moving the decimal point two places, and we have `6.25%`:

```
.intro-content {
  width: 62.5%; /* 600/960 */
  margin-right: 6.25%; /* 60/960px */
  float: left;
}
```

Next up is our call-to-action button's container, `go-premium`:

```
.go-premium {
  width: 300px;
  float: left;
  margin-top: 150px;
}
```

As the width is `300px`, it needs to be converted into a percentage as well. So let's do the same thing, in this case, 300 divided by 960—we still have the same parent here. It's 0.3125. Move the decimal point two place, add a percentage, and then put that in a CSS comment to the right in case we need it later:

```
.go-premium {
  width: 31.25%; /* 300/960 */
  float: left;
  margin-top: 150px;
}
```

Now I think we're ready to look at this in the browser. If I shrink the browser window a little, the layout no longer breaks immediately:

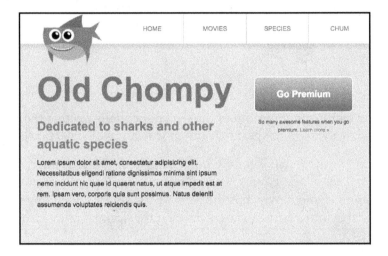

But if I shrink the browser window a little more, then it ultimately starts to look pretty terrible:

However, we did make some progress as our layout is starting to become fluid. The intro content and the call-to-action button are getting narrower as the browser window gets smaller. Eventually, they will start overlapping, but that's okay; at least we have a fluid foundation for this top section.

Now let's take a look at the three columns underneath of it; they are kind of breaking as the window gets smaller:

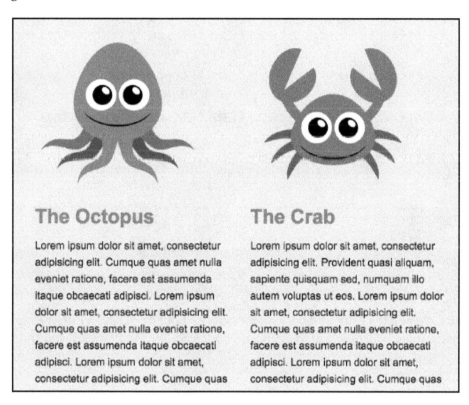

So let's take a look at the HTML for this in our `secondary-section` class. These three columns are inside of a `div` tag with a class of `wrapper` that was also originally 960 pixels wide (but is now a max-width of 960px with a width of 90%):

```
<section class="secondary-section grouping">
  <div class="wrapper">
    <div class="column">
      <figure>
        <img src="images/octopus-icon.png" alt="Octopus">
      </figure>
      <h2>The Octopus</h2>
      <p>...</p>
      <a href="#" class="button">Tenticals &raquo;</a>
    </div>
    <div class="column">
      <figure><img src="images/crab-icon.png" alt="Crab"></figure>
      <h2>The Crab</h2>
      <p>...</p>
      <a href="#" class="button">Crabby &raquo;</a>
    </div>
    <div class="column">
      <figure><img src="images/whale-icon.png" alt="Whale"></figure>
      <h2>The Whale</h2>
      <p>...</p>
      <a href="#" class="button">Stuart &raquo;</a>
    </div>
  </div><!-- end wrapper -->
</section>
```

We'll continue using it as our context while we convert our `.column` width from pixels into percentages. All the way down to the bottom of our CSS, we see that each column is `300px` wide:

```
/****************
3 columns
****************/
.column {
  float: left;
  width: 300px;
  margin-left: 30px;
}
.column:first-child {
  margin-left: 0;
}
```

Let's apply our formula here. We already know that 300 divided by 960 is 31.25 percent because that's the exact calculation we used just before this:

```
.column {
  float: left;
  width: 31.25%; /* 300/960 */
  margin-left: 30px;
}
```

The `margin-left` property is `30px`, so we're actually going to copy and paste 31.25 percent down here, but we'll move the decimal one place and add a comment stating 30 divided by 960:

```
.column {
  float: left;
  width: 31.25%; /* 300/960 */
  margin-left: 3.125%; /* 30/960 */
}
```

We do have a `margin-left` property of `0` value on the first column. We don't have to change 0 to a percentage because 0, 0 pixels, and 0 percent are all the same exact thing—nothing:

```
.column:first-child {
  margin-left: 0;
}
```

As a side note, I never changed any heights, top and bottom margins, or padding because they just didn't really matter to us. So now if we refresh this section and make it smaller, we will see our three columns shrinking proportionately as our browser window shrinks:

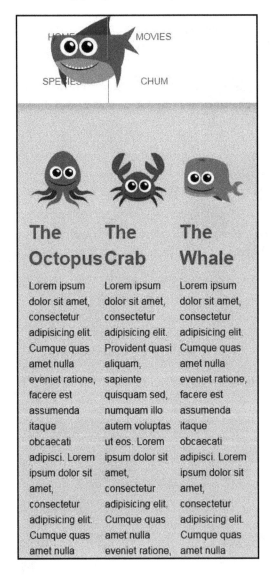

So everything in our home page is fluid now, except for our nav, which I'm going to leave as is for now. I want to handle it totally differently, so I'll leave it as a fixed width.

Changing padding to a percentage

We never had to change our padding left or right to a percentage because we didn't have any, but the process to do so is very similar. You still use the same formula – target divided by context equals result. But the context is a little different now; it's the width of the element itself and not the width of the parent element, like it is for width and margin. The only caveat to that is if the element itself doesn't have a width defined, you can use the width of its parent or determine the width itself by determining the width of the parent:

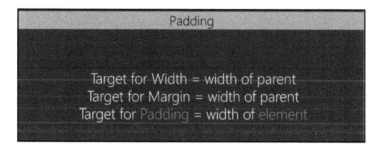

If you're using the `box-sizing` property with the border box value, padding would no longer be factored into the box model width of the element. Therefore, you can leave it as a pixel length and just convert the width and margin into a percentage, so `box-sizing: border-box` could definitely be helpful.

A fluid grid on the shark movies page

Let's search for some other non-percentage-based widths/margins/paddings. So we're not worried about anything related to vertical distance, like `height`, `margin-top`, `margin-bottom`, `padding-top` or `padding-bottom`. And we're not worried about any value of 0.

We will come across `auto` for the left and right margin in the `wrapper` rule set:

```
.wrapper {
  max-width: 960px;
  width: 90%;
  margin: 0 auto;
}
```

This doesn't need to be converted into a percentage because `auto` automatically calculates the width based on the space available, so it's as good as a percentage.

We are worried about this `margin` property in the following declaration block:

```
.content-block .figure {
  float: left;
  margin: 30px;
  border: 15px solid #fff;
  overflow: hidden;
}
```

This rule set has a `margin` of `30px`; it's using the single value syntax. This means the top, bottom, left, and right margins are all `30px`. We only want to change the left and right margins. So what we can do is use the two-value syntax. The first value refers to the top and bottom margins, and the second value refers to the left and right margins.

```
margin: 30px 30px;
```

Remember `content-block .figure` is the element that wraps around our image, as shown in the following screenshot. So we're actually trying to convert `margin-right` and `margin-left` into a percentage:

If we look in our `shark-movies.html`, we will see that the image is inside of a `wrapper`:

```
<section id="jaws" class="content-block style-1 wave-border grouping">
  <div class="wrapper">
    <a href="#" class="figure">
      <img src="images/jaws.jpg" alt="Jaws movie">
    </a>
    <h1>Jaws</h1>
    <p>...</p>
    <a href="" class="button button-narrow button-alt float-right">Learn
More</a>
  </div><!-- end of wrapper -->
</section>
```

So again, we know the `wrapper` is 960 pixels. So far, our context has been very easy to determine because our context has always been the width of the `wrapper`.

The number 30 divided by 960 is 03.125, which is 3.125%, so we'll save this:

```
.content-block .figure {
  float: left;
  margin: 30px 3.125%; /* 30/960 */
  border: 15px solid #fff;
  overflow: hidden;
}
```

On our site, except for nav, all the hard pixel lengths are percentages! Not everything has to be a percentage for responsive web design to work. We made a judgment call that we'd handle navigation without percentage widths. This is true for the fluid grid and so many other decisions for responsive web design; there really isn't a one-size-fits-all solution. Each component of your website needs to be thought out thoroughly from the desktop down to mobile, or even better yet, starting from the mobile up through to the desktop. So step one, creating fluid grids, is complete for now. This is an important step because it ensures our design will start to fit nicely on all our screen sizes. In the next section, we'll look at flexible images.

Flexible images

We've created a fluid grid, which is the first foundation of a responsive web design. Foundation two is responsive images or flexible images. We want our images or at least certain images to behave the same way as our divs and sections. We want them to be fluid or flexible.

Looking at our site, what we can notice is that the three images of `The Octopus`, `The Crab`, and `The Whale` shrink as the column they are in gets smaller. On the other hand, the shark at the top kind of stays the same size no matter what the browser width is:

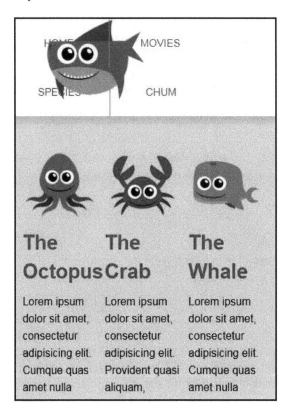

Our image in the navigation is not flexible. The three images in our columns are flexible. We'll look at the image in the navigation and see why. But first, let's go over the three things that will guarantee responsive images:

- Put the `img` tag inside of a container. The most semantic container is usually the `figure` tag, but it could certainly be any element.
- Make the container fluid; give it a percentage width.
- Assign the `max-width` property of `100%` to all the `img` tags or at least to the `img` tags you want to be fluid or flexible.

The octopus, crab, and whale images

Now let's look at one of the images in our HTML file. We can see the octopus image is inside of a container. The container is the `figure` element:

```
<figure>
    <img src="images/octopus-icon.png" alt="Octopus">
</figure>
```

The `figure` element doesn't have a width defined, but it's a block-level element that takes up the entire width of its container. So we could think of the figure width as `100%`. It's inside of the `column` div:

```
<div class="column">
    <figure>
        <img src="images/octopus-icon.png" alt="Octopus">
    </figure>
    <h2>The Octopus</h2>
    <p>...</p>
    <a href="#" class="button">Tenticals &raquo;</a>
</div>
```

If we look in our CSS column, we see the column width is `31.25%`:

```
/****************
3 columns
***************/
.column {
  float: left;
  width: 31.25%; /* 300/960 */
  margin-left: 3.125%; /* 30/960 */
}
```

So there we have our first step – we have our image inside of the container. Then we have step two – the parent is fluid. The third step is assigning a max width to all the images.

Let's scroll up to the top of our CSS file. I actually have this selector, shown in the next screenshot, as part of my reset. It targets `img`, `iframe`, `video`, and `object`, pretty much all types of media. I have assigned this selector with maximum width of 100 percent:

```
img, iframe, video, object {
  max-width: 100%;
}
```

I make this selector part of my reset or base layer of styles that I use on every project. So for fun, let's remove that property:

```
img, iframe, video, object {
 /* max-width: 100%;*/
}
```

If we save it and look at our site, as we shrink the browser window, the images wouldn't get smaller; they'll stay the same size and get squashed together:

When we add back the `max-width: 100%` declaration, these images become flexible again. This indicates that the maximum width of any image can only be 100 percent of its container. So, as the container gets smaller, the width of the image will also get smaller:

```
img, iframe, video, object {
   max-width: 100%;
}
```

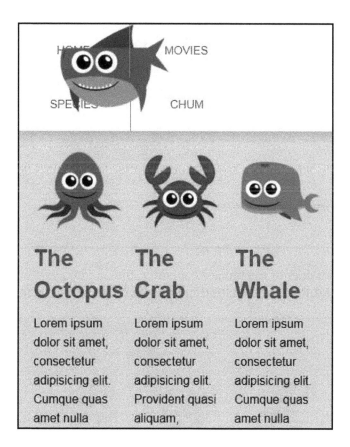

The shark image

There are two reasons why the shark image is not getting smaller. Let's inspect them. We can see that the shark image does have an immediate container element – a `figure` tag. But that container is intentionally not fluid:

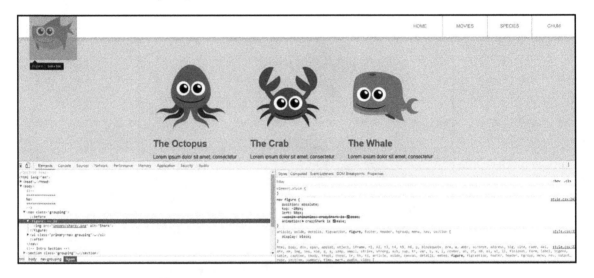

If you click on the container of the images container, the `nav` tag, you will see it expands to the full width of the browser, demonstrating how the container is not fluid:

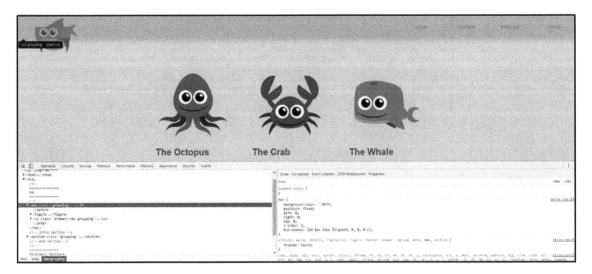

If we inspect the image itself, we see that it has a width assigned to it of 160px, which will definitely stop it from being fluid:

```
nav img {
    width: 160px;
}
```

Personally, I don't like having a width set on the image. Even if I don't want this image to be fluid, I don't want to have a width on it either. In this case, let's do a little cleanup here and change the image so the figure element has a width of 160px, which is the image's container, instead of the image itself.

```
nav img {
   width: 160px;
}
```

This is more of my preference:

```
nav figure {
   position: absolute;
   top: -20px;
   left: 50px;
   width: 160px;
   -webkit-animation: crazyShark 1s ease;
   animation: crazyShark 1s ease;
}
/* nav img {
   width: 160px;
} */
```

Intentionally we are leaving the shark image as a fixed width as it doesn't necessarily need to shrink or grow to make this design responsive. We'll handle the header section separately later in this chapter.

Shrinking images on the shark movies page

Let's take a look at the images on the movies page. They don't shrink when we resize the browser. They have fixed widths:

I think they should shrink; they're just a little too big in smaller browser sizes. The reason all three images on our movies page don't shrink is because their parent element does not have a width defined. Let's use Ethan Marcotte's formula-target divided by context equals result. We know the context of the area filled by the image, heading 1, paragraph, and learn more button is still 960px wide because it's inside of a `wrapper`:

So what is the width of the anchor tag that surrounds the image? If we look at our CSS, we have `.content-block .figure`, where there is no width defined:

```
.content-block .figure {
  float: left;
  margin: 30px 3.125%; /* 30/960 */
  border: 15px solid #fff;
  overflow: hidden;
}
```

If we look at the image that is inside of `.figure`, there is no width defined there as well:

```
.content-block .figure img {
  float: left;
  -webkit-transition: transform .25s ease-in-out;
  transition: transform .25s ease-in-out;
}
```

So we have to use the power of Chrome DevTools in order to figure out what the width of the `a` element around the `img` element is. If we hover over the actual image itself, we see the image is 200 pixels by 200 pixels:

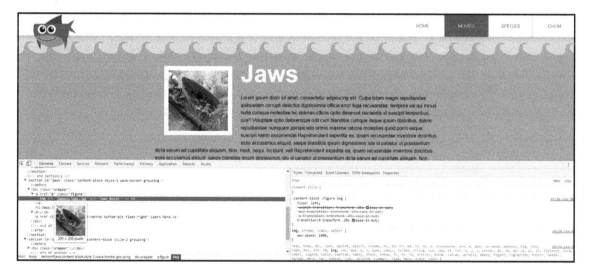

If we actually highlight the anchor, as shown in the following screenshot, DevTools tell us that the width is 230 pixels. You can see that it says in that pop-up bubble right above the image itself. Our width is 230 - 200 pixels of the image plus 15 pixels border left and 15 pixels border right. This makes sense.

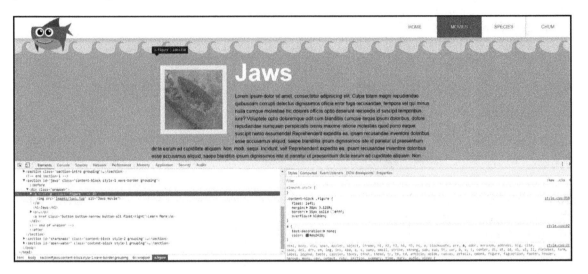

Now what we want to do is we want to use 230 as our target when we convert the pixel value into a percentage. We are also going to have to use `box sizing: border-box`. Remember that, as you learned in *The box model and block versus inline elements* section in `Chapter 1`, *CSS Foundations*, if you set an element to `box-sizing: border-box`, then the `border` and `padding` get calculated into the `width` that you define:

```
.content-block .figure {
  float: left;
  margin: 30px 3.125%; /* 30/960 */
  border: 15px solid #fff;
  overflow: hidden;
  box-sizing: border-box;
}
```

230 divided by 960 equals 0.23958333333333, so we'll convert that into a percent and we get `23.98333333333%`:

```
.content-block .figure {
  float: left;
  margin: 30px 3.125%; /* 30/960 */
  border: 15px solid #fff;
  overflow: hidden;
  box-sizing: border-box;
  width: 23.958333333333%; /*230/960*/
}
```

Now if we refresh the browser and make it smaller, we can see our images get smaller. It may look a little odd at the moment, but believe it or not, that's what we were shooting for, so that's great!

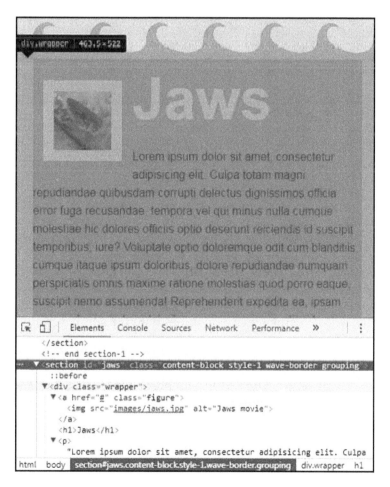

Let's head back to the CCS code now. This technique we're using is very helpful, but we could potentially be repeating `box-sizing: border-box` a lot throughout our code. Let's remove it altogether from our `.content-block` `.figure` rule set and add it to our reset a little differently, where it should be. Let's add this to our reset section of our stylesheet:

```
html {
  box-sizing: border-box;
}
*, *:before, *:after {
  box-sizing: inherit;
}
```

As part of our reset, every element will get `box-sizing: border-box`. We can see where we've added it to our HTML element and used the universal (star) selector, which, as you'll remember from our section on specificity rules, applies to all elements. We're applying `box-sizing: border-box` on the `html` element only, but everything else is going to get `box-sizing: inherit`. `html` is the parent of every element; therefore, you're inheriting the `border-box` property to every element. Alright, we took a little detour from flexible images, but we needed to do this to create a positive path forward.

So, in summary, our images are now flexible, but our site isn't perfect at very small browser widths (think smaller devices like phones or tablets). In the next section, we'll figure out how to handle this using media queries.

Media queries

The first two foundations of responsive web design can only get you so far. The most important foundation is the media query. Media queries are basically "if" statements or conditional logic inside your CSS. For instance, *if* the width of the browser is less than 500 pixels, we can then apply different rule sets based on these conditions. Media queries are extremely powerful because at certain points, our website really breaks down and looks bad, and we're going to need to fix this with . In this section, we'll figure out what a media query is, and we'll use it to fix the remaining issues with the site, especially at narrower widths.

Another thing to consider is this – since we're going to shrink our browser window to kind of emulate a tablet or mobile, we won't have a lot of room to look at DevTools. You can click on the 3-vertical-dots icon to open up a drop down menu to shift DevTools over to the right:

 Chrome changes its UI from time to time as it updates, so the icon may look different for you.

Now we can shrink our browser window to any smaller width we want and still have plenty of room for the developer tools:

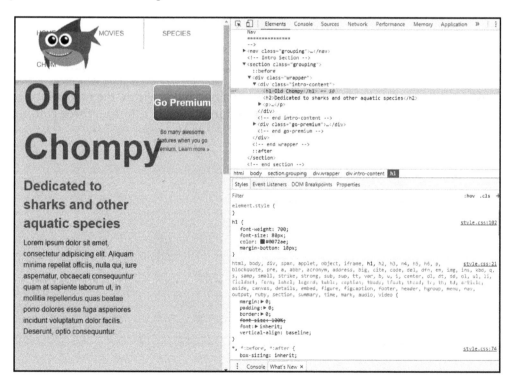

Quick tip
If you use Chrome DevTools and shrink your browser window, in the top-right corner it will show you the width and height of the browser's viewport. So, in the following image, you can see it's providing information about the width, which is at **691px**.

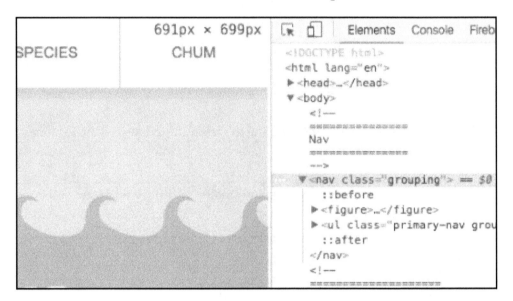

The problem with our site right now is if we reach a narrower width, the nav will be behind the shark, the call-to-action button will be smushed into the site title, and three columns are way too narrow as well:

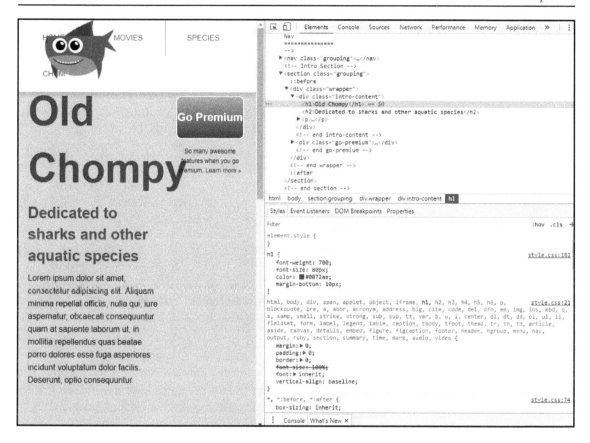

So we'll skip the nav and circle back to it at the end of this section. The main site title and call-to-action button are floated. At 1,023 pixels, let's "defloat" these two sections and stack them on top of each other using a media query.

Anatomy of a media query

I'm going to put all the media queries at the bottom of the style sheet. You don't have to do this, but that's what I'll do. Media queries always start with @media. Then, they have two parts. The first part is the *media type*. For example:

```
@media screen
```

You could plug in `print` , `screen`, `all` and a few other options as well. `print` would only be applied to print style sheets, whereas, `screen` would only be applied to computer screens (but not print outs). `all` would apply to both. If we left out the `media type` altogether - which is perfectly acceptable - it defaults to `all`.

The second part of a media query is called the *media feature* and determines when to use the media query. We need to separate this from the `@media screen` with the word "and". For instance:

```
@media screen and (max-width: 1023px) { }
```

Again, this is conditional logic similar to an if-statement in JavaScript. If both the *media type* and the *media feature* evaluate to true then what's inside the media query will be applied (Yes, we'll be putting stuff inside the media query's curly braces shortly).

`(max-width: 1023px)` means that if the browser window is 1,023px or lower then this media query will apply (or evaluate to true). Once the screen width is more than 1,023px, then the media query will no longer apply (or evaluate to false). You can also use `min-width`; it has the reverse effect, applying to everything 1,023px and greater:

```
@media screen (min-width: 1023px) { }
```

In fact, you can use any length value as well as many other values. Commonly though, `max-width` and `min-width` work just fine with what we're trying to do and we'll stick with `max-width` for now. Notice the curly braces at the end. It's almost like we just built a CSS rule set:

```
@media screen (max-width: 1023px) { }
```

Inside the curly braces of the media query, we can start writing plain old CSS that will only be applied if the browser window is both (1) a screen and (2) 1,023px or less. Let's add `float: none` and `width: auto` to both the `intro-content` and `go-premium`:

```
@media screen and (max-width: 1023px){
  .intro-content {
    float: none;
    width: auto;
  }
  .go-premium{
    float: none;
    width: auto;
  }
}
```

The `auto` value is the default for the `width` property, so it effectually makes these block elements span the full width available, which will be 100 percent of the `wrapper`. The `auto` keyword means it will automatically calculate the value. `auto` has different values based on the property it's paired with. In this case, it basically the same as `100%`.

Now we can see our intro content is no longer floated, the width is the full width, and the `go-premium` button is the same:

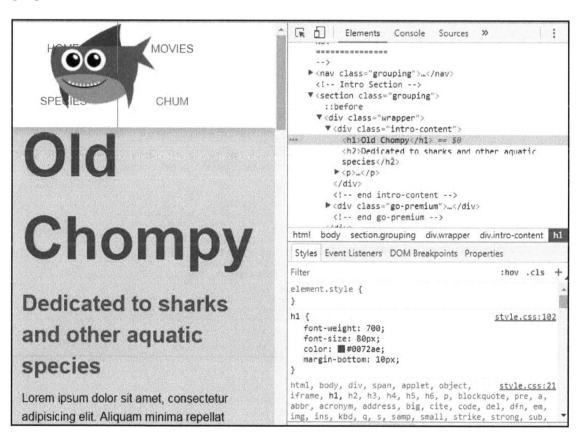

However, we have a big space between the `go-premium` button and the `intro-content` that we need to get rid of:

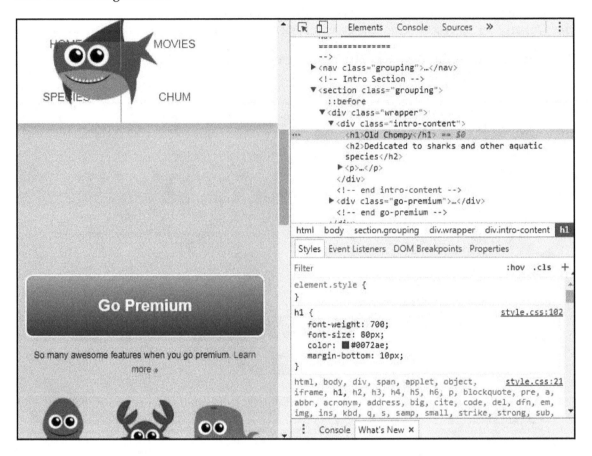

To fix this, we're going to add:

```
@media screen and (max-width: 1023px){
  .intro-content {
    float: none;
    width: auto;
    padding-bottom: 0;
    margin-bottom: 30px;
  }
  .go-premium {
    float: none;
    width: auto;
  }
}
```

On the `go-premium` button itself, we'll remove the top margin:

```
@media screen and (max-width: 1023px){
  .intro-content {
    float: none;
    width: auto;
    padding-bottom: 0;
    margin-bottom: 30px;
  }
  .go-premium {
    float: none;
    width: auto;
    margin-top: 0;
  }
}
```

We've got our title, our subtitle, our text, and our button, and everything's looking good:

 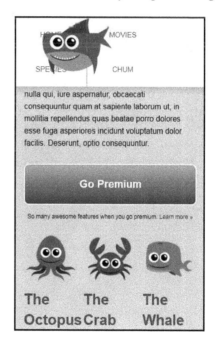

Considering iPads and other tablet dimensions

We chose 1,023 as the break point because that is just one pixel under the width of an iPad held in landscape orientation.

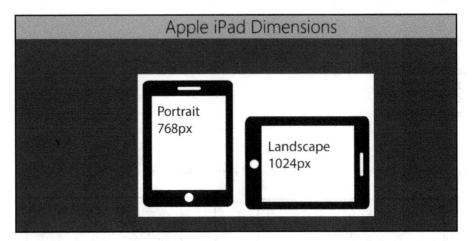

This way, our media query will apply to all the widths and devices lesser than 1,024p. As of 2017, I would *guess* that the iPad is - if not the most popular tablet - one of the most popular. I can say with more certainty that the iPad is definitely not the only popular tablet. In fact, it is amazing just how many different tablet devices and widths there are out there, so you may not want to necessarily use 1,024 and 768, respectively, as the basis for your media queries. Figure out where your layout generally starts to break or look funny and determine the logical placement of your media queries from there. Then, test your site on an iPad and any other device or emulator you can find in order to make sure your site looks good. We'll just use 1,023 as our baseline since, in our case, the layout still looks good at 1,024.

Adding our three columns to the media query

So now, we just need to add all of the CSS to our media query in order to get the rest of the site looking good, starting with the three column area. As you can see in the following screenshot, these are just too tight:

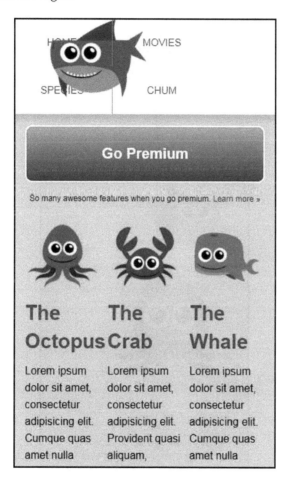

It's kind of standard practice to create a tube of content for smaller devices, getting rid of any multicolumn, floated layout. So we'll remove the float again from .column and make the width the full width of the parent by specifying the keyword of auto. Let's go to the bottom of our CSS and update the media query:

```
@media screen and (max-width: 1023px){
    .intro-content {
      float: none;
```

```
        width: auto;
        padding-bottom: 0;
        margin-bottom: 30px;
    }
    .go-premium {
      float: none;
      width: auto;
      margin-top: 0;
    }
    .column {
      float: none;
      width: auto;
    }
}
```

Now when we go to our site, each of these three columns will have a full width and will not be floated:

The problem is that we should probably center this text and the image itself. So first we'll target `.column figure` first inside the media query to center the image:

```
@media screen and (max-width: 1023px){
  .intro-content {
    float: none;
    width: auto;
    padding-bottom: 0;
    margin-bottom: 30px;
  }
  .go-premium {
    float: none;
    width: auto;
    margin-top: 0;
  }
  .column {
    float: none;
    width: auto;
  }
  .column figure {
    margin: 0 auto;
    max-width: 250px;
    width: 100%;
  }
}
```

By using the `auto` keyword for the left and right margin and setting not only `width: 100%` but also `max-width: 25px` we are able to center the images:

Adding width: `100%` ensures that if the `wrapper` container is ever less than 250px (the max-size of the image) then the image width will be `100%` of its container; sort of a safety net for really narrow widths.

Next, let's center the heading, simply using `text-align: center`:

```
@media screen and (max-width: 1023px){
  .intro-content {
    float: none;
    width: auto;
    padding-bottom: 0;
    margin-bottom: 30px;
  }
  .go-premium {
    float: none;
    width: auto;
    margin-top: 0;
  }
  .column {
    float: none;
    width: auto;
  }
  .column figure {
    margin: 0 auto;
    max-width: 250px;
    width: 100%;
  }
  .column h2 {
    text-align: center;
  }
}
```

Looking good:

There's another approach that we could take with our responsive design – the mobile-first approach.

The mobile-first approach

Typically, this is the best practice. We want to be thinking about smaller displays at the same time or before the desktop experience, as the name suggests. This way, the content and design take into account mobile devices and all their constraints at the very beginning, so they can be fully realized in the design and build process. Mobile first relates to much more than how we code our CSS. But here's the general idea behind the code part of mobile first: Put all of your CSS targeting the smallest devices outside of any media query. Then use media queries to target larger and larger devices.

This means using `min-width` media queries to add additional CSS for larger displays. For instance, our layout wouldn't have any floats by default; instead, it would be a single tunnel of content, which is usually standard for mobile. Then our media queries, using `min-width` instead of `max-width`, would add the floats that would be applied at wider screen widths to create a multicolumn layout.

For more information on the mobile-first approach, check out Luke Wroblewski's defining book on the subject-*Mobile First*-available on the `abookapart.com` website:

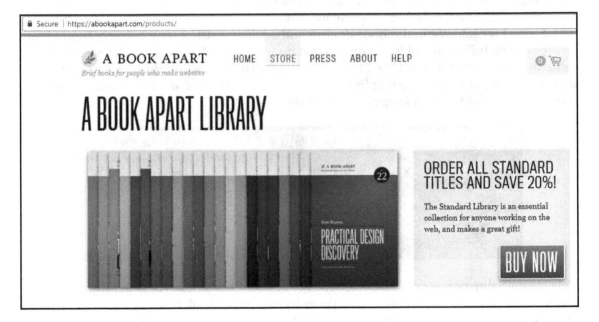

Solving the navigation problem

Let's talk about this navigation now. Solving navigation isn't as easy as solving what we just tackled using media queries. At certain widths, our shark just gets in the way of the nav, and at some point, we are going to have to do something with the dropdown as well. Also, if we were to add a few more nav items, then we'd have this problem at even wider widths.

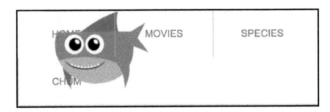

We hit our first real challenge of what to do with the navigation. There are certain responsive design patterns that have emerged. Let's talk about a site that's curated by Brad Frost – `bradfrost.github.io/this-is-responsive`:

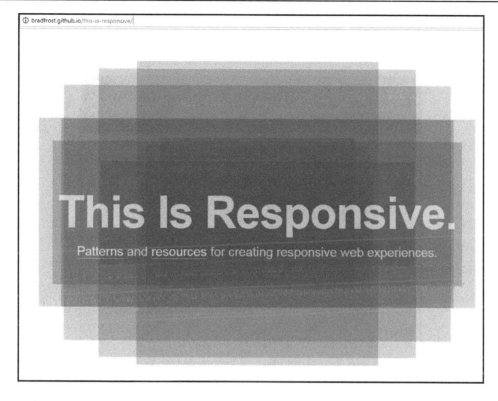

It's basically a collection of patterns to use for responsive web design. It has a bunch of different ways of handling navigation that you can explore. Let's look at the first one under *Patterns*, called **Toggle**. At a wider width, the menu kind of looks like ours; it's just some nav items up at the top:

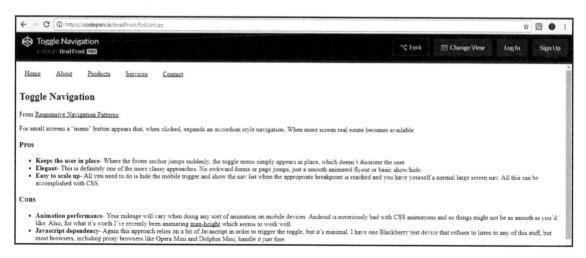

At a narrower browser width, the nav items are replaced with a menu link:

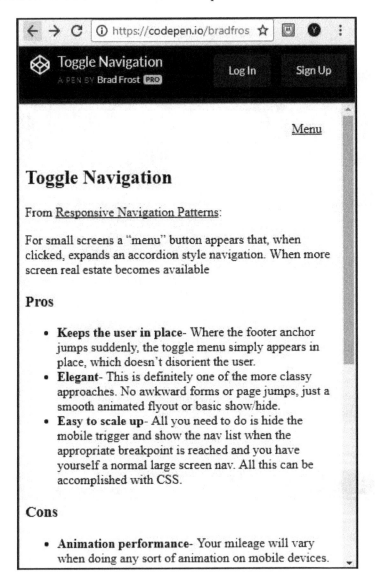

When you click on the link, it expands and hides the menu:

This is generally what we want to do with our site; this will require a little heavier use of media queries and some JavaScript or jQuery to show and hide the navigational click. Up for the challenge? Good, let's get it done!

We've used media queries to change our CSS based on the width of the screen. This is tremendously useful as it fixed most of our issues at narrower widths. We still need to remedy the navigation at smaller widths. In the next section, we are going to use media queries to drastically change our navigation so that it's hidden, except for a **Menu** icon that can be clicked to show the navigation with jQuery.

Mobile menu

So far in this chapter, you've learned about Ethan Marcotte's three fundamentals of responsive web design – fluid grids, flexible images that squish, and media queries. That's kind of the easy part in a way. The hard part is figuring out the multitude of tricky design challenges; for example, what to do with our menu on a mobile, especially as we decide to add more menus. Luckily, this is the one area where a decent design pattern has emerged. We are going to forgo the horizontal menu that shows each button on the nav in lieu of a hidden menu that is activated by a click or touch. Upon being clicked or touched, the hidden menu will slide down vertically and show all the menu choices. We'll achieve this by styling the mobile nav in its open state. Then, we'll hide the nav and add in the menu icon that triggers the mobile menu to open and close it. Finally, we'll link our HTML to the jQuery CDN and our scripts file and write a bit of basic jQuery needed to accomplish this.

Styling the mobile nav in its open state

At the very bottom of the style sheet, I'm going to add in a new media query targeting `900px` or less:

```
@media screen and (max-width: 1023px){
    ...
}/* end of media query */

@media screen and (max-width: 900px) {

}
```

Notice I also add a comment at the closing curly brace of the first media query. This is useful so we don't lose track of where our first media query ends. The new mobile nav will only be triggered at a new break point, `900px` wide. That's when it starts to look funky and starts breaking. Firstly, I don't want the nav to be fixed to the top anymore, so let's get rid of fixed positioning and replace it with the default static position:

```
@media screen and (max-width: 900px) {
  nav {
    position: static;
  }
}
```

Static, as you'll recall from an earlier section, is the default value for the `position` property so it basically turns off `fixed` positioning and returns it as an element that behaves based on the *normal flow*.

Next, let's tell all the immediate list items of `primary-nav` to float to the right instead of left. We'll also give it a full width because these floated elements are only going to take up the width needed, similar to inline elements, so we are going to tell them to take up the entire width available by setting the width to `100%`:

```
@media screen and (max-width: 900px) {
  nav {
    position: static;
  }
  .primary-nav > li {
    float: right;
    width: 100%;
  }
}/* close media query */
```

Again I also add a comment to signal the closing curly brace of this media query so to not lose track of it.

Now let's focus on the anchors. Let's align the text to the right, standardize the padding, remove the border on the left and add a border at the bottom, and give it a little smaller font size of 13px, and width of 100%:

```
@media screen and (max-width: 900px) {
  nav {
    position: static;
  }
  .primary-nav > li {
    float: right;
    width: 100%;
  }
  .primary-nav li a {
    text-align: right;
    padding: 15px 25px 15px 0;
    width: 100%;
    border-bottom: 1px solid #e7e7e7;
    border-left: none;
    font-size: 13px;
  }
}/* close media query */
```

Okay, so this is what the nav looks like before we apply this CSS:

This is what it looks like when we refresh. Now it's starting to look like mobile navigation:

The problem is that the width of 100% didn't really work. Well, actually it did; the anchors are 100 percent of their container, but it's their container also needs to be 100%. So let's assign the primary-nav with a width of 100 percent:

```
@media screen and (max-width: 900px) {
  nav {
    position: static;
  }
  .primary-nav > li {
    float: right;
    width: 100%;
  }
  .primary-nav li a {
    text-align: right;
    padding: 15px 25px 15px 0;
    width: 100%;
    border-bottom: 1px solid #e7e7e7;
    border-left: none;
    font-size: 13px;
  }
  .primary-nav {
    width: 100%;
  }
}/* close media query */
```

We can cross that off our to-do list:

This resembles a menu for sure. The big elephant in the room is that the shark is just taking up too much space in the middle. Let's fix that.

Let's add a new selector to the bottom of the media query targeting the shark. We'll make it much smaller, move it up, and hug it close to the left using the offset properties in the top and left positions since this is already an absolutely positioned element:

```
@media screen and (max-width: 900px) {
  nav {
    position: static;
  }
  .primary-nav > li {
    float: right;
    width: 100%;
  }
  .primary-nav li a {
    text-align: right;
    padding: 15px 25px 15px 0;
    width: 100%;
    border-bottom: 1px solid #e7e7e7;
    border-left: none;
    font-size: 13px;
  }
  .primary-nav {
    width: 100%;
  }
  nav figure {
    width: 100px;
    top: 0;
    left: 20px;
  }
}/* close media query */
```

That looks good:

The next thing to fix is the dropdown menu. This won't do:

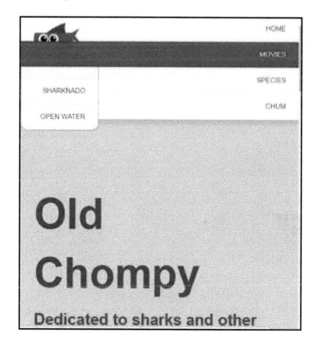

We have a design decision to make right now. Should we hide the dropdown menu and not let any mobile users have access to it? We could. But that's not fair to mobile users. We can obviously keep it as shown above, but I think we'll serve mobile users better by assimilating it into the `primary-nav`. I want to make it look like the other major menus. So we're going to target the `.has-submenu ul` selector. We'll add this rule set to the bottom of the media query. We'll change the `position` property from `absolute` to `static`, change the `display` property to `block`, remove the `border` and `border-radius` properties, and make the `width` stretch all the way across:

```
@media screen and (max-width: 900px) {
  nav {
    position: static;
  }
  .primary-nav > li {
    float: right;
    width: 100%;
  }
  .primary-nav li a {
    text-align: right;
    padding: 15px 25px 15px 0;
    width: 100%;
    border-bottom: 1px solid #e7e7e7;
    border-left: none;
    font-size: 13px;
  }
  .primary-nav {
    width: 100%;
  }
  nav figure {
    width: 100px;
    top: 0;
    left: 20px;
  }
  .has-submenu ul {
    position: static;
    display: block;
    border: none;
    border-radius: 0;
    width: 100%;
  }
}/* close media query */
```

Now we have this:

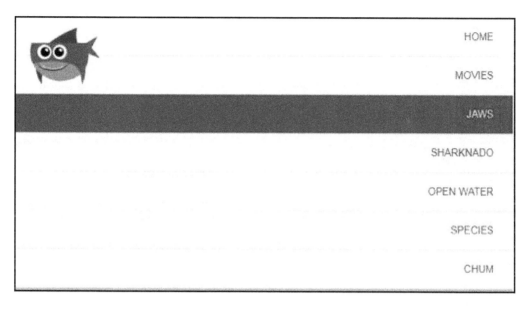

Wow! That looks pretty good. Let's also kill the animation as it's no longer needed. We'll add a new selector inside the media query and set `-webkit-animation` and `animation` to `none`; this keyword will kill the animation:

```
@media screen and (max-width: 900px) {
  nav {
    position: static;
  }
  .primary-nav > li {
    float: right;
    width: 100%;
  }
  .primary-nav li a {
    text-align: right;
    padding: 15px 25px 15px 0;
    width: 100%;
    border-bottom: 1px solid #e7e7e7;
    border-left: none;
    font-size: 13px;
  }
  .primary-nav {
    width: 100%;
  }
  nav figure {
    width: 100px;
```

```
    top: 0;
    left: 20px;
  }
  .has-submenu ul {
    position: static;
    display: block;
    border: none;
    border-radius: 0;
    width: 100%;
  }
  .has-submenu:hover ul {
    -webkit-animation: none;
    animation: none;
  }
}/* close media query */
```

We no longer get the animation. The hover-state of the "Movies" menu covers the shark in an odd way, but that will get fixed shortly when we add the hamburger menu icon:

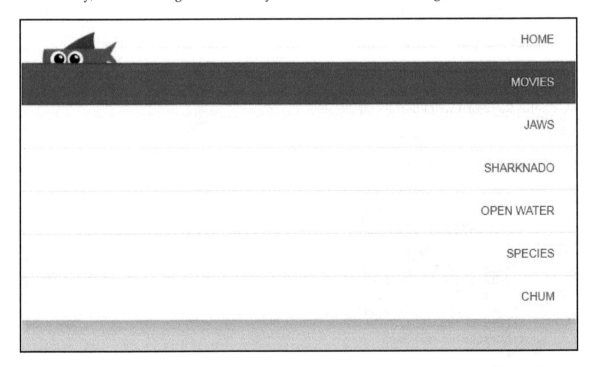

Mobile navigation in its open state is now complete; now we need to hide it and add the hamburger icon that will trigger it to open and close.

Adding the hamburger menu icon

Let's add a `div` tag right on top of the `primary-nav` in both the `index.html` file and the `shark-movies.html` file. We'll give it a class of `mobile-menu-icon`; that's going to be important:

```
<!--
===============
Nav
===============
-->
<nav class="grouping">
    <figure>
        <img src="images/sharky.png" alt="Shark">
    </figure>
    <div class="mobile-menu-icon"></div>
    <ul class="primary-nav grouping">
        <li><a href="#">Home</a></li>
        <li class="has submenu"><a href="shark-movies.html">Movies</a>
            <ul>
                <li class=""><a href="">Jaws</a></li>
                <li class=""><a href="">Sharknado</a></li>
                <li class=""><a href="">Open Water</a></li>
            </ul>
        </li>
        <li><a href="#">Species</a></li>
        <li><a href="#">Chum</a></li>
    </ul>
</nav>
```

Nothing shows up in the browser when we apply this because this is simply an empty `div` tag. Let's use a background image to add the icon. We're not going to put this in a media query; we're actually going to move all the way up to where the nav originally sits in the CSS and add this rule set:

```
/****************
nav
****************/
nav {
  background-color: #fff;
  position: fixed;
  left: 0;
  right: 0;
  top: 0;
  z-index:1;
  box-shadow: 0 8px 15px rgba(0, 0, 0, 0.1);
}
```

```
nav figure {
  width: 160px;
  position: absolute;
  top: -20px;
  left: 50px;
  -webkit-animation: crazyShark 1s ease;
  animation: crazyShark 1s ease;
}
.mobile-menu-icon {
  background: url('../images/mobile-menu-icon.png') 0 0 no-repeat;
}
```

We already have this image sitting in our images folder. We're using zero and zero as our background position and no-repeat to make sure that this image doesn't automatically repeat itself. Still nothing will show up in the browser unless we add a width and height. We know the image is 30px wide and 26px tall, so we'll use those exact dimensions:

```
.mobile-menu-icon {
  background: url('../images/mobile-menu-icon.png') 0 0 no-repeat;
  width: 30px;
  height: 26px;
}
```

Now when we save and refresh, we can see the three bar icon sitting at the top of the browser window:

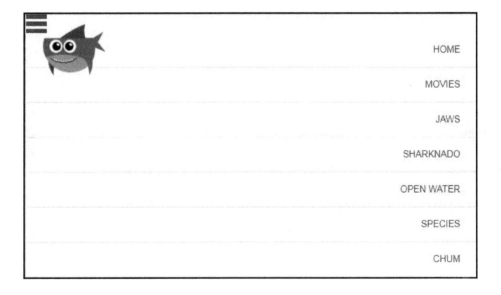

We also want to move it to the right and give it some space from the edges using some margin top, right, and bottom. We can also change the cursor, so this way it has a different look to it. Let's add these properties to `mobile-menu-icon`:

```
.mobile-menu-icon {
    background: url('../images/mobile-menu-icon.png') 0 0 no-repeat;
    width: 30px;
    height: 26px;
    float: right;
    margin: 10px 15px 10px 0;
    cursor: pointer;
}
```

Before we refresh the browser, we can see that we have just a regular cursor hovering over the icon:

After we refresh, it moves over to the right and now it has a pointer type of a cursor indicating that it's clickable:

Obviously, we won't see this on mobile devices but desktop devices or desktop browsers; that's kind of a little nice thing to have.

Hiding the menu

Now let's hide the menu by default. Instead of using `display: none`, which, as I mentioned earlier, is not great for accessibility reasons, let's explore another technique that hides the content more creatively so screen readers can still find and announce it. We'll go back down inside of our media query, inside `.primary-nav`. We're going to say the height of this element is zero:

```
@media screen and (max-width: 900px) {
  .intro-content {
    margin-top: 50px;
  }
  nav {
    position: static;
  }
  .primary-nav {
    width: 100%;
    max-height: 0;
```

```
    overflow: hidden;
    -webkit-transition: all ease-out .35s;
    -moz-transition: all ease-out .35s;
    -o-transition: all ease-out .35s;
    transition: all ease-out .35s;
  }
...
```

Following is the output of preceding code:

There you go. Now what we want to do is activate that menu on a click.

Using jQuery to trigger the menu on a click

For this stage, we have to link to jQuery and our own JavaScript file. We'll do this at the bottom of the HTML, just above our closing `</body>` and `</html>` tags. Copy a link to the jQuery CDN that's hosted on Google's site. Below this, add a link to our own JS file. We're going to put this file in the `js` folder and we're going to name that file `scripts.js`:

```
<script
src="https://ajax.googleapis.com/ajax/libs/jquery/3.2.1/jquery.min.js"></script>
<script src="js/scripts.js"></script>
</body>
</html>
```

Also, let's copy this to the same place in the `shark-movies.html`. Let's create that new JavaScript file as well.

In Sublime Text an easy way to create a new file, is to use *Cmd + N* (on Mac) or *Ctrl + N* (on Windows). *Cmd + S* (on Mac) or *Ctrl + S* (on Windows) will let you save name and save the file.

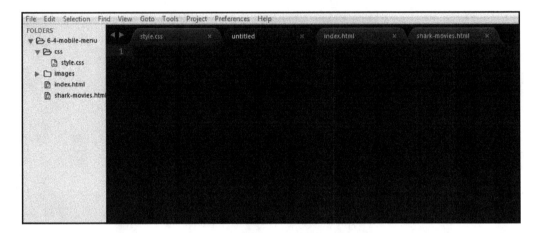

We'll save it in the `js` folder:

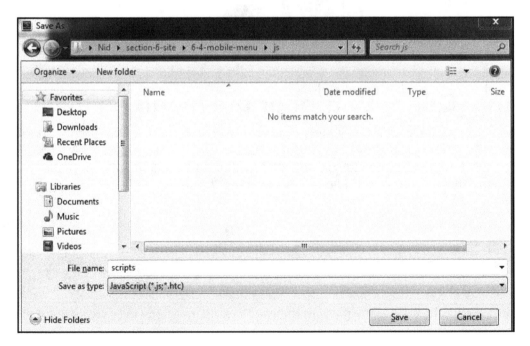

We'll name the file `scripts.js`.

Okay, great, now let's write some jQuery. Don't worry if everything here doesn't make too much sense to you. I'm not going to go into much detail as this topic is beyond the scope of this book, but it's needed for our responsive design. What we're going to paste here to our new `scripts.js` file is a function that fires when the DOM is ready:

```
$(document).ready(function() {

});//end doc ready
```

We want to put the code we write, inside this function. This simply tells the script to wait for the web page to be ready before the code inside it gets executed. It's kind of just standard fair for jQuery. So, let's paste it in our function as such:

```
$(document).ready(function() {
  $(".mobile-menu-icon").on("click", function(){
    $(".primary-nav").toggleClass("active");
    $(this).toggleClass("open");
  });
});//end doc ready
```

First, what we have here is a jQuery function that's targeting the `mobile-menu-icon` class specifically when you click on that element:

```
$(".mobile-menu-icon").on("click", function(){
```

Once that element is clicked, two lines of code are executed. We're going to hone in first on the `primary-nav` and toggle a class called `active`:

```
$(".primary-nav").toggleClass("active");
$(this).toggleClass("open");
```

So, if you click on the hamburger menu, it's going to add a class of `active` to `primary-nav`. If you click on it a second time, it's going to remove it and kind of keep doing that for us, which is nice. The next line is targeting `$(this)`. Here, `$(this)` refers to whatever we're clicking on. In this case we're clicking on `mobile-menu-icon` and toggling a class called `open` on it. Looking at the mobile menu icon and the `primary-nav` in DevTools:

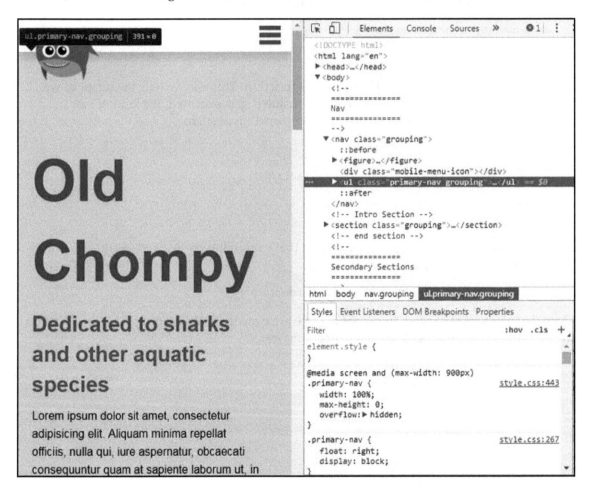

The code line in DevTools is highlighted in the following screenshot:

```
<div class="mobile-menu-icon"></div>
▶ <ul class="primary-nav grouping">…</ul>
```

Both of these should get the classes added. When we click on the hamburger menu icon, we see the `mobile-menu-icon` gets the `open` class and the `primary-nav` gets the `active` class:

```
<div class="mobile-menu-icon open"></div>
► <ul class="primary-nav grouping active">...</ul>
   ..3ft0r
```

When we click on it again, they both disappear. So now we can go ahead and target those classes how we need to. Let's go back to our CSS. We want to target the `mobile-menu-icon` in it's open state. So we add that selector to the nav section of the CSS:

```css
@media screen and (max-width: 900px) {
    ...
  .mobile-menu-icon {
    background: url('../images/mobile-menu-icon.png') 0 0 no-repeat;
    width: 30px;
    height: 26px;
    float: right;
    margin: 10px 15px 10px 0;
    cursor: pointer;
  }
  .mobile-menu-icon.open { }
}/* end of media query */
```

All we're going to do is just change the background image:

```css
.mobile-menu-icon.open {
  background-image: url('../images/mobile-menu-close-icon.png');
}
```

Now when we click on the hamburger icon, we get the **x** icon, and when we click on it again, we get the menu icon. So that's good:

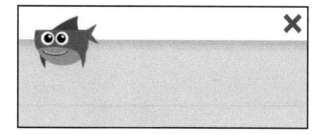

Now we want to target the `primary-nav.active` selector, so let's add that to our CSS, and give it some height:

```
@media screen and (max-width: 900px) {
  .intro-content {
    margin-top: 50px;
  }
  nav {
    position: static;
  }
  .primary-nav {
    width: 100%;
    max-height: 0;
    overflow: hidden;
  }
  .primary-nav.active {
    max-height: 350px;
  }
  ...
}
```

Now when we click on the icon, we get our menu:

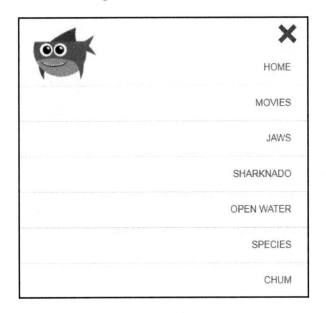

When we click on it again, it disappears:

At the moment, the image appears and disappears immediately, so we want to add a transition to that. Let's go to .primary-nav and add a transition:

```
@media screen and (max-width: 900px) {
  .intro-content {
    margin-top: 50px;
  }
  nav {
    position. static,
  }
  .primary-nav {
    width: 100%;
    max-height: 0;
    overflow: hidden;
    -webkit-transition: all ease-out .35s;
    transition: all ease-out .35s;
  }
  .primary-nav.active {
    max-height: 350px;
  }
  ...
}
```

We now should have a silky smooth transition, where the hidden navigation slides down and up as we click on the menu icon.

Our mobile navigation is done, with quite a bit of CSS and a touch of JavaScript, and our site is widely responsive now. There's just one thing we have to do – we need to test our site on a mobile device. We'll notice that the result is very different than when we resize our browser to the width of a phone or tablet. Luckily, the solution is very simple – the viewport meta tag.

Viewport meta tag

We are just about done with our responsive site. We have everything in place, except that we haven't actually tested it on a mobile device yet. In this section, let's test our design using Chrome's mobile device simulator and then look at and try to understand the `viewport` meta tag.

Testing our responsive design on a mobile device

One way to test on a mobile would be this – make your site live and test on an actual phone or tablet. An easier way to do a simple test on a phone (but possibly slightly less accurate) is to use Chrome's Device Simulator. Within DevTools there is a devices icon:

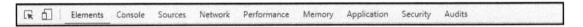

Once you click on that, you'll be able to choose a phone. We can see our site, but it doesn't look similar to when we just minimized our browser window to be about the size of a phone:

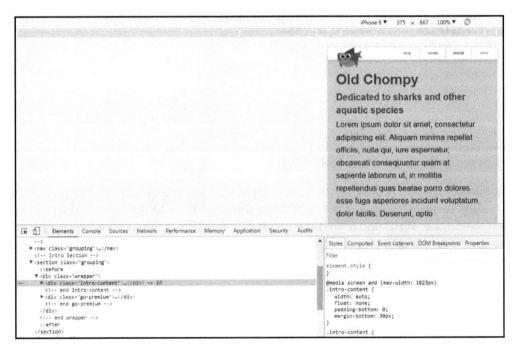

What's happening is that most mobile devices are going to try and shrink your website to fit on the phone, and then if your site isn't responsive, it will look like the desktop version, only much smaller. So one noticeable thing is I'm not seeing mobile navigation. There is a very simple solution – the `viewport` meta element. I'm going to copy and paste this into both the `index` and `shark-movies` pages:

```
<!doctype html>
<html lang="en">
<head>
  <meta charset="UTF-8">
  <meta http-equiv="X-UA-Compatible" content="IE=edge,chrome=1">

<!-- description -->
  <title>Section 6-Becoming Responsive - Mastering CSS</title>

<!-- stylesheets -->
  <link rel="stylesheet" href="css/style.css">

<!-- mobile -->
    <meta name="viewport" content="width=device-width, initial-scale=1.0,
minimum-scale=1.0">
<!-- stylesheets for older browsers -->
  <!-- ie6/7 micro clearfix -->
  <!--[if lte IE 7]>
    <style>
    .grouping {
        *zoom: 1;
    }
    </style>
  <![endif]-->
  <!--[if IE]>
    <script
src="http://html5shiv.googlecode.com/svn/trunk/html5.js"></script>
  <![endif]-->
</head>
```

It's just a `meta` element with a name of `viewport`; we'll come back to this in a second. Now, look what happens when we refresh the browser:

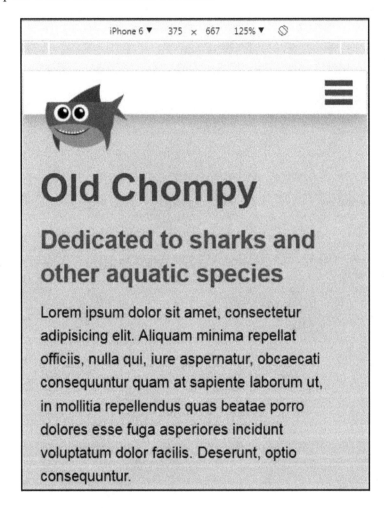

We are actually getting the mobile version, so this looks a lot better and it fixed the problem we were having.

The anatomy of the viewport meta tag

Let's examine this meta tag:

```
<meta name="viewport" content="width=device-width, initial-scale=1.0,
minimum-scale=1.0">
```

Here, I've provided the name attribute with a value of `viewport`. Then, I have a `content` attribute with a couple of different things provided inside of it. The first thing is `width=device-width`. This basically means "please don't scale my page down on mobile devices because I'm handling that with media queries. Thanks!" The second thing is `initial-scale=1.0`, which basically says this – size it to exactly the width of the device and nothing more. Lastly, we have the `minimum-scale=1.0`. This helps when you rotate your phone so the website stays exactly the width of the device after the width of the device is changed from *portrait* mode to *landscape* mode and vice versa. There's more to the `viewport` meta tag. We could add `user-scalable=no`:

The `user-scalable=no` term doesn't allow the user to zoom in or out on their phone. Sites that have this can be very annoying, which is why we're not going to include it on our site.

In conclusion, I recommend adding the `viewport` meta tag to your site's boiler plate to use it on every site. Also, there is no substitute for actual device testing as an actual phone and an emulator is never quite the same.

Summary

In this chapter, we covered the core concepts of responsive web design that will allow you to make your sites look good on any device. You learned that fluid grids and flexible images are the first steps to get a site to fit all screen sizes. We now understand how media queries can make sure the site looks good at narrower widths. We also created a mobile menu, using jQuery to trigger the menu on a click. Finally, we tested our design on Chrome's mobile device simulator and learned how to use the `viewport` meta tag to ensure our site is responsive on mobile devices. I strongly urge you, when employing these techniques yourselves, to consider the mobile experience from the very beginning, especially in the design process. In the next chapter, we will discuss web fonts.

7
Web Fonts

For a long time, we were stuck with a few basic fonts, such as Times New Roman, Georgia, and Arial. If you ever wanted to deviate farther than that, you ran the risk of the font not showing up when someone viewed your site because they probably wouldn't have had that font installed on their computer. During this period, whenever we wanted to use a fancy font, we were required to save it as an image, which used to pose many problems. Luckily for us, now web fonts have officially emerged, which gives us the ability to use a multitude of great fonts that will work on all computers. In this chapter, you're going to learn about web fonts. First you'll learn about the basic syntax of the `@font-face` rule, then we'll go over how `@font-face` can be a little tricky, followed by getting into services that provide fonts and deliver them to your website, such as Google Web Fonts and Typekit. We'll finish with icon fonts.

The @font-face property

Let's start this chapter by learning how to use the `@font-face` property to add a web font to our site. First, we'll add an OTF file to a folder on our site, then we'll define a new font in our CSS, and finally, we'll apply that CSS to the elements on our web page.

Adding font files directly to the site

In our project files for this section, we have a new folder called `fonts`. Inside this folder, there's an OTF file called `LeagueGothic-Regular`:

So now this font lives in our site's folder, and the end user visiting our website will download this font onto their computer, just like they downloaded the HTML, CSS file, and images. But first, we have to tell it to do that and look for it in our CSS.

Defining and applying new fonts in our CSS

In the CSS, right underneath our reset, let's add a new section called fonts. Add the `@font-face`; and this will allow us to declare a new font:

```
/****************
Fonts
***************/
@font-face {
    font-family: 'League-Gothic';
}
```

I'm going to declare the font name first, which can be anything. So even if the font is called `League Gothic-Regular`, you can name it `Bananas Serif` if you want. Let's call it `League Gothic` because that makes the most sense.

I've put it in single quotes for two reasons. One, it's a web font, and two, it has more than one word, which should always be quoted, just like you would quote `'Times New Roman'`. Next, we're going to declare where this font exists using the `src` property:

```
@font-face {
  font-family: 'League Gothic';
  src: url('../fonts/LeagueGothic-Regular.otf');
}
```

We want to make sure we spell that exactly right to match the name of the OTF file. Note that I used `..`/. This is an instruction to go out of the CSS folder and then go into the fonts folder and look for `LeagueGothic-Regular.otf`. Here is our projects folder structure:

So now we can add this font to any rule set using the `font-family` property that we're used to. We can specify fallbacks as well, like we normally do, in case the fonts don't get downloaded. In the "Global" section of the style sheet, there is a rule set for the h1 and another for the h2:

```
h1 {
    font-weight: 700;
    font-size: 80px;
    color: #0072ae;
    margin-bottom: 10px;
}
h2 {
    font-size: 30px;
    margin-bottom: 10px;
    color: #eb2428;
    font-weight: 700;
}
```

Beneath the h2 rule set, we'll add another, targeting h1 tags and h2 tags adding our new web font.

```
h1, h2 {
    font-family: "League Gothic", Arial, Helvetica, sans-serif;
}
```

Following is the output of preceding code:

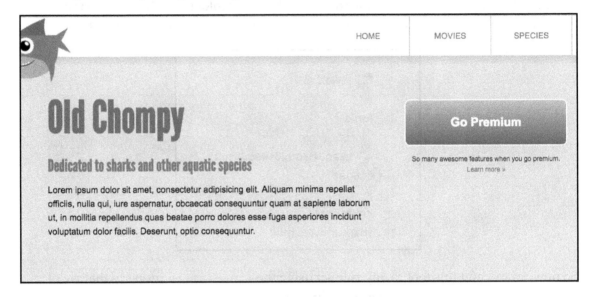

The following is what our fonts used to look like:

When we refresh, BAM! The very stylish web font is added to our website:

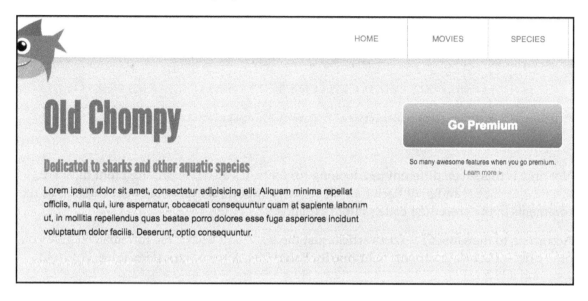

We have successfully added a web font to our website, but what we did really isn't going to work in all browsers unfortunately. Since typography may be the single most important thing on a web page, we've got to find a better solution.

@font-face: a little tricky business

On the surface, web fonts are pretty easy, but in reality, they get complicated when we want them to work in all modern browsers. Some browsers use OTF, others use WOFF, and some use EOT, RTF, and SVG. Let's go over the full setup for making a web font work using the `@font-face` property.

Making it work in all browsers

If we wanted to make this work in all browsers in the most optimal fashion, we need to provide quite a bit extra. Here's a snippet from the popular blog, *CSS Tricks*, that describes the ideal `@font-face` at-rule. (*Using @font-face* by *Chris Coyier* of `css-tricks.com`, August 25, 2016, `https://css-tricks.com/snippets/css/using-font-face/`.)

```
@font-face {
  font-family: 'MyWebFont';
  src: url('webfont.eot'); /* IE9 Compat Modes */
```

```
    src: url('webfont.eot?#iefix') format('embedded-
    opentype'), /* IE6-
    IE8 */
    url('webfont.woff2') format('woff2'), /* Super Modern
    Browsers */
    url('webfont.woff') format('woff'), /* Pretty Modern
    Browsers */
    url('webfont.ttf') format('truetype'), /* Safari,
    Android, iOS */
    url('webfont.svg#svgFontName') format('svg'); /* Legacy
    iOS */
}
```

Not only is this seven different `url` looking for fonts, it's also five different font files: `eot`, `woff2`, `woff`, `ttf`, and `svg`! Each font file format supports different browser versions as the comments in the preceding code sample explains.

According to the same *CSS Tricks* article, just the `woff` and `woff2` file formats will give you pretty decent browser support (Chrome 5+, Safari 5.1+, Firefox 3.6+, IE9+, Edge, Android 4.4+, and iOS 5.1+):

```
@font-face {
  font-family: 'MyWebFont';
  src: url('myfont.woff2') format('woff2'),
       url('myfont.woff') format('woff');
}
```

But this still means that you'll need to obtain and host both file formats, which is certainly not as challenging as five file formats, but not exactly a piece of cake either.

Web fonts are a little more involved than we would hope for. Most of the time, fonts are provided through a service, which is what we are about to see in the next two sections. Google Web Fonts, Typekit, and other services make web fonts even easier and offer high quality fonts in many different weights and styles. In the next section, we'll use a font from Google Fonts.

Google Web Fonts

Hosting your own web fonts and using proper CSS to support all browsers is slightly challenging. There are much easier ways to go about this. I really like Google Fonts; they are very easy to use and 100 percent free. The quality of the fonts is very good as well. In this section, we'll replace our hosted fonts with Google Web Fonts. The first step is to go to Google Fonts and select the two fonts we'll be using. Add a link to the CSS file in the heading of both HTML documents. Then finally, add the font name to our CSS.

Finding Google Fonts

Go to `https://fonts.google.com/` and search for our headline font: `Maven`. What's cool is that we can type in some text, say, our site title, to see how specific words will look in this font. Most font services output something like this:

So we can just type **Old Chompy** and get an idea of what this font is going to look like on our h1. We can even bump up the font size too. Let's search for and use **Maven Pro**; and do that by clicking the red plus icon. At the bottom of the screen, we should have one font family selected:

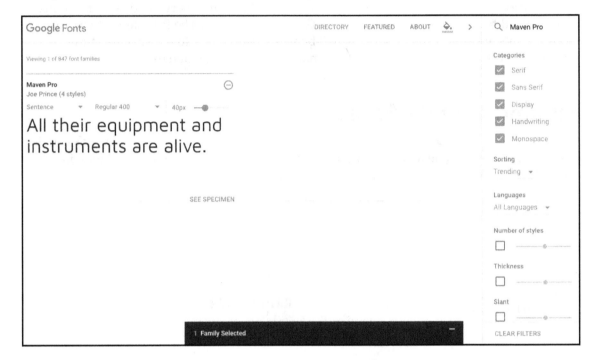

The next font we'll look for and grab **Droid Serif**. At the bottom it will show 2 families selected:

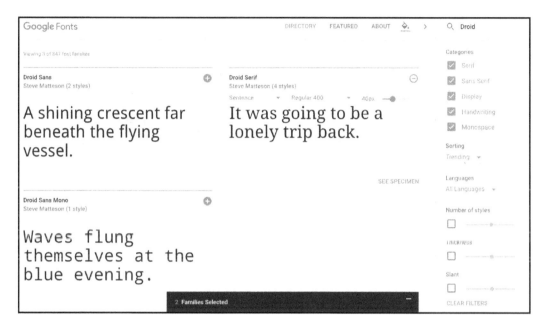

Let's open that thingy at the bottom to get more information:

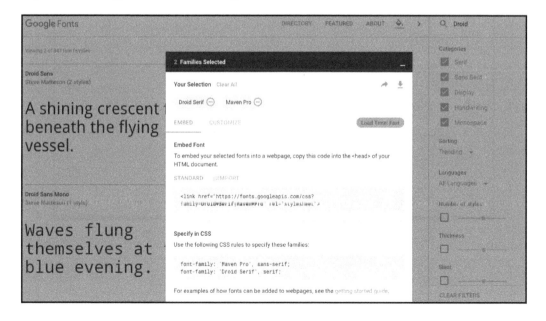

We're almost done; we're just kind of verifying and reviewing. In this panel that slid up from the bottom shows us a few interesting things:

- Load time
- How to embed the font files on our page
- How to specify these fonts in our CSS

I can add additional font-weights and font-styles by going to the *customize* tab:

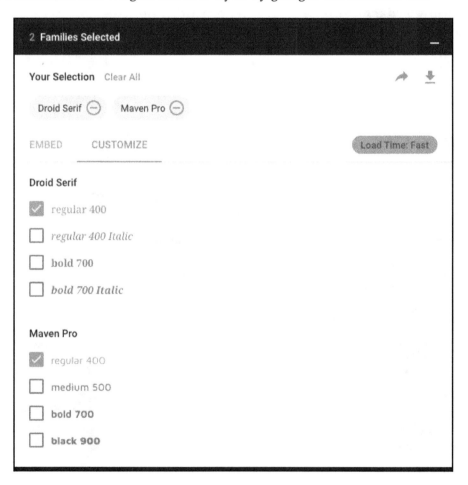

Here I can select additional font-weights and font-styles. If I select too many, the load time indicator dips to slow:

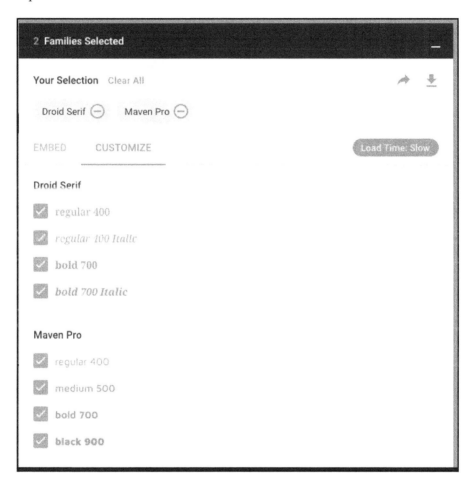

We're only going to need normal, italic, and bold for Droid Serif, and normal and bold for Maven Pro, which is goes from slow to moderate:

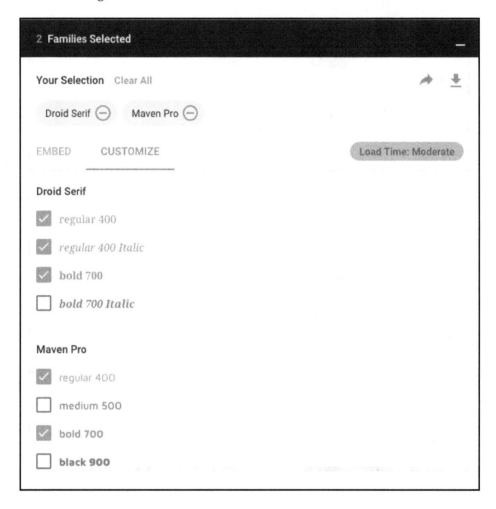

Right now, we're set to moderate load speed. I would really like to be in green, but at least we're not in red, so we'll go with that.

Let's go back to the *Embed* tab and copy the link to these font files:

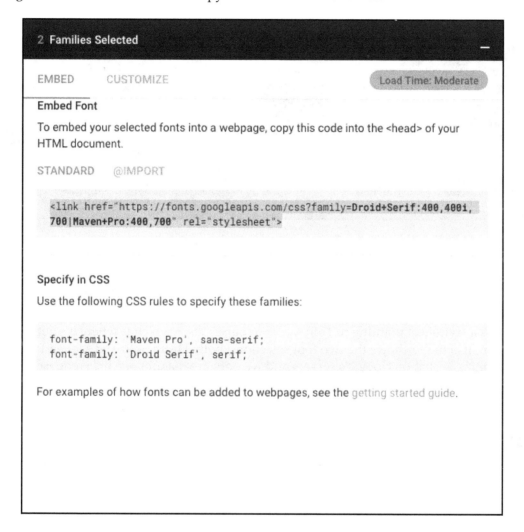

This code is really just a style sheet. Let's paste it in the `head` tag of `index.html` as well as `shark-movies.html`:

```
1  <!doctype html>
2  <html lang="en">
3  <head>
4      <meta charset="UTF-8">
5      <meta http-equiv="X-UA-Compatible" content="IE=edge,chrome=1">
6
7  <!-- mobile -->
8      <meta name="viewport" content="width=device-width, initial-scale=1.0, minimum-scale=1.0">
9
10 <!-- description -->
11     <title>Section 7-Web Fonts - Mastering CSS</title>
12
13 <!-- stylesheets -->
14     <link rel="stylesheet" href="css/style.css">
15
16 <!-- fonts -->
17     <link href="https://fonts.googleapis.com/css?family=Droid+Serif:400,400i,700|Maven+Pro:400,700" rel="stylesheet">
18
19
```

We can see that this is the same `<link/>` we use to specify our styles:

```
<link
href="https://fonts.googleapis.com/css?family=Droid+Serif:400,400i,700|Mave
n+Pro:400,700" rel="stylesheet">
```

In fact, it's a stylesheet pointing to `fonts.googleapis.com` which is where it's getting the fonts from. It actually shows the two font selections, both: Droid Serif and Maven Pro. The Google font is hosted on Google's servers and we only are making one http request, which is nice for performance.

Applying fonts in CSS

Now we want to use these fonts in our CSS. As you can see, they show us exactly how to do that:

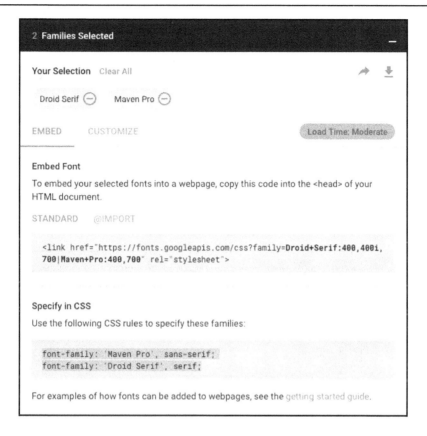

First, we replace League Gothic with Maven Pro in our h1 and h2:

```
h1 {
  font-size: 80px;
  color: #0072ae;
  margin-bottom: 10px;
  font-family: "Maven Pro", Arial, Helvetica, sans-serif;
  font-weight: 700;
}
h2 {
  font-size: 30px;
  margin-bottom: 10px;
  color: #eb2428;
  font-family: "Maven Pro", Arial, Helvetica, sans-serif;
  font-style: italic;
}
```

The next step is to add **Droid Serif**. I actually want to make sure all of our body copy, all paragraphs, anchors, and everything but `h1` tags and `h2` tags uses **Droid Serif**. We'll be a little extra cautious, so we'll add fallback fonts. We're going to specify the fallback fonts as `Georgia`, then `Times New Roman`, and then the default `serif`, as shown here:

```
body {
  background-color: #dcdcdc;
  font-family: "Droid Serif", Georgia, "Times New Roman", sans-serif;
  font-weight: 100;
  font-size: 16px;
}
```

Save these changes. Now when we go to our site, before refreshing it, we can see that we have a **League Gothic** applied to `h1` and `h2` and then our generic `Arial` for the paragraph:

When we refresh, we get our new fonts: This is very good. We have **Maven Pro** for our `h1` and our `h2`, and we have **Droid Serif** for all of our other text:

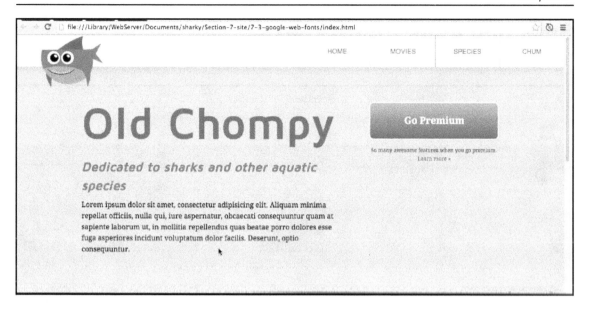

In this section, you learned how to use Google's tremendous resource of free fonts. Using Google's Web Fonts is the easiest possible way on the planet to use a font, other than not specifying a font at all. In the next section, we will look at another great font resource—*Typekit*, a subscription font library by *Adobe* that provides a very large number of high-quality fonts.

Adobe Typekit

Adobe Typekit is one of the excellent subscription font services out there. Why use Typekit, though, when there are free fonts provided by Google? I don't want to say that you get what you pay for with Google, because I think that Google's fonts are very high quality and a very large selection, but I think that the selection and quality of fonts on Typekit is outstanding as well. However, the best feature, in my opinion, is that this font service is free to all *Adobe Creative Cloud* subscribers. So if you have subscribed to the Creative Cloud suite for tools such as Photoshop and Illustrator, you have access to every font on Typekit as well. If you're not a subscriber to the Adobe Creative Cloud, you can subscribe to just Typekit as well and that's totally worth it. Another cool thing is that you can very easily sync fonts to Photoshop and Illustrator and use them for designing in those tools, which isn't as easily accomplished with Google Web Fonts. In this section, we'll add another font to our website from Typekit.

Selecting fonts from Typekit

Let's go to `https://typekit.com/`:

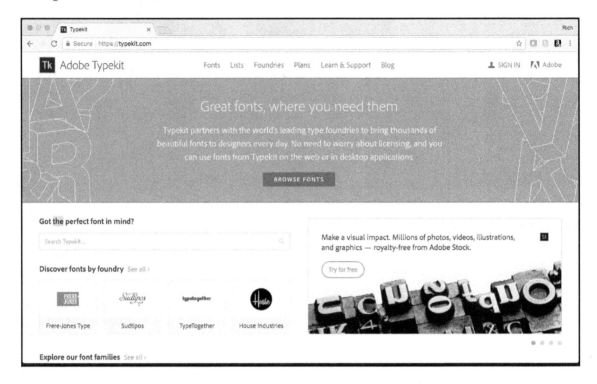

I'll sign in with my Adobe ID and password. If you don't have an Adobe ID or you're not a member of either Adobe's Creative Cloud or of Typekit as a stand alone service, you'll need to sign up in order to follow along. We can browse fonts that look good, but let's actually search for the font we want, `expo sans`:

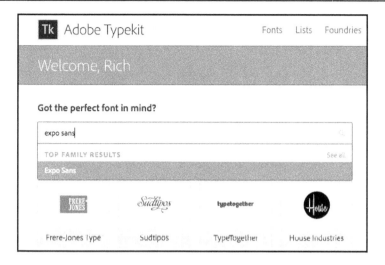

After selecting **Expo Sans**, we're at a page that shows the different weights and styles. We have two basic options that we can use, **SYNC ALL** or **ADD TO KIT**. Syncing is for syncing this font to my computer for using in Photoshop, Illustrator, and other Adobe products. Adding it to a kit allows me to use it on the Web. So let's do that and click on the **ADD TO KIT** button:

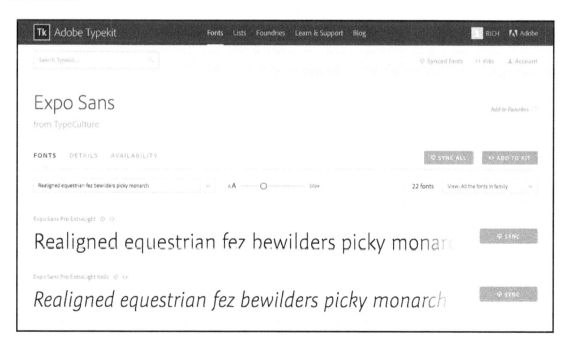

Then, we'll click on the **CREATE A KIT** button for **Expo Sans Pro**:

We'll name it `Old Chompy`, the name of our site. Then, for the domain name, I'll use `localhost:8888` and `oldchompy.com`; `localhost:8888` will be for development and `oldchompy.com` will be for later when the site goes into production, as that will be the domain name. Then we'll click on **Continue**:

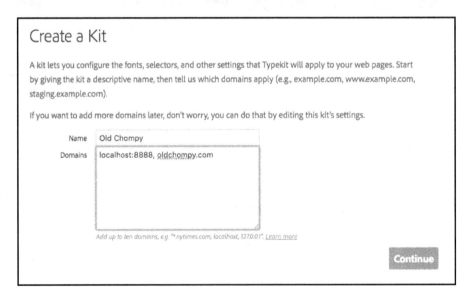

This is a minor downside of using Typekit; you have to select a domain. Throughout this course, we've been serving our pages to the browser directly through the file system. We haven't had the need to set up a local development environment. Normally, you don't have to do this until you start working with AJAX calls, server-side code, or a **content management system** (**CMS**). In order to ensure that Typekit's fonts can't be used willy-nilly anywhere, Typekit delivers them to a specific domain name.

I'll use `localhost:8888`, which is where my local server is running on my computer through MAMP. Setting up a local development environment is way beyond the scope of this project, so don't feel like you have to follow along exactly with this particular step. I'll also enter the domain where this site will theoretically will live publicly, which we'll be `localhost:8888` and `oldchompy.com`.

Before we get into this embed code, let's go back over to the site and look at the first part of the URL:

Note that I'm accessing my site differently now through `local host:8888`. This is where my local server is running. This is different from how I've been accessing it before, which is directly through the file system, going to the file library web server documents and then my site folder:

I'll do this for this one section of the entire course. Like I said before, worry if you aren't able to follow along with this part.

Adding fonts to the site

Let's head back to the embed code on Typekit; this screen gives us the JavaScript embed code:

Add your embed code

Copy the code below, and paste it into the pages on **localhost:8888** where the fonts and settings for your **Old Chompy** kit will be used. Make sure it goes into the <head> tag.

DEFAULT   ADVANCED

```
<script src="https://use.typekit.net/lac1nyi.js"></script>

<script>try{Typekit.load({ async: true });}catch(e){}</script>
```

The default embed code is simple and easy to use. It does a good job of hiding the flash of unstyled text by blocking rendering while loading. Learn more.

Continue

This code has been registered for use on **localhost:8888**. Change the domain.

I'll copy this, go over to Sublime Text, and then paste it into our HTML file's <head></head> tags. I'll do the same thing in my shark-movies.html page and save that:

```
<!doctype html>
<html lang="en">
<head>
  <meta charset="UTF-8">
  <meta http-equiv="X-UA-Compatible" content="IE=edge,chrome=1">

<!-- mobile -->
  <meta name="viewport" content="width=device-width, initial-scale=1.0,
minimum-
  scale=1.0">

<!-- description -->
  <title>Section 7-Web Fonts - Mastering CSS</title>

<!-- stylesheets -->
  <link rel="stylesheet" href="css/style.css">
```

```
<!-- fonts -->
  <link href='http://fonts.googleapis.com/css?
  family=Droid+Serif:400,700|Maven+Pro:400,700' rel='stylesheet'
type='text/css'>
<!-- Typekit -->
<script src="https://use.typekit.net/ycq4ynz.js"></script>
<script>try{Typekit.load({ async: true });}catch(e){}</script>
```

Alright, back to Typekit. I'll click on the **Continue** button to move to the next step:

On this next screen, we can do several things, including selecting which weights and styles we'd like to include. By default, regular, italic, bold, and bold italic are selected for a combined weight of 134K. I can select other weights and styles it shows me how the kit size changes. For now, I'll leave the default four weights and styles selected. Next, let's click on the **Using fonts in CSS** link near the top:

This gives us the name of the font that we want to use, which is `expo-sans-pro`:

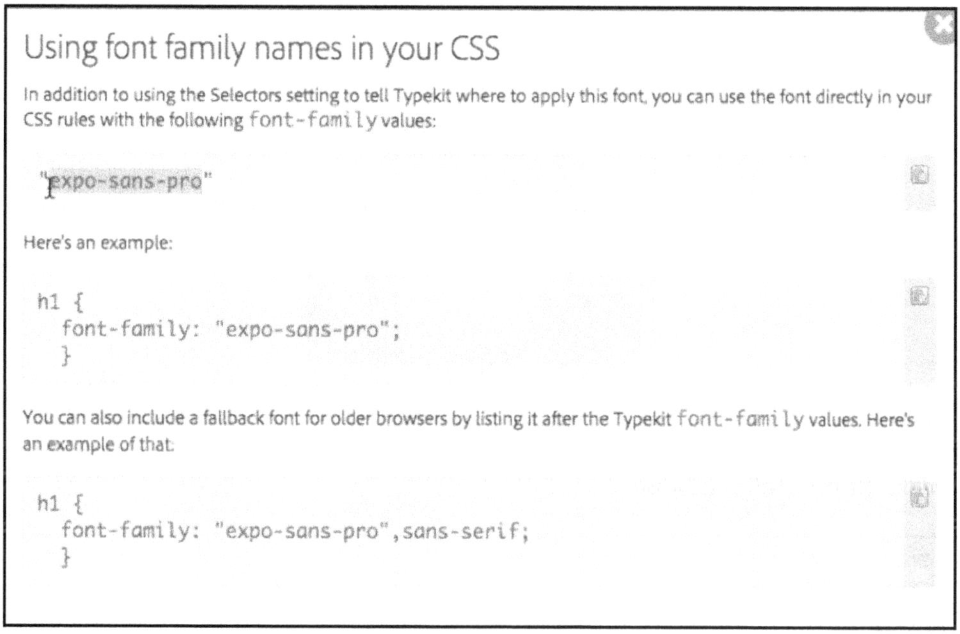

Let's copy `expo-sans-pro` and go back to the CSS file. Just for fun, paste it in our `h1` selector, right before `Maven Pro`, and save it:

```
h1 {
    font-weight: 700;
    font-size: 100px;
    color: #0072ae;
    margin-bottom: 10px;
    font-family: 'expo-sans-pro', 'Maven Pro', Arial, sans-serif;
    font-style: normal;
    font-weight: bold;
}
```

Before this is going to work though, we actually need to click on the **Publish** button:

Now, it'll tell us it may take a few minutes to be completely distributed across their network, but usually it happens a lot faster than that. If we go to our site and refresh it now, we can see a difference in the font:

This is *Expo Sans Pro*, a really gorgeous font. I almost like it better than *Maven Pro*, and that's one of the benefits of using Typekit or a paid font service: they have so many incredible high-quality fonts.

So in conclusion, we've used a beautiful font from Typekit that I'm tempted to use instead of *Maven Pro*, but I think we'll leave Maven in there. Applying fonts from a service such as Typekit involves a few extra steps, but all in all, it's still easier than hosting the fonts ourselves. In the next section, we'll look at another kind of font we can use, called icon fonts.

Icon fonts

In this section, we'll look at how we can add an icon font to our website. Icon fonts work nicely when you have solid, colored icons that are used on your site. Instead of having every image as a separate request, all icons are part of one request for the entire font—this is faster. Since we're not using images, we can use CSS to provide the color and size of the image, meaning we can make the icons larger without losing fidelity. We'll showcase our icon fonts in the footer. So first, we'll have to build the footer for both pages, then we'll download a free icon font from the ZURB Foundation. Next, we'll use CSS to add the icon fonts to our website. Last, we'll add a `:hover` state to the icons to experiment with how we can use CSS to change their appearance.

Building the footer

So here's what we're shooting for in the footer of our final website:

We want three columns of links, with each link accompanied by an icon. Traditionally, you would do this with images, but that can be a hit to performance if you have many images like we do. Traditionally, many folks have grouped all these icons into one image file called an `image sprite` and loaded it as a background image only showing the portion of the background image for the desired image using the `background-position` property. This would have made sure that you had one network request instead of 10 because you'd have been using one image file. This process was tricky because you had to use the `background-position` property to find the image you were looking for. The bigger issue was that, it came to changing a color or adding a new icon, you had to update the sprite and then the CSS. The biggest issue with an image sprite is when you have to go ahead and support HiDPI or *Retina* devices. Icon fonts aren't perfect, but they solve these tricky problems.

In both our HTML files, let's copy this code for the footer:

```
<!--
=================
Footer
=================
-->
<footer>
  <div class="wrapper grouping">
    <ul>
      <li class="list-heading">Social</li>
      <li><a href=""><span></span>Facebook</a></li>
      <li><a href=""><span></span>Twitter</a></li>
      <li><a href=""><span></span>Google+</a></li>
      <li><a href=""><span></span>Dribble</a></li>
    </ul>
    <ul>
      <li class="list-heading">Interwebs</li>
      <li><a href=""><span></span>Github</a></li>
      <li><a href=""><span></span>Stack Overflow</a></li>
      <li><a href=""><span></span>Zurb Foundation</a></li>
    </ul>
    <ul>
      <li class="list-heading">Resources</li>
      <li><a href=""><span></span>Smashing Mag</a></li>
      <li><a href=""><span></span>Treehouse</a></li>
      <li><a href=""><span></span>Designer News</a></li>
    </ul>
    <p class="legal-copy clear">Ol' Chompy - The Shark Site</p>
  </div><!-- end wrapper -->
</footer>
```

Here's what it looks like without any added CSS:

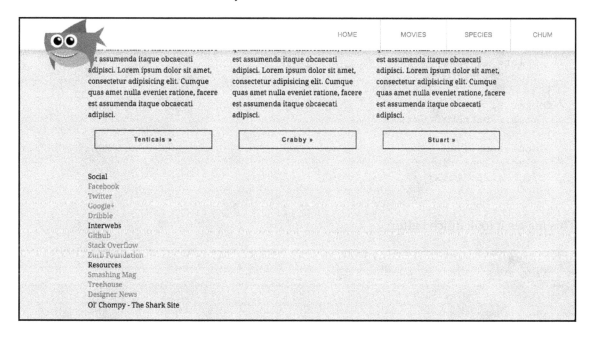

We need to clean this up. Right before the Media Queries begin, let's drop some CSS to make the footer snap into place:

```
/* * * * * * * * * * * * * * *
Footer
* * * * * * * * * * * * * * */
footer {
  background: #fff url('../images/seaweed.jpg') repeat-x 0 0;
  padding: 142px 0;
  font-size: 14px;
  line-height: 1.7;
}
footer ul {
  float: left;
  margin: 0 100px 50px 0;
}
footer .list-heading {
  text-transform: uppercase;
  color: #333;
  margin-bottom: 30px;
  font-size: 17px;
  font-family: 'Maven Pro', Arial, Helvetica, sans-serif;
}
```

```
footer a {
  color: #333;
}
footer li,
footer p {
  color: #4D4D4D;
  line-height: 30px;
}
footer li {
  margin-bottom: 10px;
}
.legal-copy {
  text-align: right;
  font-size: 10px;
}
```

This makes it look much better:

Downloading a free icon font from the ZURB Foundation

Let's go to the Zurb page for Foundation Icon Fonts 3 at `http://zurb.com/playground/foundation-icon-fonts-3`:

There's quite a few different icon fonts that come standard with this icon set. Let's click on the **Download the Font** button. In Chrome, it'll be downloaded in the bottom-left corner; we can just place the folder on the desktop and double-click on it to unzip it. Then, we can open up the Foundation-icons folder:

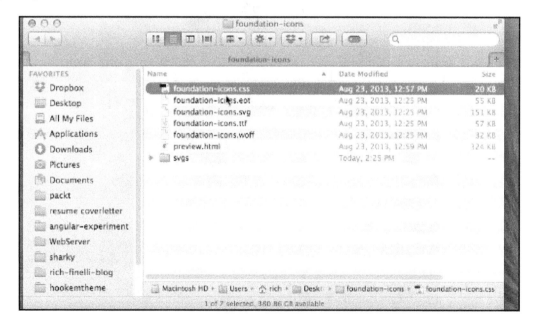

Inside this folder is a CSS file, several font files, a file called `preview.html`, and then a folder full of `svgs`. Here's what the CSS file looks like:

```css
@font-face {
  font-family: "foundation-icons";
  src: url("foundation-icons.eot");
  src: url("foundation-icons.eot?#iefix") format("embedded-opentype"),
       url("foundation-icons.woff") format("woff"),
       url("foundation-icons.ttf") format("truetype"),
       url("foundation-icons.svg#fontcustom") format("svg");
  font-weight: normal;
  font-style: normal;
}
```

Adding the icon font to our website

In our CSS, we can see the `@font-face` rule loading in different font files, just like it did with the web fonts we looked at in the second section of this chapter. Below this is the class name for every single icon font, followed by the pseudo element before:

We've learned about pseudo classes, but not pseudo elements. The pseudo elements
:before and :after are basically "make believe" elements that will appear before or after
the element you are calling. It's a neat way to add content using CSS. The content that it's
adding is the icon that relates to the class name. So if we go down to the bottom of the
selector, we can see that it actually sets up the font family, all the different font properties,
and a couple of other things:

```
...  {
  font-family: "foundation-icons";
  font-style: normal;
  font-weight: normal;
  font-variant: normal;
  text-transform: none;
  line-height: 1;
  -webkit-font-smoothing: antialiased;
  display: inline-block;
  text-decoration: inherit;
}
```

After that, in the next selector, you can see that each icon is getting content added to its
pseudo element:

The content is code that corresponds to a letter in the font family. For instance:

```
fi-address-book:before { content: "\f100"; }
```

That's the content that corresponds to the address book icon in the font family. The `fi-` prefix we're seeing in these lines of code stands for **foundation icon**. Don't worry if you don't totally understand all of this; the main thing is that we need to copy this CSS to our CSS file. It's 594 lines of code, so I don't want to include it with our existing style sheet because it will just overly bloat it more than I care to. So we have two choices. We could lint out and figure out only the icons we plan to use from the CSS file, or we could just link to the CSS file separately. Let's link to it separately—this way we have the entire icon font library at our disposal if we need it. Ideally later, we'd lint out the unused icon fonts before moving to production to as pairing that file down to just the 10 icons we're using takes it from 20kb to 1kb!

Let's save this file in our project's `css` folder and call it `icons.css`:

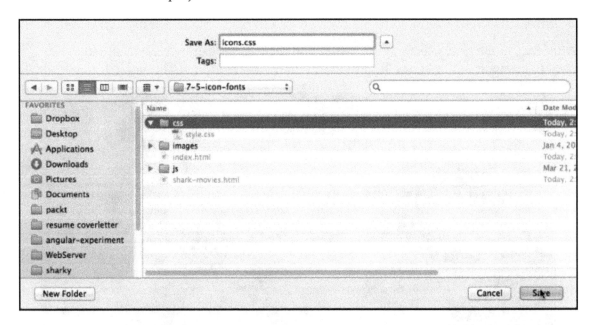

We'll now go into our `index.html` file and add a link to `foundation-icons.css` in the head of this file, right underneath the link to `style.css`:

```
<!-- stylesheets -->
  <link rel="stylesheet" href="css/style.css">
  <link rel="stylesheet" href="css/foundation-icons.css">
```

Save this, copy it, and jump over to Shark Movies to paste it in there as well, and save it.

Next, let's create a new folder called `icons`. We'll drag the four different font files to this new folder:

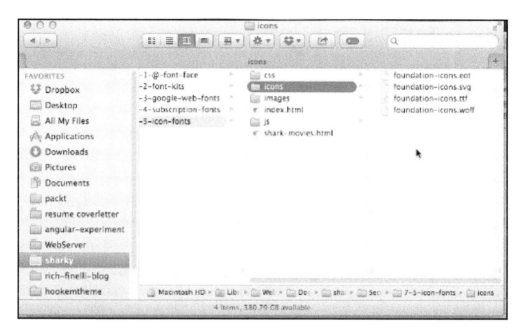

Now that these four different font files are in the `icons` folder, back in the `icons.css` file, we just have to change the source to now point to the folder where we just put those font files. Let's prepend `../icons/`, like so to the url:

```
@font-face {
  font-family: "foundation-icons";
  src: url("../icons/foundation-icons.eot");
  src: url("../icons/foundation-icons.eot?#iefix") format("embedded-
opentype"),
       url("../icons/foundation-icons.woff") format("woff"),
       url("../icons/foundation-icons.ttf") format("truetype"),
       url("../icons/foundation-icons.svg#fontcustom") format("svg");
  font-weight: normal;
  font-style: normal;
}
```

So now we have these URLs pointing to the proper folder.

We now need to add the icon classes to the elements in our HTML to load in the icon. But first we need to determine which classes to use. The `preview.html` file is a big help there, so let's open that one up from the `foundation-icons` folder:

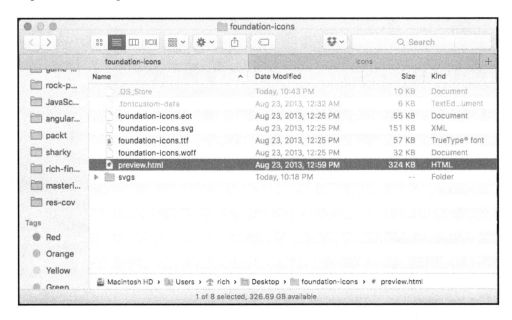

When we open it, we can see the icons displayed at different sizes. Search for Facebook, and here we can see the Facebook icon we're looking for and the class name that corresponds to it, `fi-social-facebook`:

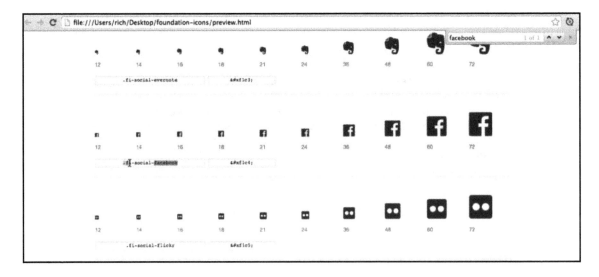

Copy everything but the period of that class name and paste that next to the link to Facebook in `index.html`:

```
<footer>
  <div class="wrapper grouping">
    <ul>
      <li class="list-heading">Social</li>
      <li><a href=""><span class="fi-social-
facebook"></span>Facebook</a></li>
      <li><a href=""><span></span>Twitter</a></li>
      <li><a href=""><span></span>Google+</a></li>
      <li><a href=""><span></span>Dribble</a></li>
    </ul>
    <ul>
      <li class="list-heading">Interwebs</li>
      <li><a href=""><span></span>Github</a></li>
      <li><a href-""><span></span>Stack Overflow</a></li>
      <li><a href=""><span></span>Zurb Foundation</a></li>
    </ul>
    <ul>
      <li class="list-heading">Resources</li>
      <li><a href=""><span></span>Smashing Mag</a></li>
      <li><a href=""><span></span>Treehouse</a></li>
      <li><a href=""><span></span>Designer News</a></li>
    </ul>
    <p class="legal-copy clear">Ol' Chompy - The Shark Site</p>

  </div><!-- end wrapper -->
</footer>
```

Save this and now, when we go to our site, we will be able to see the Facebook icon:

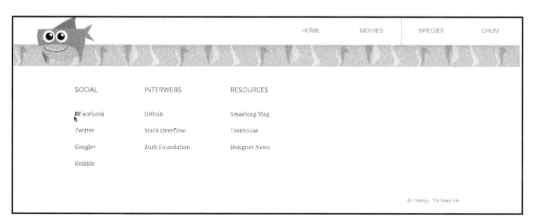

Styling icon fonts

We have two problems: one, it's too small, and two, it's really close to the word. What we should do is add `margin-right` to every icon and make it larger. This means every `span` tag in the HTML is going to need a class. Let's add `class="icon"` as follows:

```
<footer>
  <div class="wrapper grouping">
    <ul>
      <li class="list-heading">Social</li>
      <li><a href=""><span class="icon fi-social-
facebook"></span>Facebook</a></li>
      <li><a href=""><span class="icon"></span>Twitter</a></li>
      <li><a href=""><span class="icon"></span>Google+</a></li>
      <li><a href=""><span class="icon"></span>Dribble</a></li>
    </ul>
    <ul>
      <li class="list-heading">Interwebs</li>
      <li><a href=""><span class="icon"></span>Github</a></li>
      <li><a href=""><span class="icon"></span>Stack Overflow</a></li>
      <li><a href=""><span class="icon"></span>Zurb Foundation</a></li>
    </ul>
    <ul>
      <li class="list-heading">Resources</li>
      <li><a href=""><span class="icon"></span>Smashing Mag</a></li>
      <li><a href=""><span class="icon"></span>Treehouse</a></li>
      <li><a href=""><span class="icon"></span>Designer News</a></li>
    </ul>
    <p class="legal-copy clear">Ol' Chompy - The Shark Site</p>

  </div><!-- end wrapper -->
</footer>
```

Now in the CSS, in our footer section, let's add a new rule set that fixes these two issues:

```
footer .icon {
  margin-right: 10px;
  font-size: 30px;
}
```

The other thing we could do is add a transition, because we're going to have a hover effect, and this will help ease that state change. Let's add a transition:

```
footer .icon {
  margin-right: 10px;
  font-size: 30px;
  -webkit-transition: .25s color ease-in-out;
  transition: .25s color ease-in-out;
}
```

Now refresh the site and you'll see that the Facebook icon is a little bit bigger and it has some more space:

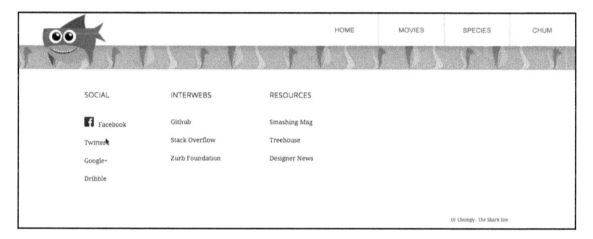

Now what we need to do is add a corresponding class for Twitter, Google, Dribble, and the other six links in the HTML:

```
<footer>
  <div class="wrapper grouping">
    <ul>
      <li class="list-heading">Social</li>
      <li><a href=""><span class="icon fi-social-facebook">
      </span>Facebook</a></li>
      <li><a href=""><span class="icon fi-social-twitter">
      </span>Twitter</a></li>
      <li><a href=""><span class="icon fi-social-google-plus">
      </span>Google+</a></li>
      <li><a href=""><span class="icon fi-social-dribbble">
      </span>Dribbble</a></li>
    </ul>
    <ul>
      <li class="list-heading">Interwebs</li>
```

```
      <li><a href=""><span class="icon fi-social-github">
      </span>Github</a></li>
      <li><a href=""><span class="icon fi-social-stack-overflow">
      </span>Stack Overflow</a></li>
      <li><a href=""><span class="icon fi-social-zurb"></span>Zurb
      Foundation</a></li>
    </ul>
    <ul>
      <li class="list-heading">Resources</li>
      <li><a href=""><span class="icon fi-social-smashing-mag">
      </span>Smashing Mag</a></li>
      <li><a href=""><span class="icon fi-social-treehouse">
      </span>Treehouse</a></li>
      <li><a href=""><span class="icon fi-social-designer-news">
      </span>Designer News</a></li>
    </ul>
    <p class="legal-copy clear">Ol' Chompy - The Shark Site</p>

  </div><!-- end wrapper -->
</footer>
```

Here's how it looks:

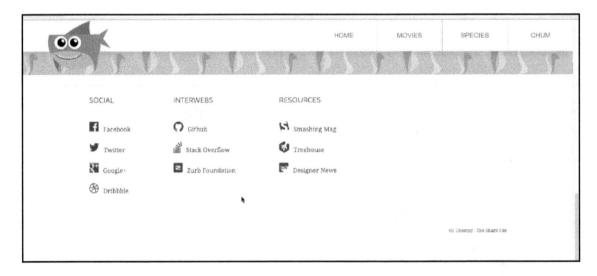

OK! So now we have all our icon-specific classes in place, and we have an icon on each link on our footer. The cool part about icon fonts is that they will be crisp and clear on HiDPI devices. Also, we can change the color and other properties on a hover state, which we couldn't do with a normal raster image. Let's add a quick hover state to all of these. In our CSS, let's add a new selector:

```
footer .icon {
  margin-right: 10px;
  font-size: 30px;
  -webkit-transition: .25s color ease-in-out;
  transition: .25s color ease-in-out;
}
footer a:hover .icon {
  color: #f00;
}
```

Apply this, and you should see that this icon transitions nicely to a totally different color:

Icon fonts are an excellent choice for your website. I recommend using icon fonts on noncritical elements of your website because, if for some reason the font doesn't load on your user's computer, there will be no fallback. The fallback usually defaults to a square, or worse, a totally unrelated character or letter. In our case, I think we're okay, because in a situation where our icon font doesn't load, we will still have descriptions of the icon right next to it. The nice part about icon fonts is that, just like any other font, they scale fluently to retina devices.

Summary

We started this chapter on web fonts by discussing the `@font-face` property, using it to add fonts to our site. We looked at how to use Google Fonts and Typekit. Finally, you learned how to use icon fonts and build a site's footer with the icon font from Zurb. In the next chapter, we'll talk about retina devices and get our pages ready for the world of HiDPI devices.

8
Workflow for HiDPI Devices

Retina devices are now almost the default for Apple computers, tablets, and phones. Also, the word "retina" is actually trademarked by Apple for computer equipment, and is their branded way of describing double(or more)-density screens and devices. I'm going to use the word "retina" loosely to describe any device that has a high-density display, whether its made by Apple or not. Everything on a retina device is sharper and crisper because there are nearly four times the pixels as there are in a CSS device's display; for every "CSS pixel", there are now four "device pixels", allowing higher quality displays. The downside is that the images we've used so far are actually not going to look so good on such a device because we haven't accounted for higher density displays.

In this chapter, we'll go over a number of techniques for images that take retina displays into account. This includes making images twice their size. We'll also look into the background image technique, using SVG, and using the `srcset` attribute on the image element to further account for retina.

2x images

2x images are twice the width and twice the height images. The basic idea is to make the image twice the width and height that we actually need. We'll then add that image to our HTML. Then we'll use CSS to constrain the image to the actual size that it will be on the screen. The way I like to do this is the same way I like to handle flexible images in responsive design: I like to make sure that the images will have a containing element with a set `width` and `height` value. Then, I make sure the image itself has its `max-width` set to 100%. Both these requirements are already in place. All my images typically have a container, and in CSS, and all my images have their `max-width` set to 100%.

Creating a retina size image (2x)

So let's get started with the raster images on the shark movies page. Right-click on the Jaws movie image and inspect this element:

We can see that these images on the shark movies page are 200 x 200 pixels. Our goal is to replace these with images that are 400 x 400 pixels. As you can see in my `images` folder, shown in the following screenshot, I've already created three images that are identical to the original images, except they are larger and suffixed with `@2x.jpg` to signify that these are the retina versions:

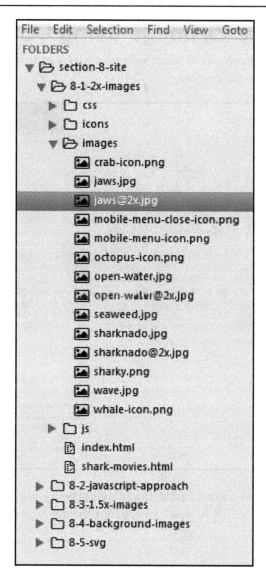

Switching over to the HTML, you can see I've added @2x to the image filename for all three images and have saved it. This is what our Open Water movie filename should look like, for example:

```
<img src="images/open-water@2x.jpg" alt="Open Water movie">
```

Sizing down the 2x image using CSS

Go over to the browser and refresh it. Now, when you look at this image of Jaws, you really wouldn't see any noticeable difference:

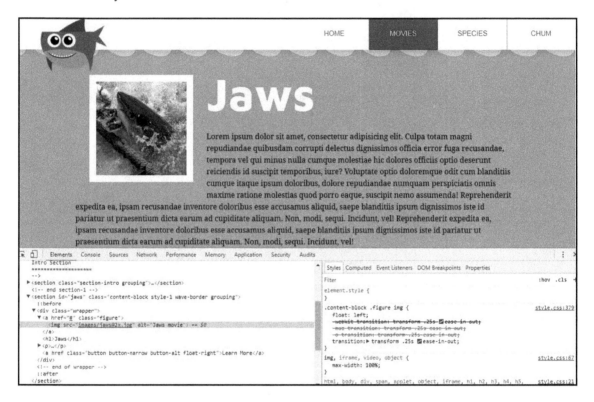

However, a quick inspection shows that a @2x image is being served, but it's being constrained to a size of 200 x 200, so you can see that the original image is 400 x 400, but it's showing as 200 x 200:

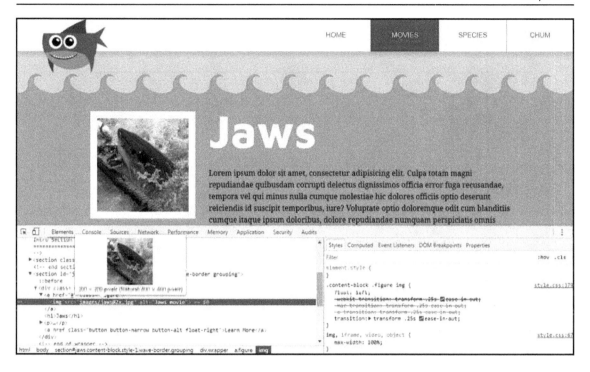

Because of our foundation of responsive design, the immediate containing element .figure already has a width set of 23.958333333333 percent (as shown in the following code), which is equal to 200 pixels in the website's widest context:

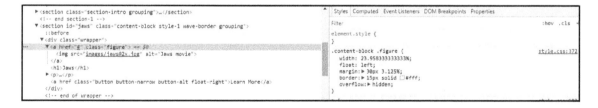

If we remove the `width` from the Styles pane of the Chrome DevTools, the image blows up to its actual size, which is `400 x 400`:

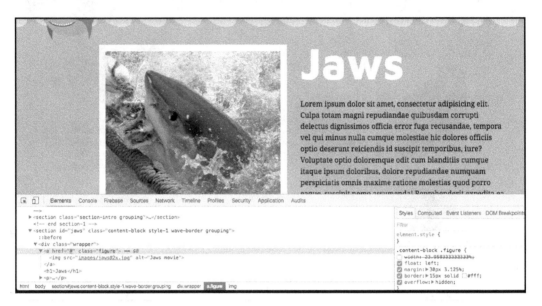

So it's the containing element, having a set `width`, along with the `max-width` set to 100%, that keeps the image constrained. If we remove this `max-width` from the Style pane of the Chrome DevTools, the image would no longer be constrained, as shown here:

The parent element has the overflow option set to hidden, which is why the image isn't getting any wider than 23.95 percent.

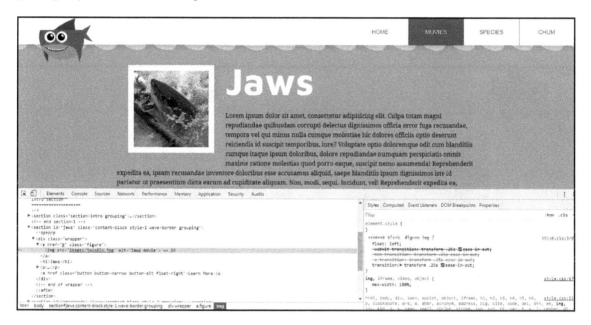

Checking the image quality on a retina device

Now how do we know that the image is going to look good on a retina device? The best thing to do is test it on a retina device, but we can also cheat a little bit and zoom Chrome to 200 percent. First, let's set this width to 200px directly in the DevTools:

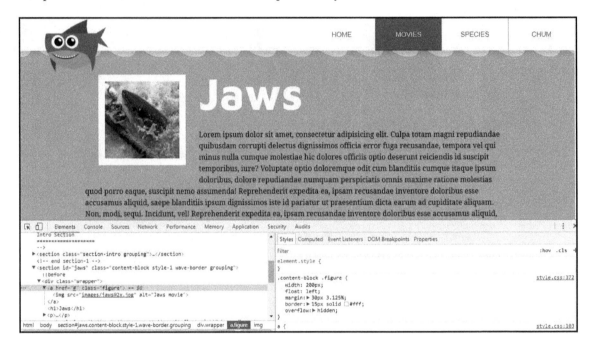

Then let's go to the Chrome toolbar and zoom in to 200%:

The preceding screenshot is supposed to demonstrate that at 200% zoom, the image is still very crisp, and this is kind of simulating a retina device.

This doesn't seem like a bad way to get your images retina ready. Well, if it were only that easy. It turns out that making your images twice the height and width really makes them about three to four times bigger than their 1x counterparts. So if you look at the Jaws image in the `images` folder, the original is 28 KB and the 2x version (the double-density version) is 105 KB. That's four times as large!

jaws	5/14/2015 12:43 AM	JPEG image	28 KB
jaws@2x	5/14/2015 12:43 AM	JPEG image	105 KB

So, in conclusion, this is just the beginning of our preparations for the retina web. Our biggest issue right now is that we are serving a huge retina-size image to all devices, even those that aren't retina. That's extra download and page weight to sites that won't get any benefit from it is not very responsible.

In the next section, we'll look at a similar technique for background images.

Background images

In order to handle background images, we can use a special media query to determine the pixel ratio and then modify the `background` property to serve up the retina image. In this section, we'll determine how we can account for background images in the sphere of retina. We'll first create a media query designed for determining the pixel ratio. Then, we'll update the image being served to be the retina version. The seaweed in the footer is a background image, and thus will be the perfect image for this task.

Targeting the seaweed in the footer

Here is the seaweed just above the footer on the movies page:

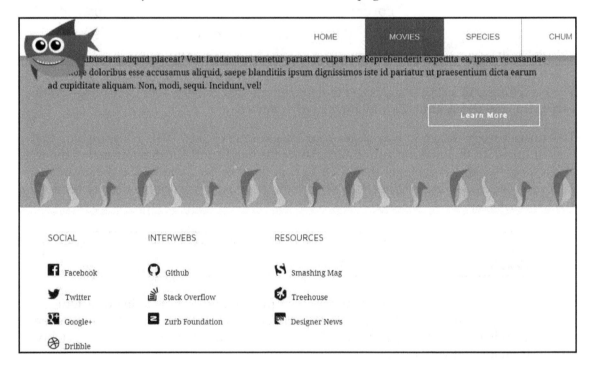

If we look at the CSS, all that's happening is that the footer has a repeating background image. The background is the seaweed, and we're getting it to repeat along the *x* axis:

```
footer {
  background: #fff url('../images/seaweed.jpg') repeat-x 0 0;
  padding: 142px 0;
  font-size: 14px;
  line-height: 1.7;
}
```

So we need to have a retina-sized version of `seaweed.jpg`. I have that in my `images` folder, and I've named it `seaweed@2x.jpg`:

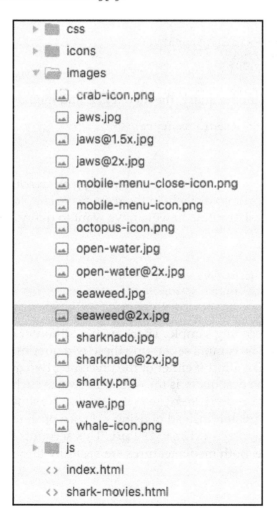

At the very bottom of the style sheet, after all our media queries, let's reserve a spot for retina background images:

```
/**************
Retina, Background Images
**************/
```

This is where we'll have the special media query to detect retina.

Media query for device pixel ratio

We remember media queries like this from Chapter 6, *Becoming Responsive*:

```
@media all and (max-width: 400px) {
  /*rule sets here*/
}
```

There are two parts to the media query, the media *type* and media *feature*:

```
@media media type and (media feature) {
  /*rule sets here*/
}
```

The media type can be keyword values such as *screen*, *print*, *speech*, and *all*. The media feature can be a number of things as well. In the responsive chapter, the feature was the max-width of the browser. For retina however, we want to query for the pixel-ratio of the screen:

```
@media
screen and (-webkit-min-device-pixel-ratio: 2),
screen and (min-resolution: 192dpi) {
}
```

A lot is going on in the preceding sample. There are two different queries targeting two different media features. The comma separating these two queries is similar to saying "or." So the media query will take affect if either of the preceding two queries are true. But why have two queries? Well, the first query is for webkit browsers such as Safari and older Chrome on devices with min-device-pixel-ratio of 2. Next, we target devices that have 192 dots per inch or greater. Instead of using a device pixel ratio, which is webkit-specific, it's just using min-resolution: 192dpi. This accounts for different browsers, such as a Windows mobile. Both media features are basically targeting retina.

Now inside of the media query, we will target the footer and change the background image to our retina version. I'll type in the footer and add an opening curly brace and then `background-image`; the URL is going to be `../images/seaweed@2x.jpg`:

```
@media
screen and (-webkit-min-device-pixel-ratio: 2),
screen and (min-resolution: 192dpi) {
    footer {
        background-image: url('../images/seaweed@2x.jpg');
    }
}
```

We see no noticeable difference though in the browser. Let's inspect the footer though, just to make sure that it's still loading up the regular `seaweed.jpg` file, and not `seaweed@2x.jpg`:

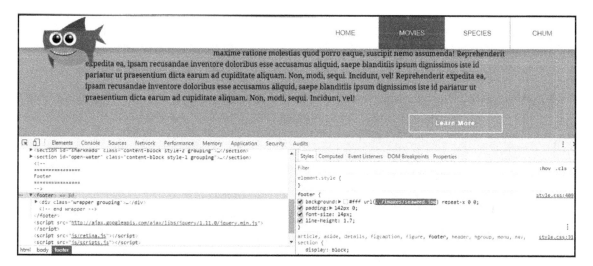

The reason we are checking this is because I'm not on a retina device. We can use some trickery to make sure this is working. Let's go to our CSS and change the device pixel ratio to `1`:

```
@media
screen and (-webkit-min-device-pixel-ratio: 1),
screen and (min-resolution: 192dpi) {
    footer {
        background-image: url('../images/seaweed@2x.jpg');
    }
}
```

Let's see what that looks like in the browser:

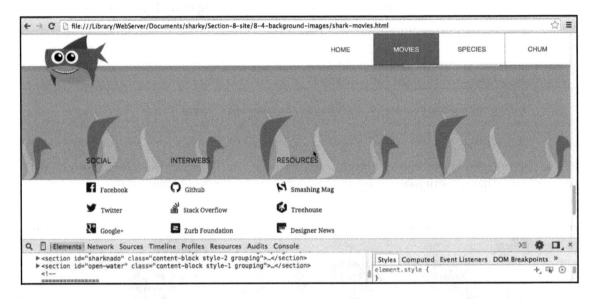

Now we are getting the 2x version, and we can see that it's noticeably larger. We have twice the size image; it visually looks like it's twice the size. It's not being constrained down to our intended display size. There's a property called `background-size` that we will use to fix this.

Serving the 2x image only to retina devices

We have to use the `background-size` property in order to ensure the seaweed is constrained appropriately. We will put the `background-size` property right in the ruleset that holds the non-retina version at the top of our footer section, not inside the media query. We could easily put it in the media query and that would be fine and dandy, but this is going to apply to non-retina devices and retina devices, so we'll just add a background size of 200px horizontally and 100px vertically, as shown in the following code:

```
footer {
  background: #fff url('../images/seaweed.jpg') repeat-x 0 0;
  background-size: 200px 100px;
  padding: 142px 0;
  font-size: 14px;
  line-height: 1.7;
}
```

Save this and go to the browser. When we refresh the site, the seaweed should shrink down to 200 x 100, back to its regular size:

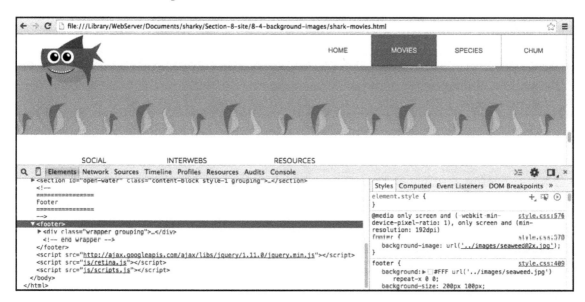

If you look at our styles in the DevTools, you can see we're getting the @2x version. You can see the way the browser is loading in the CSS—it sees the media query on top. This is what's getting used. Below it is the non-media query version that is not getting loaded. This is exactly how we want it to work, which is good.

The last thing we need to do is revert the media query to a device-pixel-ratio of two instead of one, so, we'll change that:

```
@media
screen and (-webkit-min-device-pixel-ratio: 2),
screen and (min-resolution: 192dpi) {
  footer {
    background-image: url('../images/seaweed@2x.jpg');
  }
}
```

Now it'll load the non-retina version because I'm on a non-retina device:

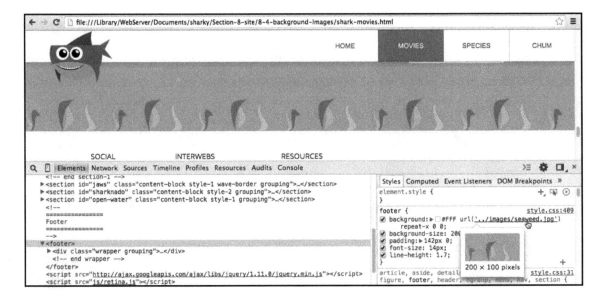

Only the retina-sized background image is downloaded by retina devices and the regular-sized background image is downloaded by non-retina devices. All is good, but this is still quite a bit of work. There's a better way that we can handle this seaweed that involves less work and only requires one image–using SVG instead of traditional raster graphics.

Scalable Vector Graphic (SVG)

A **Scalable Vector Graphic**(SVG) - is an XML-based image format for graphics. It's different than raster formats, like JPEG and PNG, because it SVG scale to any size without losing any resolution or looking pixelated. This means that we don't need multiple images for retina or responsive layouts! Another bonus with SVG's is that the file size is can be much smaller than that of the same image, saved as a JPEG or PNG. All major browsers support the SVG format as far back as IE9. SVGs aren't a replacement for every image on your site–they are particularly suited for line drawings, which are typically generated through design software, such as Adobe Illustrator.

In this section, we're going to look at how to save an Adobe Illustrator file as an SVG, and three different ways in which we can add SVG's to our website:

- Adding an SVG as a `background-image`
- Adding an SVG using the `<img>` tag
- Using an inline SVG

We've got plenty of images on our site that would lend themselves well to SVG, including the shark at the top of our site:

All the different ocean species we have in the middle of our site will also work great as SVG:

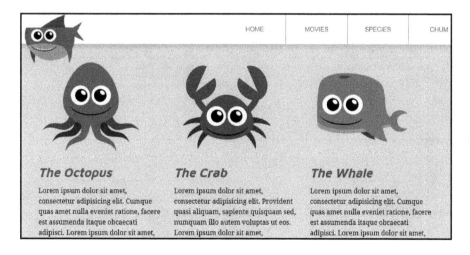

Even the seaweed we have in the footer, which we worked on in the last section is a great candidate for SVG:

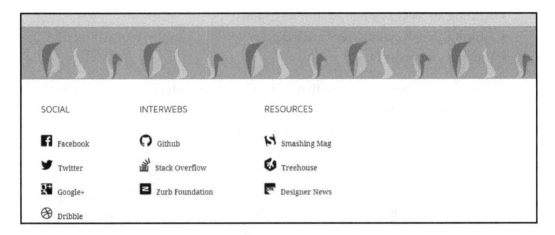

So what images aren't great candidates for SVG? Well, our raster images on the movies page are definitely not:

Saving an Illustrator file as an SVG

I have an Adobe Illustrator file called `seaweed.ai` open in Illustrator. A program like Illustrator is where SVG's can be created or drawn from scratch. Creating SVG's in Illustrator is far out of scope for this book, but I want to start here just to show where an SVG's *could* come from.

In *Illustrator CC 2017*, one of the best ways to save an AI file down to SVG for web is by using the **File** > **Export** > **Export for Screens...** option.

This option uses the `artboard` name as the name of the file, so before we export as an SVG, let's rename the artboard by going to **Window** > `Artboards`. Let's rename from **artboard1** to **seaweed**, as shown in the following screenshot:

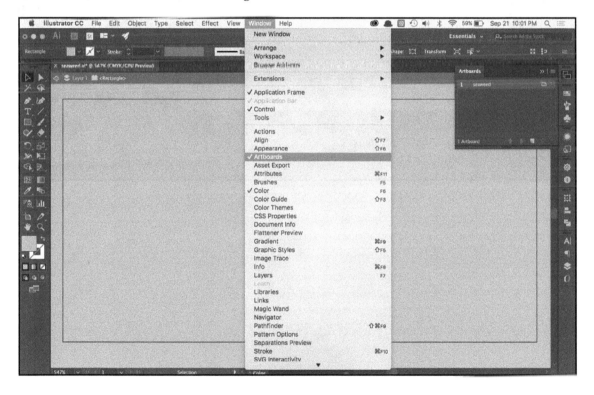

Now, by going to the **File** > **Export** > **Export for Screens...** option, we'll get an SVG file:

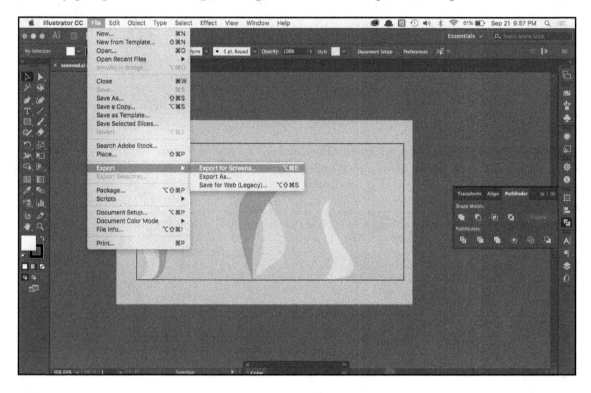

That brings up screen with a few options. Using the **Export to** field, we'll choose where to save this file, which will inevitably be in our `images` folder. We'll also change the **Format** to SVG before clicking the **Export Artboard** button in the bottom right:

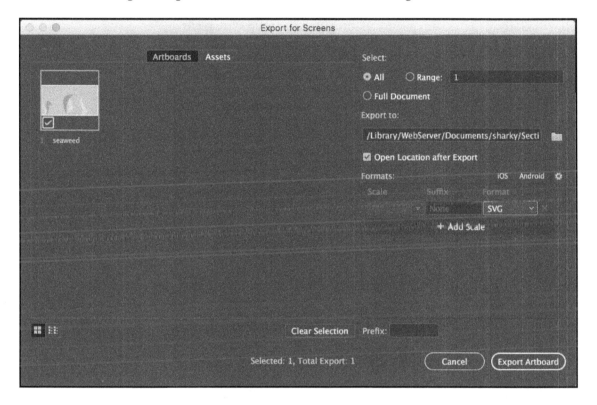

After saving, you can see that the SVG is 1 KB. The `@2x` version we used in the last section was 13 KB!

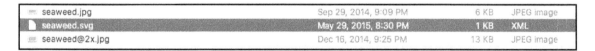

So not only is the SVG 13 times smaller than the `@2x` version, it's also six times smaller than the regular version, and that is truly amazing! Now let's integrate this into our CSS.

Adding the SVG file as a background image

In our CSS, inside the rule set targeting the footer, all I'm going to do is change the format from .jpg to .svg—that is, from ('.../images/seaweed.jpg') to ('.../images/seaweed.svg'), as shown in the following code:

```
footer {
    background: #fff url('../images/seaweed.svg') repeat-x 0 0;
    background-size: 200px 100px;
    padding: 142px 0;
    font-size: 14px;
    line-height: 1.7;
}
```

Since now we have an SVG that's going to work for both non-retina and retina devices, we'll go down to the very bottom and comment out this media query from our last section:

```
/***************
Retina, Background Images
***************/
/***********
@media
only screen and (-webkit-min-device-pixel-ratio: 2),
only screen and (min-resolution: 192dpi) {
    footer {
        background-image: url('../images/seaweed@2x.jpg');
    }
}
*************/
```

This is what we used in the last section to serve a larger image to retina devices, but we don't need all that extra code if we're using SVG. So I've gotten rid of it.

I'll refresh the browser, and it looks exactly the same. Let's inspect the element, as shown in the following screenshot. We can see that it's serving up seaweed.svg. We went from 2 images to 1. 13 KB to 1 KB. And we got rid of several lines of CSS in a complicated media query. Are you starting to understand why SVG is pure awesomeness?

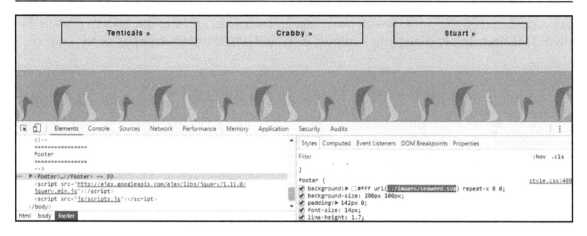

Adding the SVG as a regular ol' <img>

You can also use an SVG as a regular `<img>`. We happen to have a couple of images in the middle of our site—the different ocean species that will make perfect candidates for implementing SVG with this approach:

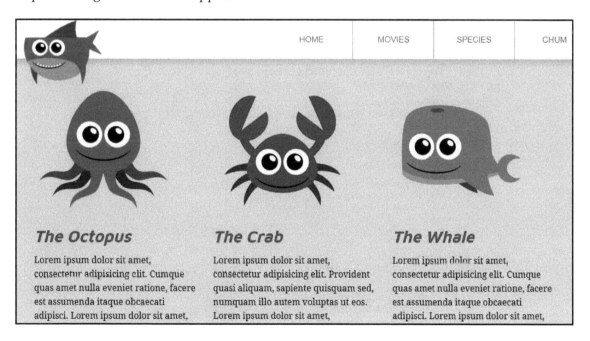

I've already saved a copy of the octopus, crab, and whale as an `.svg` file. So let's go over to the HTML and simply change the octopus, crab, and whale images from `.png` to `.svg`:

```
<!--
================
Secondary Sections
================
-->
<section class="secondary-section grouping">
  <div class="wrapper">
    <div class="column">
      <figure>
        <img src="images/octopus-icon.svg" alt="Octopus">
      </figure>
      <h2>The Octopus</h2>
      <p>Lorem ipsum dolor... </p>
      <a href="#" class="button">Tenticals &raquo;</a>
    </div>
    <div class="column">
      <figure>
        <img src="images/crab-icon.svg" alt="Crab">
      </figure>
      <h2>The Crab</h2>
      <p>Lorem ipsum dolor... </p>
      <a href="#" class="button">Crabby &raquo;</a>
    </div>
    <div class="column">
      <figure><img src="images/whale-icon.svg" alt="Whale"></figure>
      <h2>The Whale</h2>
      <p>Lorem ipsum dolor... </p>
      <a href="#" class="button">Stuart &raquo;</a>
    </div>
  </div><!-- end wrapper -->
</section>
```

The name of the files in the `images` folder are exactly the same. The only difference is that the suffix is `svg` instead of `png`:

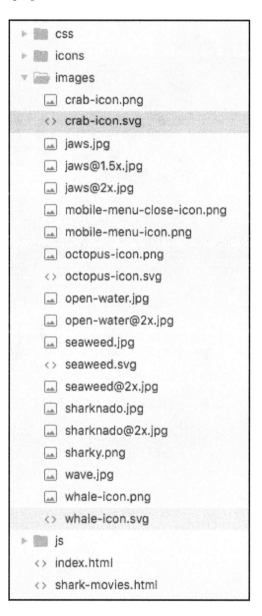

Save this. We'll get the following output:

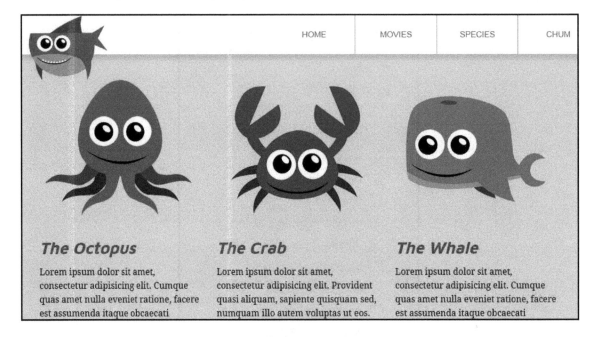

In the preceding image, we can see that the files look good; the only problem is that they appear to have gotten a little bigger. So we'll constrain these down to the size we want.

You can't stop SVG's, you can only hope to *constrain* them!

To constrain the size of images, we need to set a `width` and/or a `max-width`. We actually already did this but only inside of a media query so it isn't firing on larger screens:

```
@media screen and (max-width: 1023px){
  .intro-content {
    width: auto;
    float: none;
    padding-bottom: 0;
    margin-bottom: 30px;
  }
  .go-premium {
    width: auto;
    float: none;
    margin-top: 0;
  }
```

```
.column {
  float: none;
  width: auto;
  padding: 0 50px;
}
.column figure {
  margin: 0 auto;
  width: 100%;
  max-width: 250px;
}
.column h2 {
  text-align: center;
}
}/* end of media query */
```

Let's remove that rule set from the media query and add it up where we originally defined the 3 columns outside of our responsive media queries:

```
* * * * * * * * * * * * * * * *
3 columns
* * * * * * * * * * * * * * * */
.column {
  float: left;
  width: 31.25%; /* 300/960 */
  margin-left: 3.125%; /* 30/960 */
}
.column:first-child {
  margin-left: 0;
}
.column figure {
  margin: 0 auto;
  width: 100%;
  max-width: 250px;
}
```

And all we did there is center the `figure` element using auto margins, make sure the width is 100% of its container, as long as the width is never more than 250px (`max-width`).

Now that we have this in the right place, this is what we get:

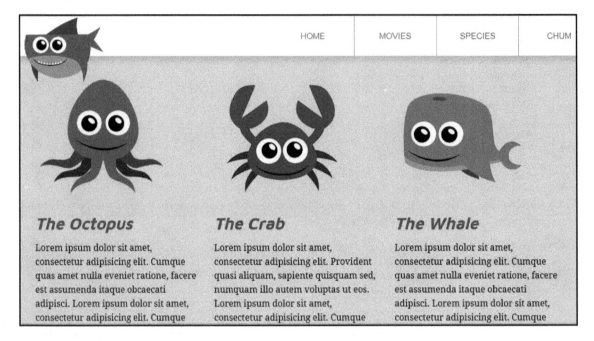

We've constrained each SVG image to a maximum width of 250px. Our crab, octopus, and whale look mighty good and are instantly retina ready.

Using an inline SVG

We have one other option for SVG, called an inline SVG. Since an SVG is really just XML inside of a text file, we can actually embed the SVG code directly into our HTML. This makes it so that we don't need to have an additional HTTP request (good for performance). Also, it allows us to alter the SVG using CSS, for example, provides a cool hover state or an animation. This really gives us a huge advantage; it just can't be overstated.

So what we're going to do is go to the `images` folder in Sublime Text and open up `crab.svg`. But first, let's look at what happens when I open `crab.png`, Sublime shows an image:

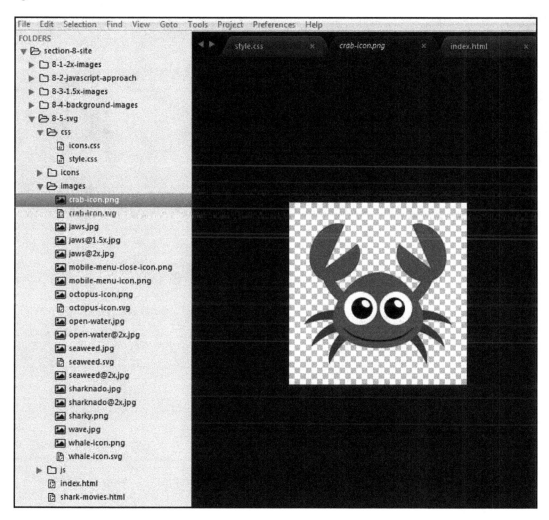

With the SVG, it actually shows the code! You can see it's XML, which is similar to HTML:

```
1  <svg xmlns="http://www.w3.org/2000/svg" viewBox="1.5 113.9 256 256">
2    <path fill="#9E2610" d="M72.1 296.8s-31.8 11.7-37.9 20.5c0 0 3.5-21.3 30.9-32.7l7 12.2zm12.1 10.7s-21.9 22.8-23.4
       32.7c0 0-5.8-19.3 12.5-40.1l10.9 7.4zm-15.9-28.7s-34 2.4-43.3 9.1c0 0 12.3-19.5 42.3-22.8l1 13.7zM185.4 295s31.8
       11.7 37.9 20.5c0 0-3.5-21.3-30.9-32.7l-7 12.2z"/>
3    <path fill="#D62D0E" d="M50.5 223.5S13 205.5 41 161c0 0 9-19.5 38-16.5L53.5 205l46-32.8s12.5 24.5-11 42.2c0 0-13.8
       10.2-20.8 9 0 0 4.5 11 12 16.2l3.5 3.2-9.5 11c.1.2-20.7-15.3-23.2-30.3z"/>
4    <path fill="#9E2610" d="M173.3 305.6s21.9 22.8 23.4 32.7c0 0 5.8-19.3-12.5-40.1l-10.9 7.4zm15.9-28.7s34 2.4 43.3
       9.1c0 0-12.3-19.5-42.3-22.8l-1 13.7z"/>
5    <path fill="#D62D0E" d="M207.9 223.5s37.5-18 9.5-62.5c0 0-9-19.5-38-16.5l25.5 60.5-46-32.8s-12.5 24.5 11 42.2c0 0
       13.8 10.2 20.8 9 0 0-4.5 11-12 16.2l-3.5 3.2 9.5 11c0 .2 20.7-15.3 23.2-30.3z"/>
6    <path fill="#D62D0E" d="M127.8 212s44-5.2 65.2 57.8c0 0 11.8 44.5-62.2 48.5 0 0-70.2 1.2-66.2-43.8-.1 0 6.6-54
       63.2-62.5z"/>
7    <circle fill="#FFFFFF" cx="103.8" cy="265.1" r="23.5"/>
8    <circle fill="#FFFFFF" cx="153.6" cy="264.1" r="23.5"/>
9    <circle cx="105.2" cy="263.8" r="14.8"/>
10   <circle cx="152.2" cy="262.5" r="14.8"/>
11   <ellipse transform="rotate(-45.37 157.15 256.57)" fill="#FFFFFF" cx="157.1" cy="256.6" rx="4.7" ry="7.2"/>
12   <ellipse transform="rotate(-45.37 110.35 257.456)" fill="#FFFFFF" cx="110.3" cy="257.4" rx="4.7" ry="7.2"/>
13   <path d="M78.5 290s12.7 20 51.6 19.5c0 0 34.2 1.5 49.2-19.5 0 0-15.8 17.5-49.2 17.2 0 0-36.1.3-51.6-17.2z"/>
14  </svg>
15
```

I'll copy and paste all of the SVG code, and go over to our `index.html` file and get rid of the entire `img` tag:

```
<div class="column">
  <figure>
    <img src="images/crab-icon.svg" alt="Crab">
  </figure>
  <h2>The Crab</h2>
  <p>Lorem ipsum dolor... </p>
  <a href="#" class="button">Crabby &raquo;</a>
</div>
```

Then we'll replace it with the SVG code:

```
<div class="column">
  <figure>
    <svg xmlns="http://www.w3.org/2000/svg" viewBox="1.5 113.9 256 256">
      <path fill="#9E2610" d="M72.1 296.8s-31.8 11.7-37.9 20.5c0 0 3.5-21.3
        30.9-32.7l7 12.2zm12.1 10.7s-21.9
        22.8-23.4 32.7c0 0-5.8-19.3 12.5-40.1l10.9 7.4zm-15.9-28.7s-34
        2.4-43.3 9.1c0 0 12.3-19.5 42.3-22.8l1
        13.7zM185.4 295s31.8 11.7 37.9 20.5c0 0-3.5-21.3-30.9-32.7l-7
        12.2z"/>
      <path fill="#D62D0E" d="M50.5 223.5S13 205.5 41 161c0 0 9-19.5
        38-16.5L53.5 205l46-32.8s12.5 24.5-11
        42.2c0 0-13.8 10.2-20.8 9 0 0 4.5 11 12 16.2l3.5 3.2-9.5 11c.1.2-20.7-15.3-23.2-30.3z"/>
      <path fill="#9E2610" d="M173.3 305.6s21.9 22.8 23.4 32.7c0 0
```

```
        5.8-19.3-12.5-40.11-10.9 7.4zm15.9-28.7s34
        2.4 43.3 9.1c0 0-12.3-19.5-42.3-22.81-1 13.7z"/>
        <path fill="#D62D0E" d="M207.9 223.5s37.5-18 9.5-62.5c0
        0-9-19.5-38-16.5l25.5 60.5-46-32.8s-12.5 24.5
        11 42.2c0 0 13.8 10.2 20.8 9 0 0-4.5 11-12 16.2l-3.5 3.2 9.5 11c0 .2
        20.7-15.3 23.2-30.3z"/>
        <path fill="#D62D0E" d="M127.8 212s44-5.2 65.2 57.8c0 0 11.8
        44.5-62.2 48.5 0 0-70.2 1.2-66.2-43.8-.1 0
        6.6-54 63.2-62.5z"/>
        <circle fill="#FFFFFF" cx="103.8" cy="265.1" r="23.5"/>
        <circle fill="#FFFFFF" cx="153.6" cy="264.1" r="23.5"/>
        <circle cx="105.2" cy="263.8" r="14.8"/>
        <circle cx="152.2" cy="262.5" r="14.8"/>
        <ellipse transform="rotate(-45.37 157.15 256.57)" fill="#FFFFFF"
        cx="157.1" cy="256.6" rx="4.7"
        ry="7.2"/>
        <ellipse transform="rotate(-45.37 110.35 257.456)" fill="#FFFFFF"
        cx="110.3" cy="257.4" rx="4.7"
        ry="7.2"/>
        <path d="M78.5 290s12.7 20 51.6 19.5c0 0 34.2 1.5 49.2-19.5 0 0-15.8
        17.5-49.2 17.2 0 0-36.1.3-51.6-
        17.2z"/>
    </svg>
  </figure>
  <h2>The Crab</h2>
  <p>Lorem ipsum dolor... </p>
  <a href="#" class="button">Crabby &raquo;</a>
</div>
```

Woah, that's a lot of code... The downside of SVG is it's a lot of code you're putting directly into your markup. You're still going to get better performance, because you don't have an HTTP request for it, but we're adding close to 30 lines of code for that.

We see no change in the Chrome; the crab looks exactly the same. So we might as well inspect this element. Now we can see that it's the inline SVG code:

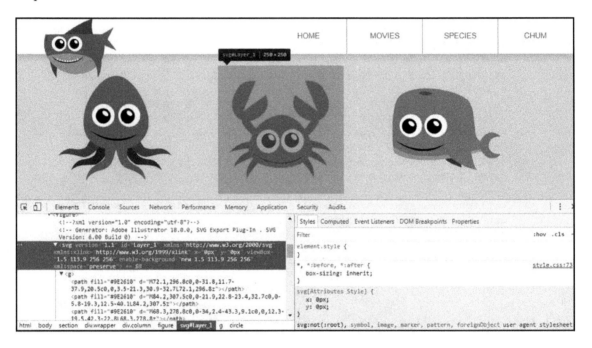

You can also see how you would think that you can use CSS to change these properties because each of these paths is literally a separate kind of node in the Dom:

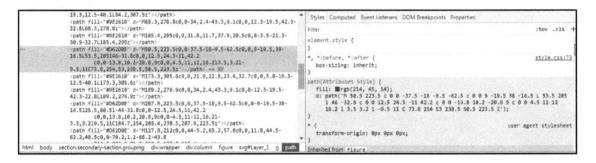

For instance, if we wanted to, we could change the fill color of this line of code:

Let's change it to green:

Now you get a green claw:

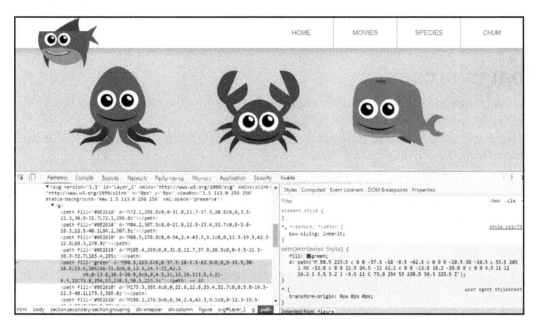

So you can see how you might be able to change the properties of the SVG, animate it, or create a cool hover state. You can't do this with SVG as a `background-image` or an `img` tag, but you can do this with an inline SVGs.

Since this is a different media format, it's not an `img` tag and not a `video` tag. It's really an `SVG` tag. Let's go to the top of the style sheet, into my reset. This is where we set `max-width: 100%` on our media as shown in the following code. We'll also add an SVG to this list:

```
img, iframe, video, object, svg {
  max-width: 100%;
}
```

In the next section, we'll go over how we can use the `srcset` attribute on an `img` tag to serve retina images to high-density displays and normal-sized images to normal density displays.

Source set attribute (srcset)

SVG is still the most preferred way to serve retina images to HiDPI devices because the file size is nearly always smaller than JPG and PNG, and you only need one image for both retina and non- retina devices. But there is another, very good option that's emerged, called `srcset`. This option isn't meant to replace SVG, but rather complement it, since SVG can't be used for traditional raster images and photos, which are more suited for JPEG and PNG.

What is srcset?

The `srcset` attribute is simply just a set of images, just like the name implies. What we can do is provide not just one image for the browser to serve, but a set of images that the browser can choose from and only fetch whichever image the browser decides is most appropriate for the device.

We're going to focus on the three movie images on our movies page, which are all raster, photographic images:

In `movies.html` we have an `img` tag and the appropriate image for each movie. So for Sharknado, we have `sharknado.jpg`:

```
<img src="images/sharknado.jpg" alt="Sharknado movie">
```

For Jaws, we have `jaws.jpg`:

```
<img src="images/jaws.jpg" alt="Jaws movie">
```

Let's update the Jaws image and add a new attribute called `srcset` and we'll put our Jaws image as the value of that attribute:

```
<img src="images/jaws.jpg" srcset="images/jaws.jpg" alt="Jaws movie">
```

Like I mentioned, `srcset` is a set of image choices to provide to the browser so it can decide which is best suited for the situation. Let's add a set of images.

Adding a set of images to srcset

To add a set of images to the `image` tag, comma separate each image. We're providing the regular-sized image first. Then we'll add `images/jaws@2x.jpg`:

```
<img src="images/jaws.jpg" srcset="images/jaws.jpg, images/jaws@2x.jpg"
alt="Jaws movie">
```

The browser actually needs something else to let it know that it's a larger image, something called the *pixel density descriptor,* or just the *X descriptor*. Let's add that, as shown in the following screenshot:

```
<img src="images/jaws.jpg" srcset="images/jaws.jpg 1x, images/jaws@2x.jpg
2x" alt="Jaws movie">
```

Following each image string, I'm going to provide a space and then the X descriptor. So the first image string will be `1x`, and the second one will be `2x`. The X descriptor is a hint we provide to the browser. This means we are using the `images/jaws.jpg` for `1x`, or normal pixel density, displays, and using `images/jaws@2x.jpg`, the larger image, for `2x`, or retina, displays.

Testing the image set

Let's see whether the image set is working. This would be tough without testing it on a retina display, which we're not doing. But let's see whether we can do some rough testing. Chrome has a nice feature where, if we inspect an image, we can see its `src` attribute and the `srcset` attribute. Check out the following code:

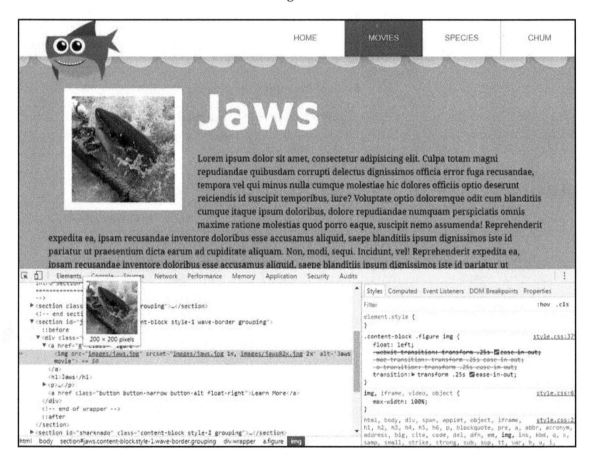

Here, if we hover the mouse over the path to each image, you can see that a popup appears over the image that's being served. But when we hover over `jaws@2x`, no popup appears because that image is not being served:

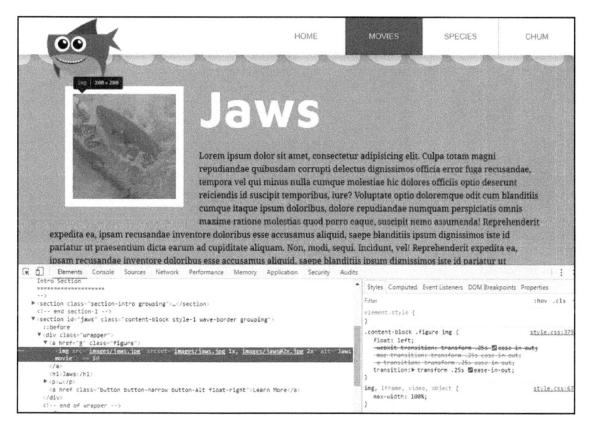

This makes sense as I'm not on a retina display, so it's using a non-retina image.

Let's use the browser zoom trick, which we used in earlier sections, to see whether we can fake a retina device. Let's zoom up to 200 percent:

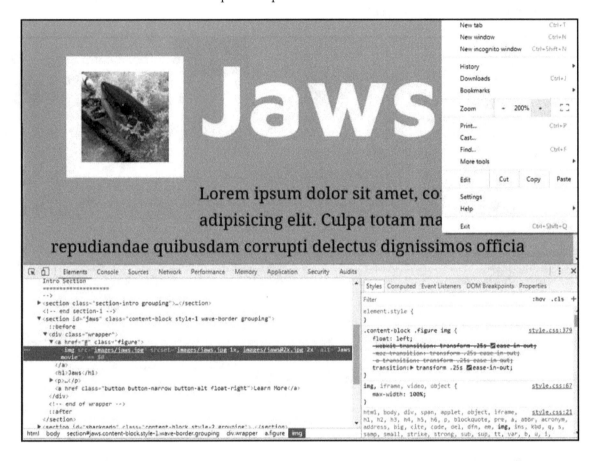

Then, refresh the page so that it goes and fetches the image it thinks is best:

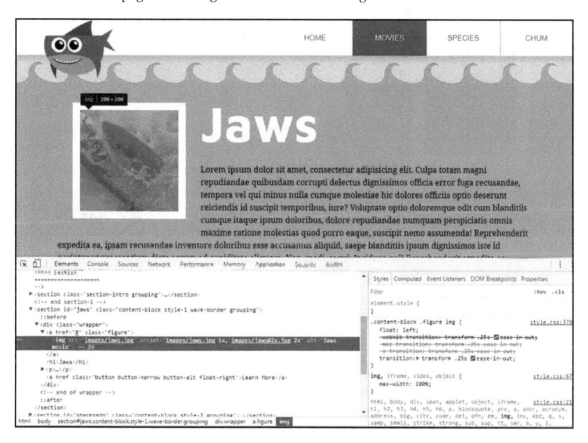

When I hover over `jaws.jpg` in the `src` and `srcset`, we don't get a popup. But we do get it when we hover over the path to `jaws@2x.jpg`, as shown here:

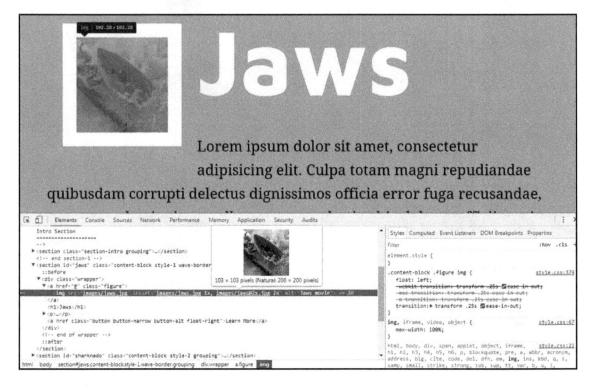

This tells me that the larger image is getting fetched. That's good stuff.

Simplifying the srcset attribute

Let's take a look at the code a little bit more to simplify the `srcset` attribute:

```
<img src="images/jaws.jpg" srcset="images/jaws.jpg 1x, images/jaws@2x.jpg
2x" alt="Jaws movie">
```

We need to keep the original `src` there as a fallback for browsers that don't support `srcset`. We'll talk about how awesomely good browser support is later in the section, but it's important to keep in mind that the `src` attribute is there so that unsupported browsers aren't left out in the lurch.

The one other thing to note is that we can simplify this code equation. The W3C spec mentions that for new user agents, the `src` attribute participates in the resource selection as if it were specified in the `srcset` with a `1x` descriptor. Since we have the traditional `src` attribute that will serve the `1x` version of the image, we can remove the first image string from our `srcset` attribute and simplify our markup:

```
<img src="images/jaws.jpg" srcset="images/jaws@2x.jpg 2x" alt="Jaws movie">
```

In other words, we can remove the regular size image string with the `1x` descriptor from the `srcset` attribute since this is already being specified in the `src` attribute. This simplifies it, which is good.

Now let's update our other two movies with similar markup starting with Sharknado:

```
<img src="images/sharknado.jpg" srcset="images/sharknado@2x.jpg 2x"
alt="Sharknado movie">
```

We'll do the same thing for the movie, Open Water:

```
<img src="images/open-water.jpg" srcset="images/open-water@2x.jpg 2x"
alt="Open Water movie">
```

Browser support

Let's discuss browser support `caniuse.com` shows an awful lot of green browsers:

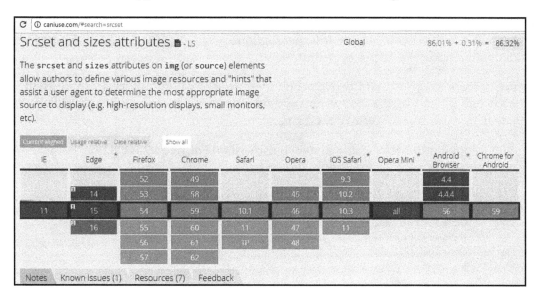

Microsoft Edge supports `srcset` and Chrome, Firefox, Safari, Opera, and starting with iOS Safari 8.

Changing the option to *Date Relative* shows the support goes farther back for iOS:

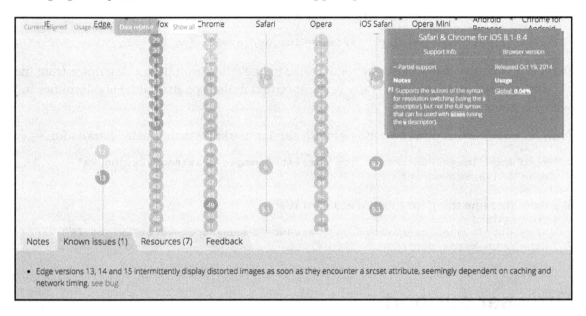

It provides partial support from Safari 8.1 through to 8.4. It supports "resolution switching", which is what we're doing using the X descriptor; however, it doesn't support the full syntax, which I'll talk about a little bit more later in the section. One notable non-supported browser is IE as recent as IE11. But, Internet Explorer will get the regular-sized image we specified in the traditional source attribute.

The nice part about this is that the overwhelming majority of high-density devices will ultimately end up getting the `2x` version, and unsupported browsers which are likely non-retina devices anyway, will receive the `1x` version.

I'm going to point out that you don't have to use just one or two image paths. I'm going to copy and paste in three image paths, as shown here:

```
<img src="images/sharknado.jpg"
srcset="images/sharknado@1.5x.jpg 1.5x,
        images/sharknado@2x.jpg 2x,
        images/sharknado@4x.jpg 4x"
alt="Sharknado movie">
```

As you can see in the preceding code, I've specified an `image` that I can use for `4x` displays, `2x` displays, and `1.5x` displays. This brings me to another point–you don't necessarily have to use whole numbers. You can use 1.5 or 1.325 if you want.

Moreover, we're only providing hints to the browser, so even though we have what looks like a great amount of control over which image gets served, ultimately it's up to the browser to decide which is the most suitable to use. This is based on factors other than users' screen pixel density, for example, zoom level, as we saw already, and other factors, such as the user's network conditions.

So, in theory, if a user has a retina device but poor internet, the browser would serve a smaller image because it would prioritize the speedy loading of images—the loading will be faster, but not as crisp. We've likely seen this type of prioritization in other technologies. For instance, a Netflix may show a fuzzy version of a movie until it gets enough bandwidth to show you the HD version of the same movie. We like this, because we'd rather get something to view faster than waiting for the best version of something to view.

Using the W descriptor and sizes attribute of the srcset attribute

Note that the `srcset` attribute is not a one-trick pony; we have talked about how it works for handling retina images easily. But there is another use case of the `srcset` attribute that uses the `W` descriptor and the `sizes` attribute:

```
<img src="images/medium.png"
    srcset="images/big.png 1600w,
            images/small.png 600w"
    sizes="(min-width: 1000px) 1600px,
            600px" />
```

It allows you to handle the serving of different images based on the width of the browser. A gigantic, hero, full-page image looks beautiful on a desktop, but would be bad for performance, if you just shrink it down and serve it on much smaller mobile devices, since small devices don't need a super large image.

The `w` descriptor is a hint to the browser about the size of the image; here `w` stands for the width. The `sizes` attribute adds media queries and a dimension telling the browser our preferred render size of the image if the browser width matches the media query and finally the preferred render size of the image if the browser width doesn't match the media query.

My intention isn't to explain the details, of this alternate usage of the `srcset` attribute but to let you know that there is more depth to the `srcset` attribute. If you'd like to dive deeper, I've written an article on my site at `richfinelli.com/srcset-part-2/`. I've also written an article on the X descriptor, available at `richfinelli.com/srcset-part-1/` if you're still hungry to learn more about what we just talked about.

Summary

Developing for retina is extra effort. My recommendation is to use SVG when possible as your first choice for serving super crisp images to retina devices. In instances when SVG is not possible - that is photographs - use the `srcset` attribute of the `img` tag to enable your browser to make smart decisions about serving images. Browser support for `srcset` is great, and non-supporting browsers will fall back to the `src` attribute. The browser makes the final decision of which image is best to use, based on pixel density, zoom level, and other factors, such as network conditions.

In the next `Chapter 9`, *Flexbox, Part 1*, we'll look at an alternate and better solution for laying out parts of our web page using flexible boxes.

9
Flexbox, Part 1

Flexbox is a module for laying out portions of a page, and it currently has great browser support, starting with Internet Explorer 10. Technically, it's not designed for full-page layout; it's more for layout of portions of your page, or a given component.

For instance, the following three columns (**The Octopus**, **The Crab**, and **The Whale**) were laid out using floats, but we're going to use flexbox to do the exact same thing:

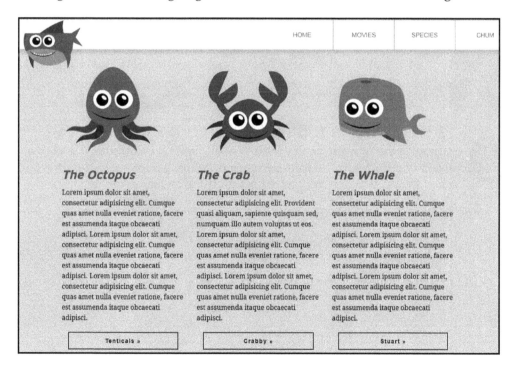

Flexbox is a big topic, so we're going to be covering it across two chapters. This chapter will cover the basics, we'll tackle implementing flexbox, switching from floats to flexbox, and go through all the flexbox properties and shorthands. In the next chapter we'll build a new section—the following product listing—to demonstrate how we can build different things with flexbox:

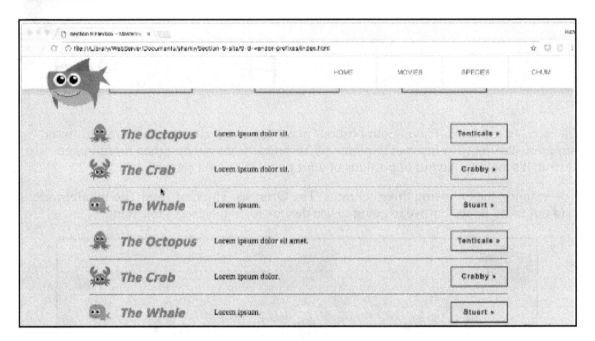

 I'm going to code in the latest version of Chrome, which as of now supports the non-prefixed versions of all flexbox properties. This is going to un-complicate the learning experience. But, before we're done we'll need to add vendor prefixes for maximum browser compatibility.

We are going to cover the following topics:

- Overview of the flexible box layout module of CSS
- Switching from floats to flexbox
- Flexbox properties and shorthands

Overview of the flexible box layout module

What is flexbox? Commonly referred to as flexbox, it's real name is *flexible box layout module*. It provides a more efficient way to lay out, align, and distribute space among child elements of a parent element, even when their size and quantity is unknown or dynamic. Flexbox defines a whole new layout mode.

Traditionally, there is *block mode*, which was designed for document layout. There is *inline mode*, which was designed for text; *table mode*, which was designed for tabular data (tables); and *positioned mode*, which was designed for explicit positioning without much regard for other elements around it. Now there is *flexbox mode*. So what does flexbox do? It can do a lot of really useful things. At the core, flexbox is for layout and alignment. The following list illustrates its more common use cases:

- Layout of elements vertically or horizontally.
- Alignment of elements to the left or right, like you can with floats but without all the extra baggage that comes along with floats. You can also center elements, horizontally or vertically.
- Also, you have control over the display direction. For instance, you can have the elements displayed in the source order by default or in reverse direction.
- Furthermore, you can take explicit control of elements and change their display order.
- Another thing it does easily is it gives you equal height columns, which could only be achieved previously using hacks
- Its real delight is how it can distribute elements in a parent in regards to the available space.
- Geared towards responsive design

Flex terminology

So this is all exciting stuff and I'm sure you want to start seeing it in action, but before we jump in, we need to do some homework and learn the flex terminology.

Flex container and flex items

First of all, there is something called a *flex container*, which is essentially an element that contains all the *flex items*. In other words, it's the parent of a collection of elements; flex items are child elements of their parent, or flex container.

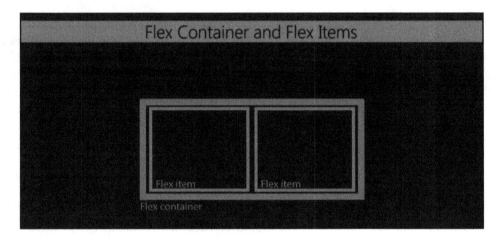

Main size and cross size

There's something called the *main size* and *cross size*, as shown here:

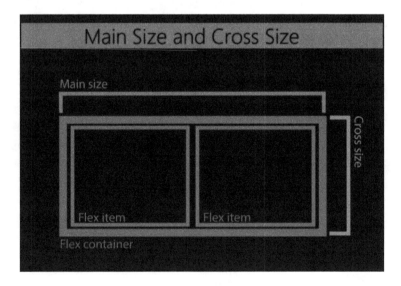

By default, the main size is the width and cross size is the height, but this can change if you modify the `flex-direction`, something we'll learn about in the next section.

Main axis and cross axis

Furthermore, there is something called the *main axis*, which runs horizontally by default, and *cross axis*, which runs vertically by default, as shown in the following image:

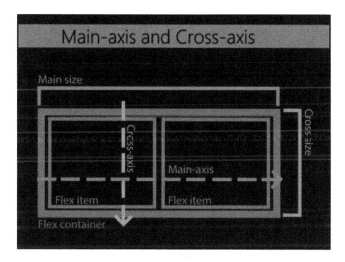

Justify-content and align-items

There's a property you'll learn about later in this chapter called `justify-content`, which controls alignment along the main axis; the `align-items` property controls alignment along the cross axis. Here's an important concept. The main axis and cross axis can be toggled based on the `flex-direction` being set to either a `column` or `row`. So the main axis is always the horizontal axis by default, unless you use `flex-direction: column` and the vertical axis becomes the main axis!

If this is your first taste of flexbox your probably saying, "Hey, slow down!" Not to worry, this is just an introduction to the terminology and a few of the properties and concepts; don't expect to have all this sink in right away. We'll refer more to the preceding diagrams as we start using different properties throughout the next sections, and we'll cover every single property in depth in the upcoming sections.

From floats to flexbox

In this section, we'll get to work and change our columns module from a float-based layout to a flexbox-based layout (I'm excited!).

First, we'll remove all the float-related properties from the columns and break them down to square one; then, we'll use `display: flex` to transform the float layout into our flexbox-based layout to see immediate results. Finally, we'll explore how `flex-direction` will be useful in a responsive design; we'll discuss this when we get down to smaller screen sizes.

Removing float-related properties from the columns section

OK, here's our three-column layout:

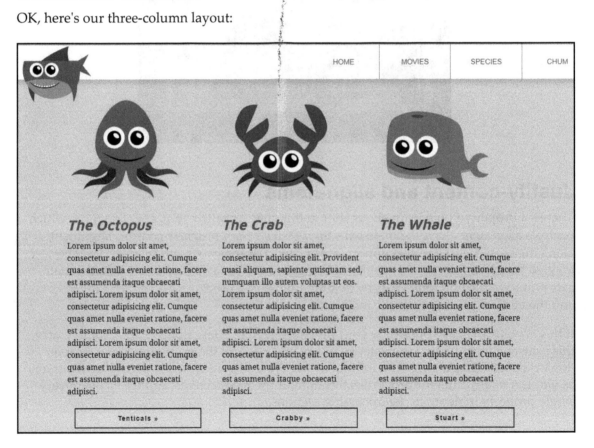

Let's recall how it moves to a one-column tube at smaller widths:

Alright, let's go to the CSS file. Now we'll remove all the float-based properties from our columns.

Starting with this:

```
* * * * * * * * * * * * * * * *
3 columns
* * * * * * * * * * * * * * * */
.column {
  float: left;
  width: 31.25%; /* 300/960 */
```

```
    margin-left: 3.125%; /* 30/960 */
  }
  .column:first-child {
    margin-left: 0;
  }
  .columns figure {
    margin: 0 auto;
    width: 100%;
    max-width: 250px;
  }
```

Let's basically remove everything to make it look like this:

```
* * * * * * * * * * * * * * * *
3 columns
* * * * * * * * * * * * * * * */
.column {
}
```

Next, there let's rip out the float-based code in the responsive media query. So starting with this:

```
@media screen and (max-width: 1023px){
  .intro-content {
    width: auto;
    float: none;
    padding-bottom: 0;
    margin-bottom: 30px;
  }
  .go-premium {
    width: auto;
    float: none;
    margin-top: 0;
  }
  .column {
    float: none;
    width: auto;
    padding: 0 50px;
  }
  .column figure {
    margin: 0 auto;
    width: 100%;
    max-width: 250px;
  }
  .column h2 {
    text-align: center;
  }
}/* end of media query */
```

Let's change it to this:

```
@media screen and (max-width: 1023px){
   .intro-content {
      width: auto;
      float: none;
      padding-bottom: 0;
      margin-bottom: 30px;
   }
   .go-premium {
      width: auto;
      float: none;
      margin-top: 0;
   }
}/* end of media query */
```

And inside one more media query for very small widths, let's remove the last reference to the column. So, starting with this:

```
@media screen and (max-width: 550px) {
   h1 {
      font-size: 40px;
   }
   h2 {
      font-size: 26px;
   }
   .column {
      padding: 0;
   }
   .content-block .figure {
      width: 200px;
      display: block;
      margin-left: auto;
      margin-right: auto;
      float: none;
   }
   .content-block h1 {
      text-align: center;
   }
   .button-narrow {
      width: 100%;
   }
}/* end of media query */
```

Let's remove the `.column {}` rule set, so it looks like this:

```
@media screen and (max-width: 550px) {
  h1 {
    font-size: 40px;
  }
  h2 {
    font-size: 26px;
  }
  .content-block .figure {
    width: 200px;
    display: block;
    margin-left: auto;
    margin-right: auto;
    float: none;
  }
  .content-block h1 {
    text-align: center;
  }
  .button-narrow {
    width: 100%;
  }
}/* end of media query */
```

Alright, if we refresh the browser and widen it, we will be back to a stacked layout:

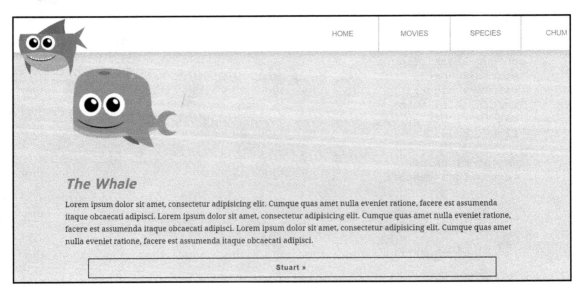

We've successfully remove our float-based layout from this section as our three columns are gone.

Turning on flexbox using display: flex

Now we'll rebuild the columns using flexbox. We'll take a look at our index.html file. Here's are markup for this area we are calling columns:

```
<!--
===============
Secondary Sections
===============
-->
<section class="secondary-section grouping">
  <div class="wrapper">
    <div class="column">
      <figure>
        <img src="images/octopus-icon.png" alt="Octopus">
      </figure>
      <h2>The Octopus</h2>
      <p>Lorem ipsum dolor...</p>
      <a href="#" class="button">Tenticals &raquo;</a>
    </div>
    <div class="column">
      <figure>
        <img src="images/crab-icon.png" alt="Crab">
      </figure>
      <h2>The Crab</h2>
      <p>Lorem ipsum dolor...</p>
      <a href="#" class="button">Crabby &raquo;</a>
    </div>
    <div class="column">
      <figure><img src="images/whale-icon.png" alt="Whale"></figure>
      <h2>The Whale</h2>
      <p>Lorem ipsum dolor...</p>
      <a href="#" class="button">Stuart &raquo;</a>
    </div>
  </div><!-- end wrapper -->
</section>
```

Each of these `<div class="column"></div>` will be our flex items; `<div class="wrapper">` will be our flex container. For ease of understanding, I'm going to simplify our markup down to this:

```
<div class="wrapper"> <!--flex container-->
  <div class="column">...</div> <!--flex item-->
  <div class="column">...</div> <!--flex item-->
  <div class="column">...</div> <!--flex item-->
</div> <!--end of flex container-->
```

Let's add a new class to the flex container called "columns" that we'll use to target the flex container with our flexbox code:

```html
<div class="wrapper columns"> <!--flex container-->
  <div class="column"></div> <!--flex item-->
  <div class="column"></div> <!--flex item-->
  <div class="column"></div> <!--flex item-->
</div> <!--end of flex container-->
```

Let's add a new rule set targeting our would-be flex container. To convert something into a flex container, simply add display: flex:

```css
/****************
3 columns
****************/
.columns {
  display: flex;
}
.column {

}
```

The children of a flex container will automatically become flex items.

 Note the grandchildren and great-grandchildren elements will not be considered flex items, only the immediate children.

Here's what we get:

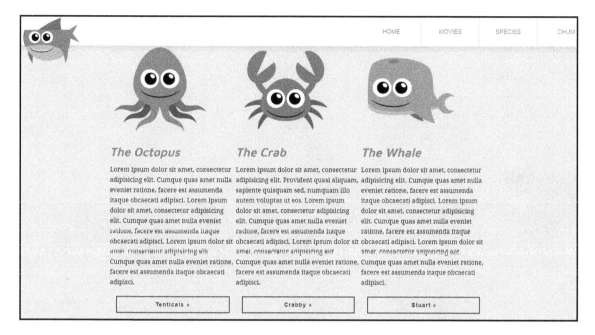

We've basically achieved our float layout with one simple property: `display: flex`. The spacing is a little tight, but we have a horizontal layout nonetheless.

Flex overrides floats. Let's say we have many floats, namely `float: left`, `float: right`, and `float: none`; whatever it might be, flex items ignore floats, that is, they have zero impact. So once a container element gets `display: flex`, making the children elements flex items, floats are now ignored on those flex items. I can float to my heart's delight, but it will have zero impact on flex items. .

Also, another thing to keep in mind is that each column are now of equal height. But let's just do one thing. Let's add a border around the flex items:

```
/***************
3 columns
***************/
.columns {
  display: flex;
}
.column {
  border: 1px solid pink;
}
```

Here's what that looks like:

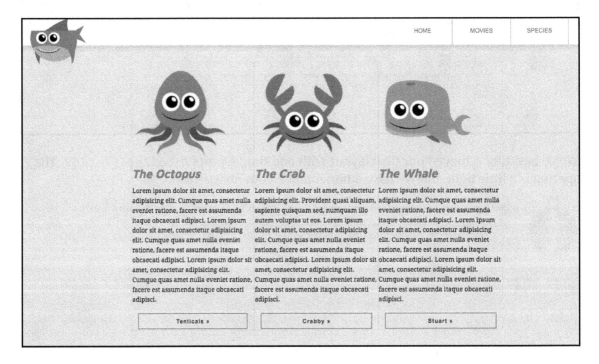

Equal-height columns right? Well, each column has the exact same amount of content. So even if we were using floats for layout, we'd have equal-height columns. The unequal height comes when the amount of content varies in each column. I'll remove some of the paragraph text in the crab column:

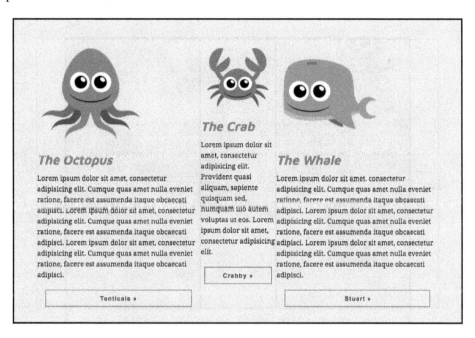

After doing this, you can see that even though it has a lot less content, it still has the same height. Albeit, a few other things happened here, namely the crab column is a different width than the other 2 columns. We'll talk about this later in the chapter, but we do get equal height by default, which is a quick win that is difficult to accomplish using a float-based layout.

Changing the flex-direction

Let's look at how easy it is to change the layout direction by adding the `flex-direction` property with a value of `column`. This property applies to the `.columns` flex container. I've also removed the pink `border` as well.

```
/****************
3 columns
****************/
.columns {
  display: flex;
```

```
    flex-direction: column;
}
.column {
}
```

We'll save this and boom! We went from horizontal to vertical:

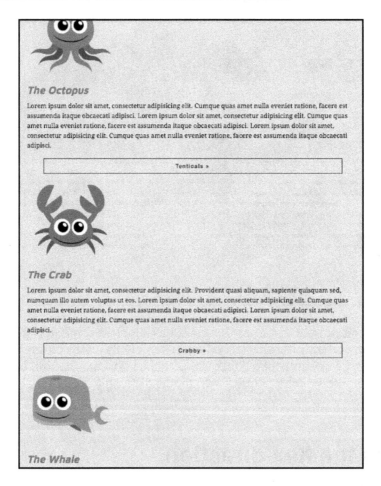

Some of our center alignment, which we probably wanted, has gone; however, the layout is vertical nonetheless. So that's interesting.

Another thing we can is set the `flex-direction` to be `column-reverse`:

```
/*****************
3 columns
*****************/
.columns {
  display: flex;
  flex-direction: column-reverse;
}
.column {
}
```

Earlier, our octopus appeared first; now if we refresh the browser, our whale comes first and the octopus comes last:

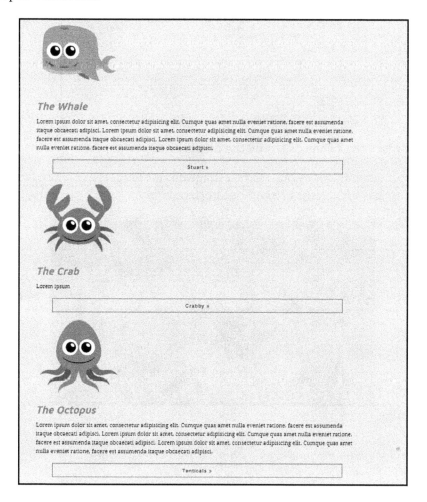

If we look at our DevTools, though, we will see that the octopus is still first in the source order but the last one to be displayed:

```
▼<div class="wrapper columns">
  ▼<div class="column">
    ▶<figure>…</figure>
      <h2>The Octopus</h2> == $0
    ▶<p>…</p>
      <a href="#" class="button">Tenticals »</a>
  </div>
  ▼<div class="column">
    ▶<figure>…</figure>
      <h2>The Crab</h2>
    ▶<p>…</p>
      <a href="#" class="button">Crabby »</a>
  </div>
  ▼<div class="column">
    ▼<figure>
        <img src="images/whale-icon.png" alt="Whale">
      </figure>
      <h2>The Whale</h2>
    ▶<p>…</p>
      <a href="#" class="button">Stuart »</a>
  </div>
</div>
```

So the source order hasn't changed, only the display order.

This is a good time to talk about our flexbox diagram. When `flex-direction` is set to `row`, this diagram applies—flex items are laid out horizontally:

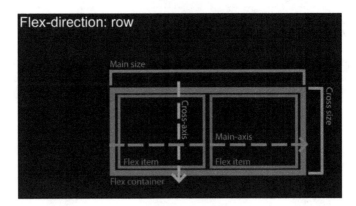

However, when `flex-direction` is changed to a `column`, the diagram changes:

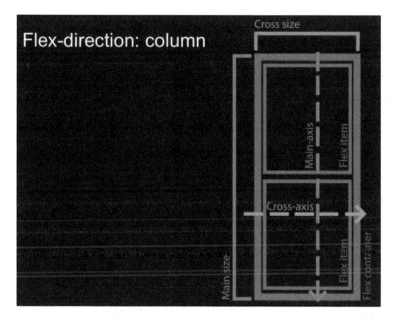

The cross axis now runs from left to right and the main axis runs from top to bottom, and the flex items are now stacked on top of each other.

 The default value of `flex-direction` is row; `flex-direction: row`.

We can also set `flex-direction` to `row-reverse`, which does what you think it does: it lines the flex items horizontally but in reverse order. Let's take a look at the following image; we have the whale, crab, and octopus in reverse order:

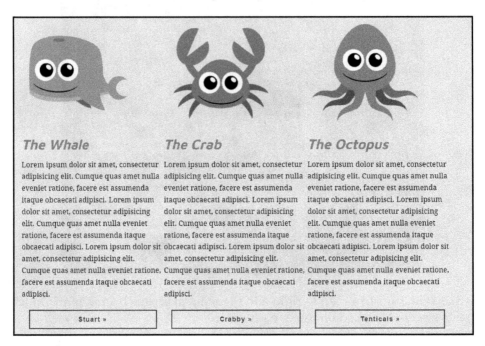

Let's remove the `flex-direction` property from the `.column` flex container, and it will default to row, which is what we want:

```
/ * * * * * * * * * * * * * * * *
3 columns
* * * * * * * * * * * * * * * * /
.columns {
  display: flex;
}
.column {
}
```

Browser shrinking

Now let's think about smaller devices by shrinking our browser. It gets a little tight down near tablet dimensions:

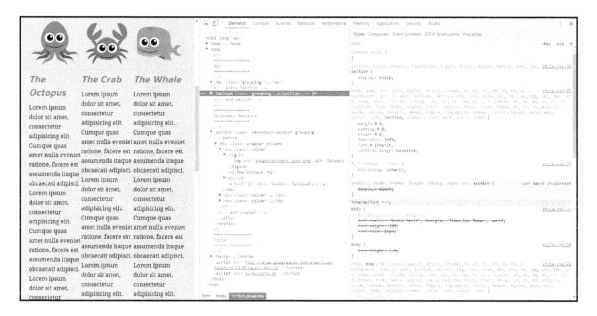

In our media query, where we had originally removed all of the `float` stuff. Let's change the `flex-direction` to `column`:

```
@media screen and (max-width: 550px) {
  h1 {
    font-size: 40px;
  }
  h2 {
    font-size: 26px;
  }
  .columns {
    flex-direction: column;
  }
  .content-block .figure {
    width: 200px;
    display: block;
    margin-left: auto;
    margin-right: auto;
    float: none;
  }
  .content-block h1 {
```

```
      text-align: center;
    }
    .button-narrow {
      width: 100%;
    }
}/* end of media query */
```

We're back to a one-column-stacked layout for narrower browser widths:

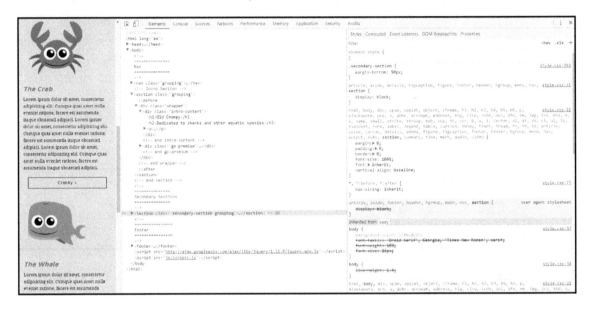

As you can see, there are still some issues with spacing and alignment, which we'll address with flexbox in the next section.

In summary, we removed all our float-based layout CSS from our column section, and we added a flexbox layout using `display: flex`. We also changed `flex-direction`, which as we saw determines the direction of the main axis and cross axis.

Understanding flex-grow, flex-basis, flex-shrink, and flex

Let's take a crack at understanding flexbox's sizing properties. In this section, we'll look at sizing flex items with `flex-grow`, `flex-shrink`, `flex-basis`, and the shorthand for them all; `flex`. All of these properties apply to flex items, not to flex containers.

Using flex-grow

First, we'll look at a new page—`flexbox.html`. As you might have guessed, there's a `<section>` that will be the flex container, and 5 `<div>`'s which will be the flex items. :

```
<!--
====================
Flexbox Demo
====================
-->
<section class='flex-container'>
    <div class="flex-item flex-item1">item 1</div>
    <div class="flex-item flex-item2">item 2</div>
    <div class="flex-item flex-item3">item 3</div>
    <div class="flex-item flex-item4">item 4</div>
    <div class="flex-item flex-item5">item 5</div>
</section>
```

Here's the CSS we'll start with before adding flexbox properties:

```
/***************
Flexbox demo
***************/
.flex-container {
  margin-top: 200px;
}
.flex-item {
  padding: 20px;
}
.flex-item1 { background: deeppink;}
.flex-item2 { background: orange; }
.flex-item3 { background: lightblue; }
.flex-item4 { background: lime; }
.flex-item5 { background: olive; }
```

Here's what it looks like in the browser:

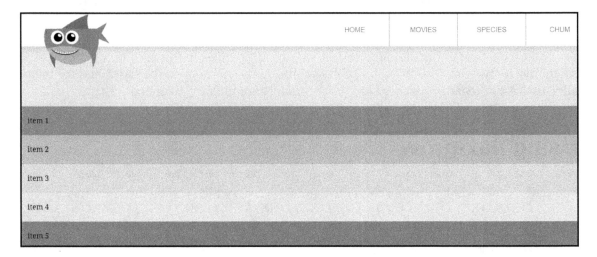

Let's switch on flexbox by adding `display: flex` to the flex container in our CSS file:

```
.flex-container {
  margin-top: 200px;
  display: flex;
}
```

Alright, if we refresh our browser, this creates a horizontal row for us, as shown in the following screenshot:

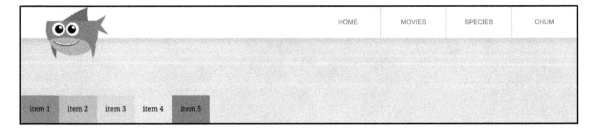

The first flexbox sizing property we'll look at is `flex-grow`, which is a factor. It determines how to distribute "leftover space" along the main axis of the flex container. Let's be clear on what I mean when I say, "leftover space". That is the unfilled space inside of the flex container that the flex items don't occupy. In our case, that is this empty space on the right:

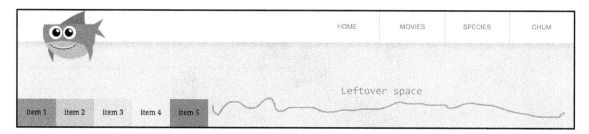

Again, `flex-grow` determines how to distribute that leftover space to the flex items. Let's apply it to our flex items using a value of `1`:

```
.flex-container {
  margin-top: 200px;
  display: flex;
}
.flex-item {
  padding: 20px;
  flex-grow: 1;
}
```

`flex-grow: 1` will force the leftover space to be evenly distributed to all the flex items. Each flex item gets an equal amount of the space that was previously unoccupied:

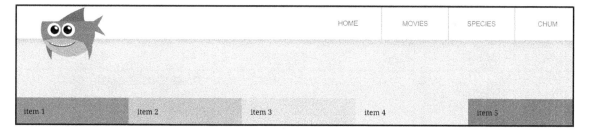

As I shrink the browser, we can see that we achieved a perfectly fluid grid without using the `width` property and calculating the exact percentage of how 100 divides equally into 5!

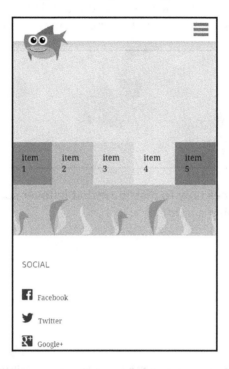

Let's create a new ruleset for just the second flex item (each flex item has a unique class, the second one being `flex-item2`). And we'll add a `flex-grow` property with a value of `2`, and this will distribute twice as much of the leftover space to that second flex-item:

```
.flex-container {
  margin-top: 200px;
  display: flex;
}
.flex-item {
  padding: 20px;
  flex-grow: 1;
}
.flex-item2 {
  flex-grow: 2
}
```

If we refresh the browser, it should look something like this:

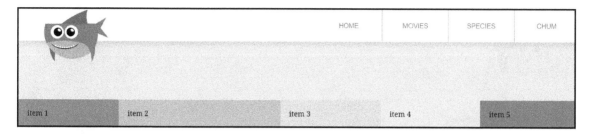

Notice that `flex-item2` isn't necessarily twice the width of the others; it's just getting twice the leftover space as the others. That's a notable distinction. And, if we shrink the browser window, we can see how it gets narrower as the browser window shrinks until we get down to a certain width, then they're all roughly the same. When there is extra space, it tries to distribute more to `flex-item2` since it has a higher `flex-grow` factor:

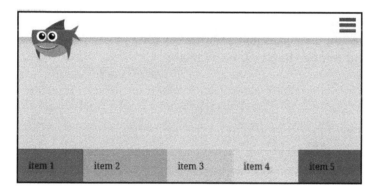

We could also set `flex-grow` of `flex-item2` to 0, which is the default value for `flex-grow`. This basically says don't distribute any of the leftover space to this flex item:

```
.flex-item2 {
  flex-grow: 0
}
```

The second flex item doesn't grow to take up any of the extra space; the remaining four items take the extra space available:

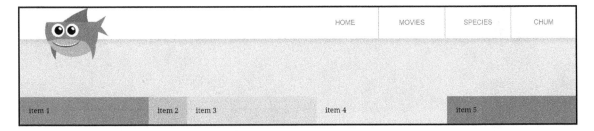

Using flex-basis

Let's check out another property for flex items: `flex-basis`. Note that `flex-basis` is the initial main size of the flex item, before leftover space is distributed according to the flex factors, which are `flex-grow` and `flex-shrink`; we'll talk about the latter shortly. For now, let's think of `flex-basis` as just a width. So, for `flex-item2`, let's give it `flex-basis` of `400px` and remove its `flex-grow` factor:

```
/**************
Flexbox demo
**************/
.flex-container {
  margin-top: 200px;
  display: flex;
}
.flex-item {
  padding: 20px;
  flex-grow: 1;
}
.flex-item2 {
  flex-basis: 400px;
}
```

If you refresh the browser, it will size the second flex item to `400px`. But if we really look at this, it's sizing it to a little more than 400 pixels:

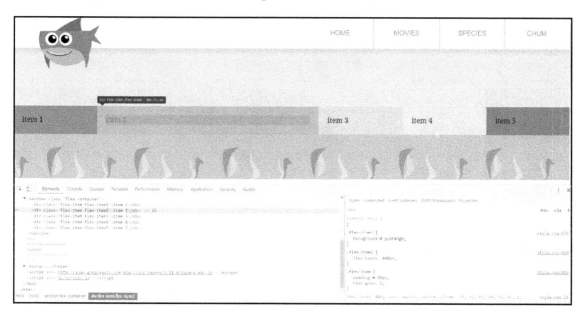

However, I'm still applying `flex-grow` as 1 to all flex items including this one. Let's change this to make it so our second flex item has the default value `flex-grow: 0;`:

```
.flex-item2 {
    flex-grow: 0;
    flex-basis: 400px;
}
```

Now when you refresh your browser, you can see it's exactly 400 pixels:

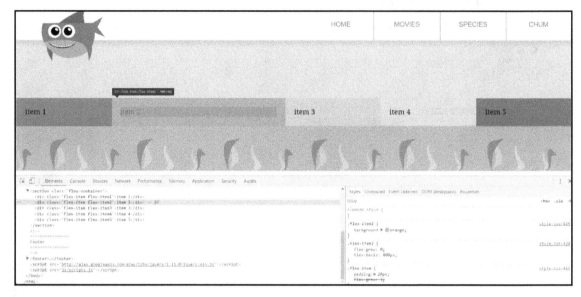

It'll be exactly 400 pixels until we start shrinking the browser; at some point, it's going to start giving way. Once space starts to get very limited, it decides to make it less than 400 pixels; this is where the *initial main size* part of the `flex-basis` definition comes into play. We're telling flexbox we want a width of 400 pixels for the second flex item, and flexbox will obey that until the flex container runs out of space to accommodate that. Then, it starts to reduce the width of the second flex item to less than the `flex-basis: 400px` to entertain the best layout that it can.

Let's remove `flex-grow` again:

```
.flex-item2 {
  flex-basis: 400px;
}
```

Note that `flex-basis` is not just a width: it's the width when `flex-direction` is set to `row`, which is the default, and it's the height when `flex-direction` is set to `column`. And technically speaking, since it's not width or height, it's the main size.

> Are you starting to understand why we spent all that time going over flex terminology? If any of this is not making sense to you, I recommend going back to the start of this chapter to review flex terminology.

So let's change `flex-direction` to `column`. We'll do this on the flex container:

```
.flex-container {
  margin-top: 200px;
  display: flex;
  flex-direction: column;
}
.flex-item {
  padding: 20px;
  flex-grow: 1;
}
.flex-item2 {
  flex-basis: 400px;
}
```

A `flex-basis` of `400px` is now the height of the second flex item, now that the main axis is running vertically. You can see this in the following screenshot:

So `flex-basis` overrides any heights that are set. Let's take an example and enter a `height` of `800px` for the second flex item:

```
.flex-item2 {
  flex-basis: 400px;
  height: 800px;
}
```

We see that the height is still 400 pixels. Really, I should say the main size is 400 pixels, and it should look something like this:

So, `flex-basis` also accepts two keywords: `auto` and `content`. The `auto` keyword means, "go look at the `width` or `height` property". Since `flex-direction` is currently `column`, when we change `flex-basis` to `auto`, the `height` of `800px` should no longer be ignored:

```
.flex-item2 {
  flex-basis: auto;
  height: 800px;
}
```

And the height is now 800 pixels:

So, again, `auto` is the default value of `flex-basis`. There's also another keyword available called `content`; this means the size of the flex item is based on the size of the flex item's content. This is currently not supported by the most recent version of Chrome, so I won't demo it; however, it sounds like it could be useful in future once browsers start implementing it.

Alright, I'll remove the `height` and `flex-basis`. I'll also remove the `flex-direction` ending up with our CSS in this state:

```
.flex-container {
  margin-top: 200px;
  display: flex;
}
.flex-item {
  padding: 20px;
  flex-grow: 1;
}
.flex-item2 {

}
```

Here's what that looks like:

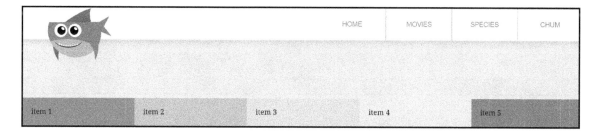

Using flex-shrink

A `flex-shrink` can be thought of as the opposite of `flex-grow`. While `flex-grow` determines how much of the extra space a flex item should consume, proportionate to others when there is leftover space, `flex-shrink` determines how much the flex item itself should shrink proportionately to others when there isn't any leftover space. So, let's see this in action and step this out.

First, let's add `flex-basis` of `200px` to each flex item and temporarily remove `flex-grow`:

```
.flex-container {
  margin-top: 200px;
  display: flex;
}
.flex-item {
  padding: 20px;
  flex-basis: 200px;
}
.flex-item2 {

}
```

So if `flex-basis` is set to 200 pixels, each flex item will be 200 pixels wide and any extra space is not allowed in any of the flex items because `flex-grow` was removed. Here's how it should look:

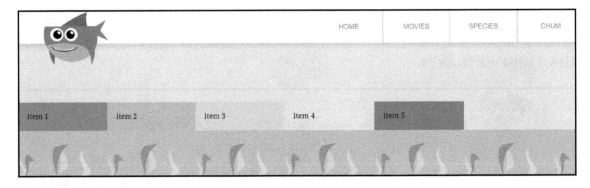

Let's add `flex-grow` of 1 back to our `flex-item` class:

```
.flex-item {
  padding: 20px;
  flex-basis: 200px;
  flex-grow: 1;
}
```

Again, the extra space is distributed to each flex item. The `flex-basis` property was just a starting point for the initial main size (notice I didn't said "initial main size" and not "width"). But each flex item got wider to eat up the extra space that was allocated evenly to each item. This is how your page should look at the moment:

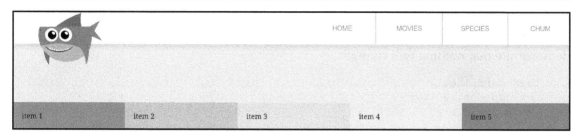

Let's throw a `flex-shrink` property on the second flex item. We'll use a factor of `2`, as shown in the following code:

```
.flex-container {
  margin-top: 200px;
  display: flex;
}
.flex-item {
  padding: 20px;
  flex-basis: 200px;
  flex-grow: 1;
}
.flex-item2 {
  flex-shrink: 2;
}
```

As we decrease the browser size, all the items shrink. Except for the second flex item, which shrinks twice as much as other flex items, as shown in the following screenshot:

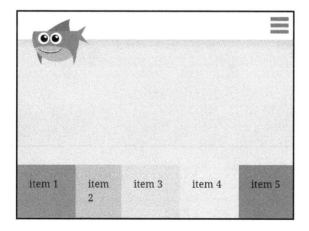

If not specified for a flex item, `flex-shrink` defaults to `1`. So let's add `flex-shrink: 1` to all the flex items except for the second flex item, which has `flex-shrink` set to `2`, just to demonstrate that nothing will change:

```
.flex-container {
  margin-top: 200px;
  display: flex;
}
.flex-item {
  padding: 20px;
  flex-basis: 200px;
  flex-grow: 1;
  flex-shrink: 1;
}
.flex-item2 {
  flex-shrink: 2;
}
```

We can see that when we make the browser smaller, there really is no change; the second flex item is still shrinking more than the others, as shown in the following samples:

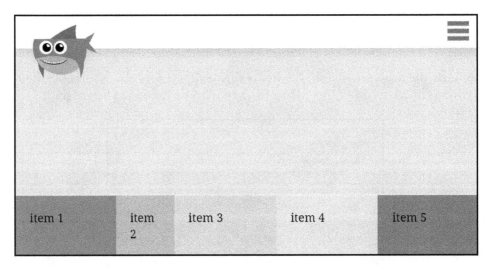

Another neat thing you can do is set `flex-shrink` to 0 to ensure that an item does not shrink. Let's do this for the second flex item:

```
.flex-container {
  margin-top: 200px;
  display: flex;
}
.flex-item {
  padding: 20px;
  flex-basis: 200px;
  flex-grow: 1;
  flex-shrink: 1;
}
.flex-item2 {
  flex-shrink: 0;
}
```

Refresh the browser now. All the other flex items shrink when space is limited, except for item 2; it maintains its `flex-basis: 200px`:

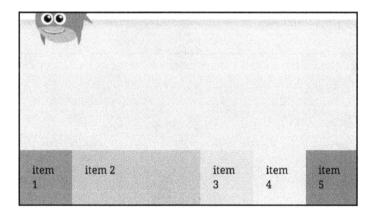

Using the flex shorthand

There's also a shorthand property, called `flex`, that we can substitute for using `flex-grow`, `flex-shrink`, and `flex-basis`. Let's swap out `flex-basis`, `flex-grow`, and `flex-shrink` for just `flex`:

```
.flex-container {
  margin-top: 200px;
  display: flex;
}
```

```
.flex-item {
  padding: 20px;
  flex: 1 1 200px;
}
.flex-item2 {
  flex-shrink: 0;
}
```

So, the order of the values in `flex` is as follows: `flex-grow`, `flex-shrink`, and `flex-basis`:

```
.flex-container {
  margin-top: 200px;
  display: flex;
}
.flex-item {
  padding: 20px;
  flex: 1 1 200px; /* order: flex-grow, flex-shrink, flex-basis */
}
```

If we refresh the browser, it will do exactly the same thing it was doing when we used the non-shorthand properties:

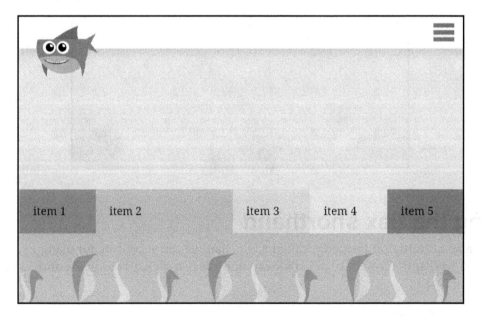

For the second flex item, all it has is `flex-shrink`, so we can use a shorthand of `flex: 1 0`. The `flex-basis` will be intelligently set to its default of `auto` and can be omitted. We need to make the value `1 0` though because the default value for `flex-grow` is `1`, so even though we didn't have a `flex-grow` set explicitly we need to add it's value to our shorthand. We'll also delete the existing `flex-shrink`:

```
.flex-container {
  margin-top: 200px;
  display: flex;
}
.flex-item {
  padding: 20px;
  flex: 1 1 200px; /* order: flex-grow, flex-shrink, flex-basis */
}
.flex-item2 {
  flex: 1 0; /* order: flex-grow, flex-shrink */
}
```

Again, we see no change in the browser, which is what we wanted from our little refactor:

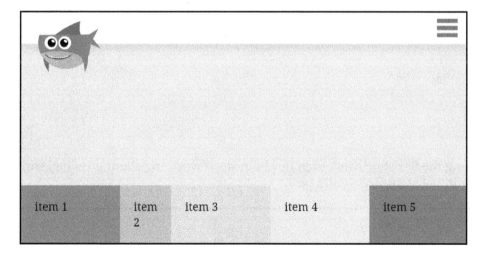

So `flex: 1 0` means `flex-grow = 1` and `flex-shrink = 0`. As mentioned, `flex-basis` defaults to `auto`, so we don't need to add that here. There's also a keyword of `none`, which basically says don't grow, don't shrink, and look at my width or height for the main size, in other words, don't flex. The shorthand is nice and compact, but when getting started with flexbox I recommend using each property on its own, until you gain a full understanding of what each one is doing.

More layout, more positioning

This section is on more layout and more positioning with flexbox. Here, we'll check out a new property, `justify-content`, as well as how to nest flexboxes within each other, and finally using automatic margins.

Before we get started, let's reset some of our `flex` properties by getting rid of our flex shorthand:

```
.flex-container {
  margin-top: 200px;
  display: flex;
}
.flex-item {
  padding: 20px;
}
.flex-item2 {

}
```

By removing the flex shorthand, each flex item stops worrying about growing, shrinking, or what their initial main size should be:

Using the justify-content property

First up is `justify-content`, which is a flex container property that determines whether the content is justified - or positioned - at the start of the main axis, the end of the main axis, or somewhere in between. Let's add `justify-content` and set it to `flex-start`, as shown in the following code snippet:

```
.flex-container {
  margin-top: 200px;
  display: flex;
  justify-content: flex-start;
}
```

`flex-start` is the default value for `justify-content`, so nothing changes:

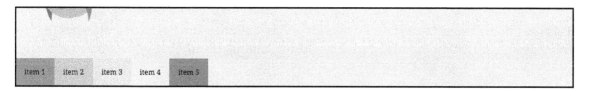

`flex-start` positions the flex items at the start of the main axis. Remember, when `flex-direction` is not specified, or specified as `row`, the main axis runs from left to right horizontally. So `flex-start` would be the left edge and `flex-end` would be the right edge:

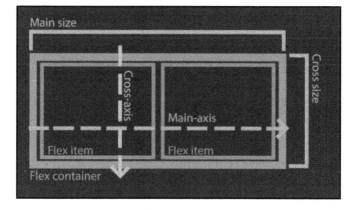

Now let's change the value to `flex-end`:

```
.flex-container {
  margin-top: 200px;
  display: flex;
  justify-content: flex-end;
}
```

The content is now positioned to the right:

This is a lot like using `float:right`, except without all the extra baggage and issues that come along with floats: no clearing, no collapsing, and no reshuffling of the floated items. Essentially, we just position the flex items to the right.

That's pretty useful and all, but the real magic happens when we use `justify-content: center`:

```
.flex-container {
  margin-top: 200px;
  display: flex;
  justify-content: center;
}
```

Oh my gosh, we've just centered the flex items!

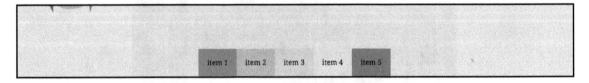

There was never a `float: center`. Admittedly, we could center things by setting the left and right margins to `auto` on the container. But the problem with that was we always had to specify the `width` of the container when we do this; therefore, if the number of items in the container changed, we would have to change the `width` property as well. There are other tricks to centering things, but none this easy and flexible.

Flexbox is inherently more prepared for dynamic content and doesn't need any `width` defined; let's add another flex item to the HTML to prove this:

```
<section class="flex-container">
    <div class="flex-item flex-item1">item 1</div>
    <div class="flex-item flex-item2">item 2</div>
    <div class="flex-item flex-item3">item 3</div>
    <div class="flex-item flex-item4">item 4</div>
    <div class="flex-item flex-item5">item 5</div>
    <div class="flex-item flex-item1">item 6</div>
</section>
```

Now we have six items and all of them are still centered:

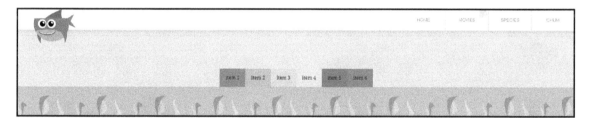

But wait, there's more! There's a keyword called `space-between` that we can use:

```
.flex-container {
  margin-top: 200px;
  display: flex;
  justify-content: space-between;
}
```

This keyword, `space-between`, redistributes the extra space evenly between each item. So there's "space between" each element:

Notice that the first and last elements are hugging the edge; the first flex item hugs the left-most edge of its container; and the last flex item hugs the right-most edge of its container.

There's another value, though, `space-around` that does something slightly different:

```
.flex-container {
    margin-top: 200px;
    display: flex;
    justify-content: space-around;
}
```

Note that `space-around` redistributes the extra space of the container around all the flex items, even the first and the last, whereas `space-between` inserts extra space only between each item.

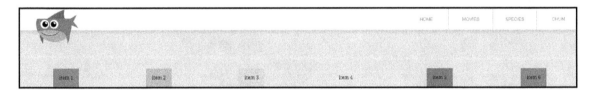

Let's revisit the **Home** page and implement this in a more practical example, that is, our three columns:

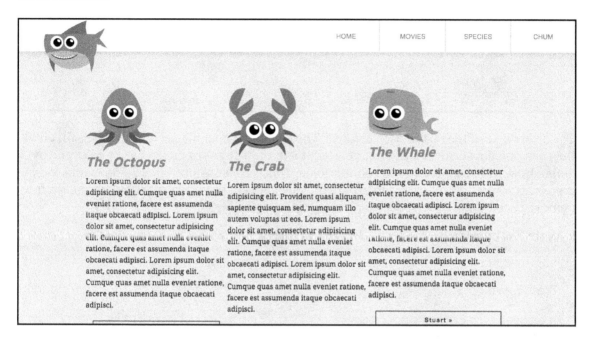

Our three columns are set to `display: flex` but no other flex properties are applied. The flex items are kind of centered already because the flex container is centered. However, we want some space between each flex item. So in our area of the CSS for our columns, let's say `justify-content: space-between`. Unrelated to what we're currently doing. I am also setting `max-width: 50%` on our sea creatures so they are not so big. But more important is the `justify-content`:

```
.columns {
  display: flex;
  justify-content: space-between;
}
.column {

}
.column figure {
  max-width: 50%;
}
```

Nothing changes!

This is because of the text in each column. The content is pushing each flex item to fill out the space available. So we need to add a `width` to these items or `flex-basis` to explicitly define how wide we prefer each column to be. This is because since there's no extra space, there's no way for flexbox to redistribute the flex items to put extra space between each flex item. We need some extra space.

Let's do this by adding `flex-basis: 30%` to each column:

```css
.columns {
  display: flex;
  justify-content: space-between;
}
.column {
  flex-basis: 30%;
}
.column figure {
  max-width: 50%;
}
```

Refresh the page and this is what you should see:

Notice the space is evenly distributed between each item. Lovely! We still have a little cleaning to do, though. The button at the bottom is not consistently at the bottom of each column; this is not so noticeable now because the content within each column is relatively the same; however, it will become more apparent if we make the amount of content in each column a lot different:

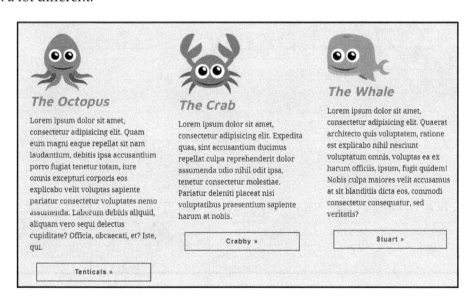

How do we fix this? Well, remember, in our case, the flex container is the columns, and each column is a flex item. The button is not a flex item because it is within the column. This is where nested flexboxes come into play.

Nesting Flexboxes

Let's convert the column into a nested flex container:

```
.columns {
  display: flex;
  justify-content: space-between;
}
.column {
  flex-basis: 30%;
  display: flex;
}.column figure {
  max-width: 50%;
}
```

Of course, the flex items of a container are set as `flex-direction:row` by default, so they all sit next to each other horizontally, which totally destroyed things:

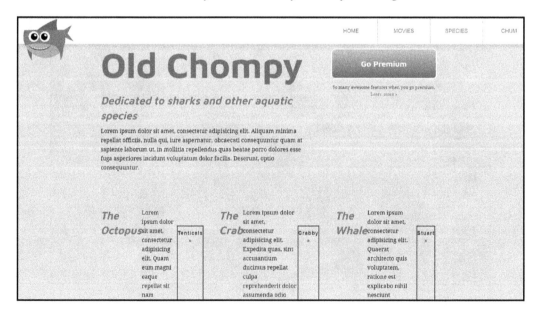

That's not what we want it to look like, obviously, but we can easily remedy this. Let's change `flex-direction` to `column`, as shown in the following code snippet:

```
.column {
  flex-basis: 30%;
  display: flex;
  flex-direction: column;
}
```

Nice, we're back in business. Looks identical to what it did before we made the columns a flex container:

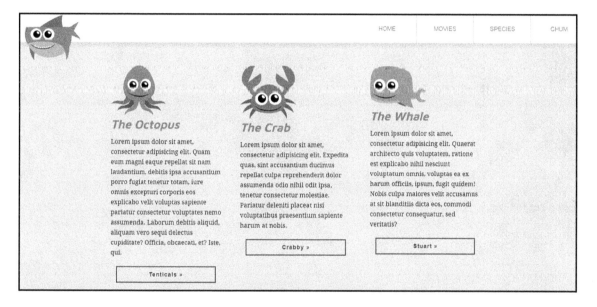

How does this help us? Well, we could start using `justify-content` and maybe we could say `justify-content, space-between`:

```
.column {
  flex-basis: 30%;
  display: flex;
  flex-direction: column;
  justify-content: space-between;
}
```

This makes the button sit nicely at the bottom but now in the middle of the content. The space between each flex item is spaced out evenly, which ends up being different for each column, and thus not looking great:

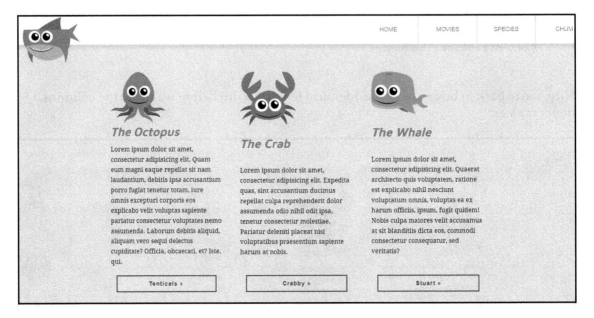

Let's revert back to the default value for `justify-content`:

```
.column {
  flex-basis: 30%;
  display: flex;
  flex-direction: column;
  justify-content: flex-start;
}
```

This moves everything back to the top because `flex-direction` is `column`, and the main axis now runs up and down:

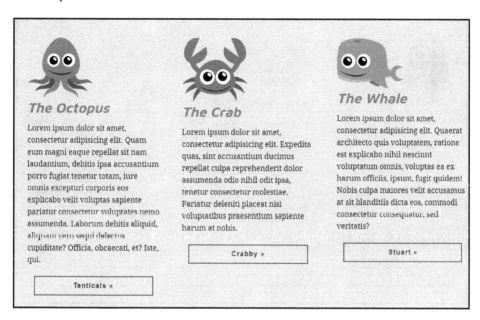

Using automatic margins

Something notable about flexbox is that it does a fresh take of the `auto` keyword for `margin`. Automatic margins are now working very closely with flexbox. I can now target my button as the selector and give it `margin-top` of `auto`:

```
.columns {
  display: flex;
  justify-content: space-between;
}
.column {
  flex-basis: 30%;
  display: flex;
}
.column figure {
  max-width: 50%;
}
.column .button {
 margin-top: auto;
}
```

Boom! The space above the button is now automatically calculated, and the button is positioned at the bottom of each column:

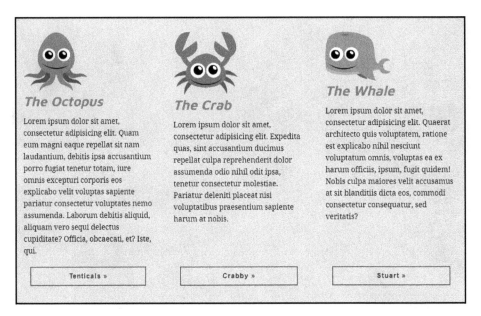

This also works when flex-direction is row; you can use `margin-left: auto;` or `margin-right: auto` to hug flex items to the outer edges of their flex container.

To illustrate an example of this, let's go back to our flexbox demo sample, and we can change `justify-content` of the flex container to `flex-start` and then add another rule set that pushes the final flex item to hug the right edge using `margin-left: auto`:

```
/ * * * * * * * * * * * * * *
Flexbox demo
* * * * * * * * * * * * * * /
.flex-container {
  margin-top: 200px;
  display: flex;
  justify-content: flex-start;
}
.flex-item {
  padding: 20px;
}
.flex-item:last-child {
  margin-left: auto;
}
```

All of the flex-items are lined up on the left -at their `flex-start` - except for the last flex item, which is hugging the right -or at the `flex-end` - because we're calculating it's left margin automatically:

Let's go back to the **Home** page and look at our columns. One last thing about these columns: the red headline is not aligned at the same vertical position for each one because each of our sea creature SVG's are of a slightly different height:

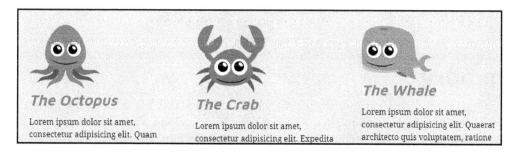

Let's give each sea creature a `flex-basis` of `150px`. Since, `flex-direction` is `column`, `flex-basis` can be thought of as the height; therefore, we're basically giving each figure the same height of `150px`:

```
.columns {
  display: flex;
  justify-content: space-between;
}
.column {
  flex-basis: 30%;
  display: flex;
  flex-direction: column;
}
.column figure {
  max-width: 50%;
  flex-basis: 150px;
}
.column .button {
  margin-top: auto;
}
```

Now those red headlines will all sit neatly together:

In summary, `justify-content` positions and redistributes extra space along the main axis. You can nest flexboxes all day long, and automatic margins are pretty sweet and allow you to position content to hug the opposite edge of a flex container, which is an enormously common UI pattern.

Summary

We've covered a ton of ground with flexbox in this chapter including all of the basic flexbox properties. We'll carry that on in the next chapter when we look at how to align and flow flexbox content, and the properties that are required to do that. We'll also create a new UI pattern—a product listing—and see how flexbox can help there.

10
Flexbox, Part 2

Let's carry on our exploration of flexbox and the power it offers. You should have the basics under your belt now, so in this chapter we'll go ahead and build a new section—the product listing that you see below—to get some practical experience of building things with flexbox:

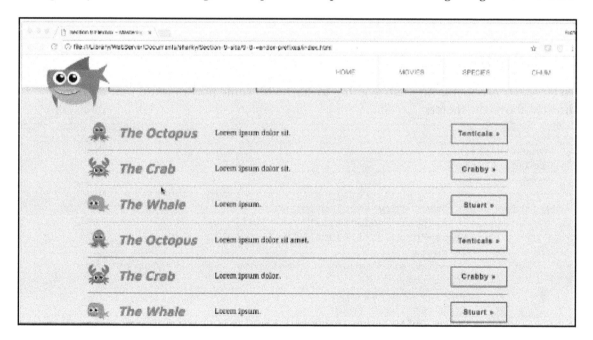

We'll also talk about what needs to be prefixed when using flexbox, and how to add prefixes in the easiest way possible.

We are going to cover the following topics:

- Building a new section using flexbox
- Using flex-wrap and align-content
- Changing the display order of flex items
- Handling vendor prefixes

Building the product listing

Let's build a product listing with flexbox. We're going to see what else we can build with flexbox by creating a product listing. We'll explore two new flexbox properties: `align-items` and `align-self`.

Using align-items

To build the product listing, we're going to start with some new markup that will sit directly above the footer:

```
<!--
===============
Product Listing
===============
-->
<section class="secondary-section grouping">
    <ul class="wrapper product-list">
        <li class="product-list-item">
            <figure>
                <img src="images/octopus-icon.svg" alt="Octopus">
            </figure>
            <h2>The Octopus</h2>
            <p>Lorem ipsum dolor sit.</p>
            <a href="#" class="button">Tenticals &raquo;</a>
        </li>
        <li class="product-list-item">...</li>
        <li class="product-list-item">...</li>
        <li class="product-list-item">...</li>
        <li class="product-list-item">...</li>
        <li class="product-list-item">...</li>
    </ul><!-- end wrapper -->
```

```
</section>
<!--
================
Footer
================
-->
```

There's quite a bit of markup, but it's not very complex. There's an unordered list with six list items (`<li>` tags). Each list item has an SVG image (`<figure><img></figure>`), a headline (`<h2>`), a paragraph (`<p>`), and an anchor (`<a>`). In the previous code snippet, I've omitted the guts of all the list items except for the first one.

We're also starting with some CSS that bootstraps this section:

```
/****************
Product Listing
****************/
.product-list-item {
  border-bottom: 1px solid #766e65;
}
.product-list-item figure {
  width: 50px;
  margin-right: 20px;
}
.product-list-item h2 {
  margin: 0;
}
.product-list-item p {
  margin: 0;
}
.product-list-item .button {
  transform: scale(1);
  width: 130px;
}
```

Here's what we're starting with in our product listing:

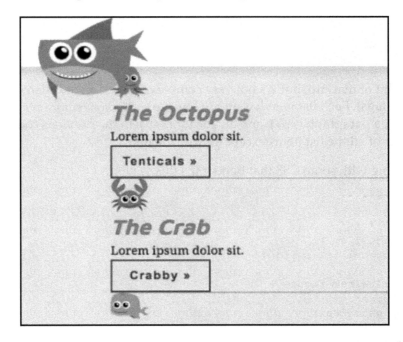

We want each list item to have its contents laid out horizontally. We can target the class, `product-list-item`, and use `display: flex`:

```
.product-list-item {
  border-bottom: 1px solid #766e65;
  display: flex;
}
```

This ruleset is targeting six different `li` tags with the class of `product-list-item`. This is important because we have six different flex containers. Adding `display: flex` should lay out all the different flex items in each flex container—horizontally. Because that's what flexbox does. By default `flex-direction` is `row`, so everything is laid out in a row:

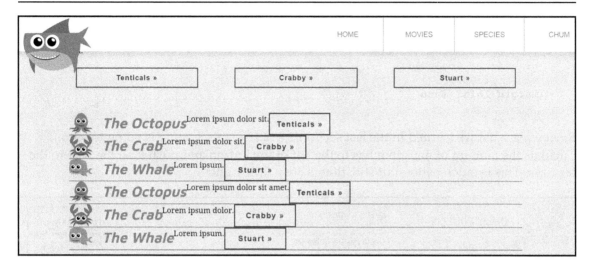

Alright, so things don't look great. One of the things we can do is add `flex-basis` with a value of `250px` to the h2:

```
.product-list-item h2 {
  margin: 0;
  flex-basis: 250px;
}
```

This should add some semblance of organization and it does:

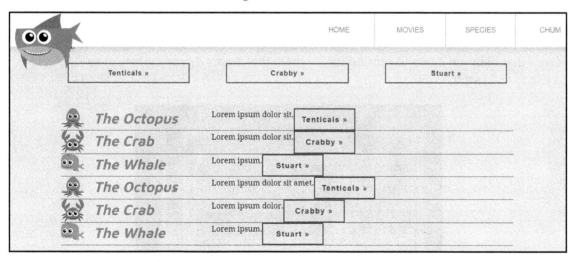

Now, let's use automatic margins to align the button to the far right edge:

```
.product-list-item .button {
  transform: scale(1);
  width: 130px;
  margin-left: auto
}
```

Reviewing what we learned in the last section, `margin-left: auto` is going to auto calculate the amount of margin it has to the left of the button and push it all the way to the far right. This is much better, but still, things are a little tight:

🐙	*The Octopus*	Lorem ipsum dolor sit.	Tenticals »
🦀	*The Crab*	Lorem ipsum dolor sit.	Crabby »
🦑	*The Whale*	Lorem ipsum.	Stuart »
🐙	*The Octopus*	Lorem ipsum dolor sit amet.	Tenticals »
🦀	*The Crab*	Lorem ipsum dolor.	Crabby »
🦑	*The Whale*	Lorem ipsum.	Stuart »

Let's fix this with a new property called `align-items`. So these buttons are way too close to each other and this paragraph sits up high. We want the images, the headline, the paragraph and the button all centered vertically. The `align-items` is a property that can be used on flex containers that controls the positioning of flex items along the cross axis. Here's that diagram again to remind us of where the cross axis runs when `flex-direction` is set to `row`:

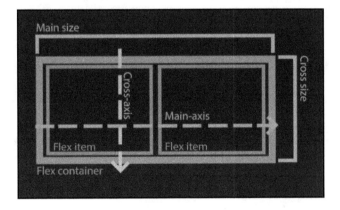

As we can see, the cross axis runs from top to bottom when `flex-direction` is row. We'll add `align-items` with a value of `center`. And that really won't do much noticeably unless we add a `height` of `80px`. So let's do that too:

```
.product-list-item {
  border-bottom: 1px solid #766e65;
  display: flex;
  align-items: center;
  height: 80px;
}
```

So, using `align-items: center` will align items in the middle of the cross axis:

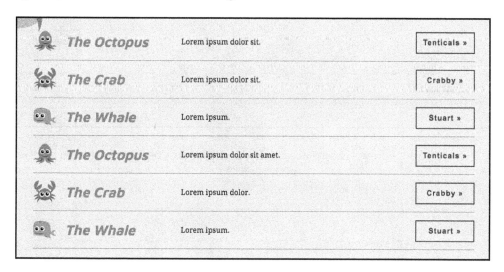

Okay, not bad! All our flex items are centered vertically, with one property, and each item has a different height. Also, I want to note that the default value of `align-items` is `stretch`, which forces the flex item to stretch from the start of the cross axis to the end of it. This is the reason why flexbox comes standard with equal height columns.

We can also use `flex-start`, which aligns all the flex items to the top of the flex container or the start of the cross axis:

```
.product-list-item {
  border-bottom: 1px solid #766e65;
  display: flex;
  align-items: flex-start;
  height: 80px;
}
```

Following is the output of preceding code:

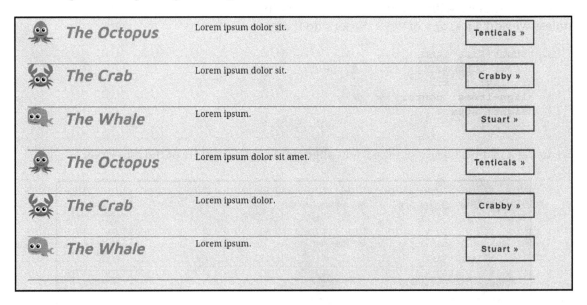

Let's try `flex-end`, which will align all the flex items—you guessed it—to the bottom or the end of the cross axis:

```
.product-list-item {
  border-bottom: 1px solid #766e65;
  display: flex;
  align-items: flex-end;
  height: 80px;
}
```

Our flex items are now aligned to the end of the cross axis—the bottom:

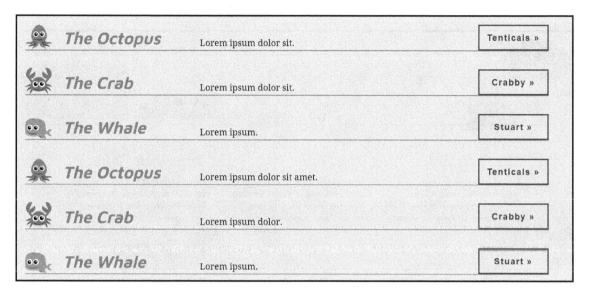

Let's change this back to `center`:

```
.product-list-item {
  border-bottom: 1px solid #766e65;
  display: flex;
  align-items: center;
  height: 80px;
}
```

Now let's go back to our three columns; we still have problems with our images and headlines aligned to the left, and we want them to be centered:

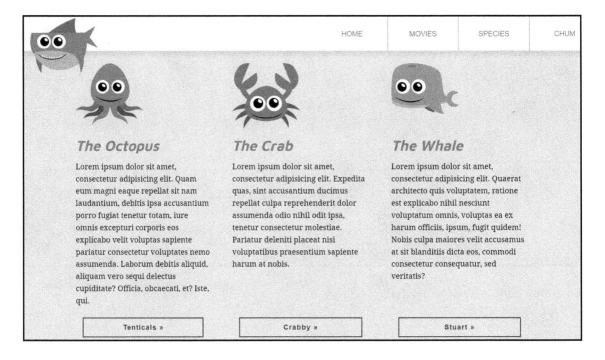

Let's see how we can use `align-items` to center our sea creatures and headlines, when the `flex-direction` is set to `column`. In this use case, the cross axis runs horizontally.

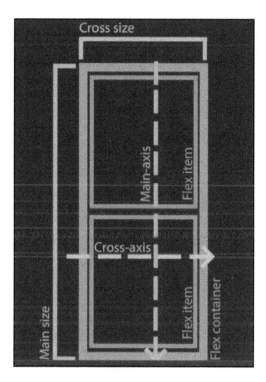

This is good news. Since `align-items` is used for alignment on the cross axis, which runs horizontally for `flex-direction: column`, this should center our sea creature images and headlines.

Remembering that each `.column` is a flex item of `.columns`, but also its own flex container for its own flex items. Those flex items being things like the sea creature image, the headline, the paragraph, and the button. So each column is its own flex container. We can use `align-items: center`:

```
/****************
3 columns
****************/
.columns {
  display: flex;
  justify-content: space-between;
}
.column {
  flex-basis: 30%;
```

```
  display: flex;
  flex-direction: column;
  justify-content: flex-start;
  align-items: center;
}
.column figure {
  max-width: 50%;
  flex-basis: 150px;
}
.column .button {
  margin-top: auto;
}
```

So here's what we end up with:

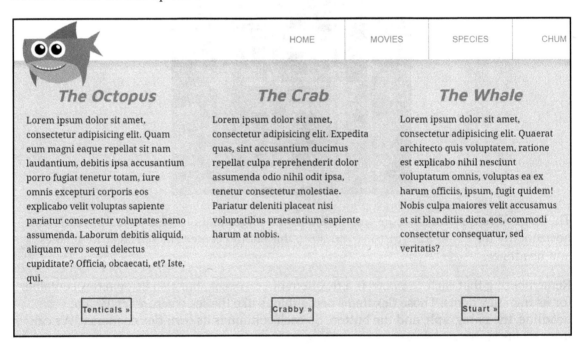

Things are centered, like the headline and the button at the bottom, but our sea creature images have totally disappeared and our buttons have shrunk. Let's tackle these problems one at a time, starting by thinking about why our sea creatures have disappeared. Let's inspect in the general vicinity of where the sea creatures would be and find the images:

Inspecting the `figure` element that holds the `img` element in the DevTools shows that the width is 0 and the height is 150. So why would the width be 0 if we have this CSS in place?

```
.column figure {
  max-width: 50%;
  flex-basis: 150px;
}
```

Well, we don't have an explicit `width` set for these SVGs. We have a `max-width` set but that really doesn't force a width. Recall that `max-width` just says, "never be wider than x number of pixels", but doesn't enforce any width below that threshold. And our `flex-basis` of `150px` is controlling the height because the `flex-direction` is `column`. We never set a true width at all. When we set `align-items: center`, it forces the elements to only take up as much width or height as they need, almost like when you `float` a block-level element to the `left` or `right`. Also, SVG is unique in the universe of images. Traditional images like PNG's and JPG's have set dimensions even if nothing is specified in the CSS. SVG's, since they are scalable to any size big or small, don't have a baseline size. Since there are never any widths or heights set for the `figure` or `img`, the `align-items` property kind of squeezes the width to 0, which is why they vanished on us.

This is easily fixable; we'll just add a `width`. Let's make it even a little smaller than they were before, about 50 percent of their container:

```
.column figure {
  max-width: 50%;
  flex-basis: 150px;
  width: 50%;
}
```

Our sea creatures are back!

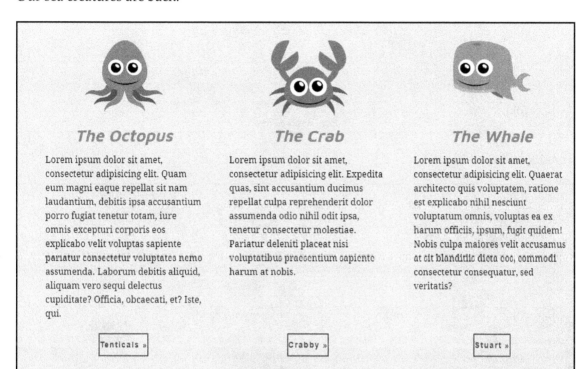

The buttons at the bottom have the same problem as our images just had; they don't have any `padding` or `width` set, so `align-items` forces the width to only be as wide as the content, hence why they look all squished and small.

The solution for this is the same: just set a `width`. Let's have the `width` as `90%` in this case:

```
/****************
3 columns
****************/
.columns {
  display: flex;
  justify-content: space-between;
}
.column {
  flex-basis: 30%;
  display: flex;
  flex-direction: column;
  justify-content: flex-start;
  align-items: center;
```

```
}
.column figure {
  max-width: 50%;
  width: 50%;
  flex-basis: 150px;
}
.column .button {
  margin-top: auto;
  width: 90%;
}
```

That fixes that problem:

The Octopus

Lorem ipsum dolor sit amet, consectetur adipisicing elit. Quam eum magni eaque repellat sit nam laudantium, debitis ipsa accusantium porro fugiat tenetur totam, iure omnis excepturi corporis eos explicabo velit voluptas sapiente pariatur consectetur voluptates nemo assumenda. Laborum debitis aliquid, aliquam vero sequi delectus cupiditate? Officia, obcaecati, et? Iste, qui.

Tenticals »

The Crab

Lorem ipsum dolor sit amet, consectetur adipisicing elit. Expedita quas, sint accusantium ducimus repellat culpa reprehenderit dolor assumenda odio nihil odit ipsa, tenetur consectetur molestiae. Pariatur deleniti placeat nisi voluptatibus praesentium sapiente harum at nobis.

Crabby »

The Whale

Lorem ipsum dolor sit amet, consectetur adipisicing elit. Quaerat architecto quis voluptatem, ratione est explicabo nihil nesciunt voluptatum omnis, voluptas ea ex harum officiis, ipsum, fugit quidem! Nobis culpa maiores velit accusamus at sit blanditiis dicta eos, commodi consectetur consequatur, sed veritatis?

Stuart »

Using the align-self Flexbox property

Looks good, but what if I don't want all the flex items to be centered? I might prefer the h2 to be aligned to flex-start (in fact I do). The align-items is a property used on the flex container to control the cross axis alignment of all flex items. Another, flexbox property called align-self controls alignment along the cross axis but is a property used directly on flex items. This will help us aligning only our h2 to the left.

Let's create a new selector for the h2 and add align-self: flex-start:

```
/****************
3 columns
****************/
.columns {
  display: flex;
  justify content: space between;
}
.column {
  flex-basis: 30%;
  display: flex;
  flex-direction: column;
  justify-content: flex-start;
  align-items: center;
}
.column figure {
  max-width: 50%;
  width: 50%;
  flex-basis: 150px;
}
.column h2 {
  align-self: flex-start;
}
.column .button {
  margin-top: auto;
  width: 90%;
}
```

Note that align-self is a property only for flex items; its default value is auto, which means tells it to check the value of align-items for cross axis alignment. It also accepts stretch, flex-start, flex-end, center, and baseline. It allows us to override the align-items value for a single flex item.

If we refresh the browser now, we will see that our `h2` tags are aligned to the left - at their `flex-start`:

The Octopus

Lorem ipsum dolor sit amet, consectetur adipisicing elit. Quam eum magni eaque repellat sit nam laudantium, debitis ipsa accusantium porro fugiat tenetur totam, iure omnis excepturi corporis eos explicabo velit voluptas sapiente pariatur consectetur voluptates nemo assumenda. Laborum debitis aliquid, aliquam vero sequi delectus cupiditate? Officia, obcaecati, et? Iste, qui.

Tenticals »

The Crab

Lorem ipsum dolor sit amet, consectetur adipisicing elit. Expedita quas, sint accusantium ducimus repellat culpa reprehenderit dolor assumenda odio nihil odit ipsa, tenetur consectetur molestiae. Pariatur deleniti placeat nisi voluptatibus praesentium sapiente harum at nobis.

Crabby »

The Whale

Lorem ipsum dolor sit amet, consectetur adipisicing elit. Quaerat architecto quis voluptatem, ratione est explicabo nihil nesciunt voluptatum omnis, voluptas ea ex harum officiis, ipsum, fugit quidem! Nobis culpa maiores velit accusamus at sit blanditiis dicta eos, commodi consectetur consequatur, sed veritatis?

Stuart »

We're looking good now. Let's take a minute to quickly fix a bug we created a little while back. We'll take a look at this bug as we inspect the page by right-clicking and choosing **Inspect**; we'll move the DevTools to the right in Chrome. I'll just resize it to tablet size; we can see the problem now, our sea creatures are out of control!

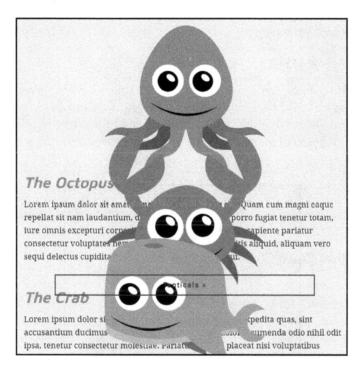

Our columns are all jumbled up on top of each other. So we've got to figure out why that's happening. This is because we have `flex-basis` set to `30%` for each column. It worked great when `flex-direction` was row, but as you may recall from the section *Floats to Flexbox*, we changed `flex-direction` to `column` inside a media query for smaller devices. When `flex-direction` is `column`, `flex-basis` controls the height instead of the width because the main axis runs vertically instead of horizontally in this scenario.

So let's fix this inside of our media query. Let's create a new selector and set `flex-basis` to `auto`:

```
@media screen and (max-width: 1023px){
  .column {
    flex-basis: auto;
    margin-bottom: 50px;
  }
}/* end of media query */
```

You'll recall that setting `flex-basis` to `auto` implies this: look at my width or height. Because we don't have a height set explicitly; the height is determined by the content, exactly what we want—just have the height be the size of the content. Also, I snuck in a `margin-bottom` of 50px to provide each one with a little breathing room between each other:

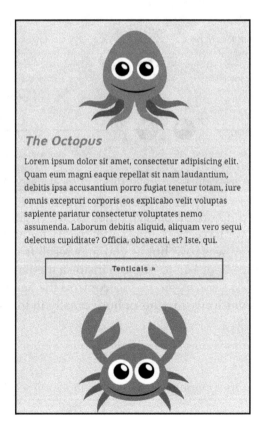

In this section, we built our product listing using flexbox and introduced two new flex properties: `align-items` and `align-self`. In the next section, I'll introduce two more properties: `flex-wrap` and `align-content`.

Using flex-wrap and align-content

The `flex-wrap` property allows us to determine whether we are going to wrap our content to a second row or squeeze all the flex items into a single row; `align-content` determines the alignment of a row that is being wrapped to multiple lines, thus becoming multiple rows. They are basically best friends.

Using flex-wrap

We'll return and use our flexbox sample page (`flexbox.html`) as a playground for testing these properties. Here's our CSS we ended up with in this area:

```
/***************
Flexbox demo
***************/
.flex-container {
  margin-top: 200px;
  display: flex;
  justify-content: flex-start;
}
.flex-item {
  padding: 20px;
}
.flex-item:last-child {
  margin-left: auto;
}
.flex-item1 { background: deeppink; }
.flex-item2 { background: orange;  }
.flex-item3 { background: lightblue; }
.flex-item4 { background: lime;  }
.flex-item5 { background: olive;  }
```

The flex container has all of the content justified to `flex-start`, or in our case, to the left. This is because `flex-direction` is not set, and hence it defaults to `row`. The last flex item is being pushed to the far right with `margin-left: auto;`. This is how our `flexbox.html` page should look at the moment:

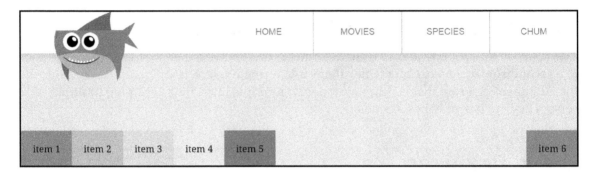

In `flexbox.html`, let's add quite a few more flex items and save them:

```
<section class='flex-container'>
    <div class="flex-item flex-item1">item 1</div>
    <div class="flex-item flex-item2">item 2</div>
    <div class="flex-item flex-item3">item 3</div>
    <div class="flex-item flex-item4">item 4</div>
    <div class="flex-item flex-item5">item 5</div>
    <div class="flex-item flex-item1">item 6</div>
    <div class="flex-item flex-item1">item 1</div>
    <div class="flex-item flex-item2">item 2</div>
    <div class="flex-item flex-item3">item 3</div>
    <div class="flex-item flex-item4">item 4</div>
    <div class="flex-item flex-item5">item 5</div>
    <div class="flex-item flex-item1">item 6</div>
    <div class="flex-item flex-item1">item 1</div>
    <div class="flex-item flex-item2">item 2</div>
    <div class="flex-item flex-item3">item 3</div>
    <div class="flex-item flex-item4">item 4</div>
    <div class="flex-item flex-item5">item 5</div>
    <div class="flex-item flex-item1">item 6</div>
</section>
```

Now we see how flexbox is really squishing the flex items to fit on one single row inside the flex container.

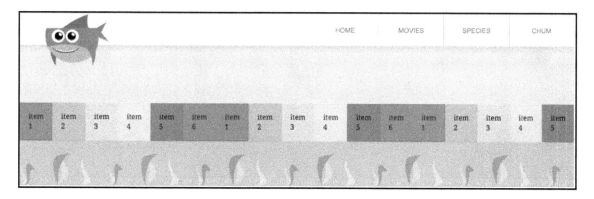

So what we'll do is wrap multiple rows by adding the `flex-wrap` property to the flex container with the value of `wrap`. Also, let's get rid of `margin-left: auto` on our last flex item by just removing that entire rule set:

```
/ * * * * * * * * * * * * * *
Flexbox demo
* * * * * * * * * * * * * * * /
.flex-container {
  margin-top: 200px;
  display: flex;
  justify-content: flex-start;
  flex-wrap: wrap;
}
.flex-item {
  padding: 20px;
}
.flex-item1 { background: deeppink; }
.flex-item2 { background: orange; }
.flex-item3 { background: lightblue; }
.flex-item4 { background: lime; }
.flex-item5 { background: olive; }
```

So all the flex items, which were previously shrinking to fit on one row, now expand to their natural size; this implies the width of the text plus `20px` of `padding` on each side of the text. This creates two rows of content. Good, exactly what we want!

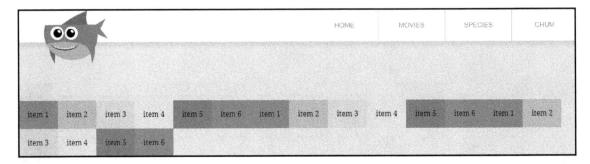

The default for `flex-wrap` is `nowrap;`. That makes sense because before we set it to `wrap` it was forcing all our flex items to fit on one row. As if we omitted `flex-wrap` altogether. Let's swap in `nowrap` to test this out:

```
.flex-container {
    margin-top: 200px;
    display: flex;
    justify-content: flex-start;
    flex-wrap: nowrap;
}
```

As if we never specified a `flex-wrap` at all:

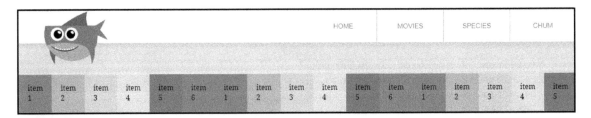

There's also `wrap-reverse;` let's try that:

```
.flex-container {
  margin-top: 200px;
  display: flex;
  justify-content: flex-start;
  flex-wrap: wrap-reverse;
}
```

The last item is now the first, and the first item is the last. Technically, the last item is now the fourth on the first row:

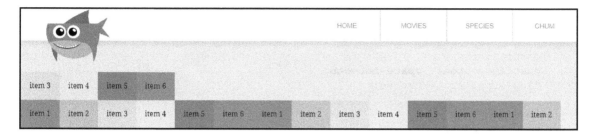

The cool thing about using `flex-wrap` is that each row now works independently of other rows when it comes to properties like `flex-grow`, `flex-shrink`, and `justify-content`.

Let's test it out and add `flex-grow: 1`:

```
.flex-container {
  margin-top: 200px;
  display: flex;
  justify-content: flex-start;
  flex-wrap: wrap-reverse;
}
.flex-item {
  padding: 20px;
  flex-grow: 1;
}
```

This redistributes any extra space between the flex items to make sure they fill all the leftover space:

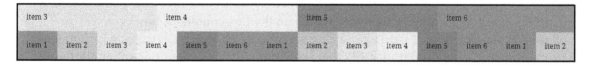

Each row has their flex items expanded to occupy the extra space. As you can see, the first row has its flex items stretched farther to fill up the extra space than the row below. In these other two rows underneath it, the flex items are only stretched a tiny bit to fill up the extra space.

Let's take another look at how these rows work independently of each other by changing `justify-content` to `space-between` the flex container. We'll also get rid of `flex-grow` on the flex item:

```
.flex-container {
  margin-top: 200px;
  display: flex;
  justify-content: space-between;
  flex-wrap: wrap-reverse;
}
.flex-item {
  padding: 20px;
}
```

So there's this extra space allocated between each flex item:

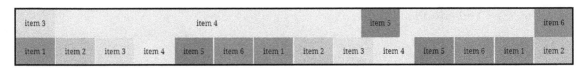

The first row has a lot of extra space, while the second row has only a little extra space between each flex item. Again, each row functions independently of each other on how to handle `flex-grow`, `flex-shrink`, and `justify-content`. This is the sort of stuff that works extremely well with dynamic, unknown quantities of content coming from a **content management system** (**CMS**).

Using align-content

Alright, let's take a look at another property called `align-content`. Like `flex-wrap`, `align-content` is a property that only works on the flex container; however, `align-content` is dependent on `flex-wrap` being set to `wrap` or `wrap-reverse`, which means `align-content` is ignored under all other scenarios. Also, `align-content` is similar to `align-items` because it controls arrangements or alignments along the cross axis. The only difference is that instead of redistributing each *flex item* along the cross axis, it redistributes each *row* along the cross axis.

Let's set a `align-content` to `space-between`. We'll also give it a height of `300px` and a dark gray border:

```
.flex-container {
  margin-top: 200px;
  display: flex;
  justify-content: space-between;
  flex-wrap: wrap-reverse;
  align-content: space-between;
  height: 300px;
  border: 1px solid #777;
}
```

And I'm also going to double the number of flex items to keep things interesting:

```
<!--
====================
Flexbox Demo
--------------------
-->
<section class='flex-container'>
    <div class="flex-item flex-item1">item 1</div>
    <div class="flex-item flex-item2">item 2</div>
    <div class="flex-item flex-item3">item 3</div>
    <div class="flex-item flex-item4">item 4</div>
    <div class="flex-item flex-item5">item 5</div>
    <div class="flex-item flex-item1">item 6</div>
    <div class="flex-item flex-item1">item 1</div>
    <div class="flex-item flex-item2">item 2</div>
    <div class="flex-item flex-item3">item 3</div>
    <div class="flex-item flex-item4">item 4</div>
    <div class="flex-item flex-item5">item 5</div>
    <div class="flex-item flex-item1">item 6</div>
    <div class="flex-item flex-item1">item 1</div>
    <div class="flex-item flex-item2">item 2</div>
    <div class="flex-item flex-item3">item 3</div>
    <div class="flex-item flex-item4">item 4</div>
    <div class="flex-item flex-item5">item 5</div>
    <div class="flex-item flex-item1">item 6</div>
    <div class="flex-item flex-item1">item 1</div>
    <div class="flex-item flex-item2">item 2</div>
    <div class="flex-item flex-item3">item 3</div>
    <div class="flex-item flex-item4">item 4</div>
    <div class="flex-item flex-item5">item 5</div>
    <div class="flex-item flex-item1">item 6</div>
    <div class="flex-item flex-item1">item 1</div>
    <div class="flex-item flex-item2">item 2</div>
    <div class="flex-item flex-item3">item 3</div>
```

```
            <div class="flex-item flex-item4">item 4</div>
            <div class="flex-item flex-item5">item 5</div>
            <div class="flex-item flex-item1">item 6</div>
            <div class="flex-item flex-item1">item 1</div>
            <div class="flex-item flex-item2">item 2</div>
            <div class="flex-item flex-item3">item 3</div>
            <div class="flex-item flex-item4">item 4</div>
            <div class="flex-item flex-item5">item 5</div>
            <div class="flex-item flex-item1">item 6</div>
    </section>
```

Now we have 3 rows and we have space between each row thanks to `align-content`:

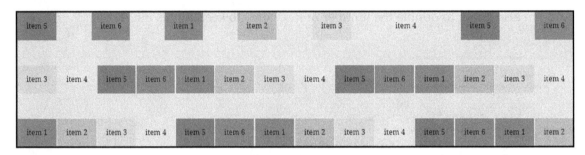

The `height` property is relevant because if omitted, the height of the flex container will only be as tall as its flex items; therefore, `align-content` wouldn't do anything because there wouldn't be any extra vertical space to play with. Other values aside from `space-between` for `align-items` include `flex-start`, `flex-end`, `center`, and `space-around`. These values should be familiar from when we studied the `justify-content` property. The default value is `stretch`. The `space-around` value redistributes the extra space around all the items evenly, including the first and the last.

So let's change it from `space-between` to `space-around`:

```
.flex-container {
  margin-top: 200px;
  display: flex;
  justify-content: space-between;
  flex-wrap: wrap-reverse;
  align-content: space-around;
  height: 300px;
  border: 1px solid #777;
}
```

You can see with space-around, there is a space between the top of the flex container and the first row and the bottom of the container and the last row:

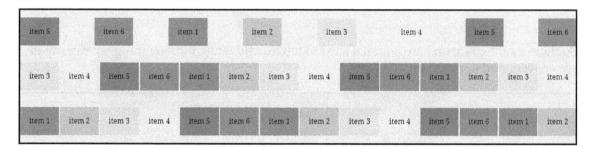

Whereas `space-between` had the first and last rows hugging tightly to the flex container, which is a subtle difference. Again we've noticed this subtlety from before when we studied `justify-content`.

Now let's change the value of `align-content` to `center`:

```
.flex-container {
  margin-top: 200px;
  display: flex;
  justify-content: space-between;
  flex-wrap: wrap-reverse;
  align-content: center;
  height: 300px;
  border: 1px solid #777;
}
```

As we would expect, our rows are centered:

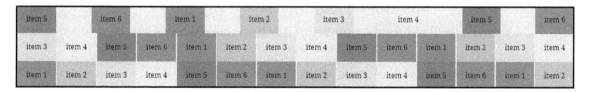

Let's change `flex-direction` to column now to see how `flex-wrap` and `align-content` work together in this use case:

```
.flex-container {
  margin-top: 200px;
  display: flex;
  justify-content: space-between;
  flex-direction: column;
```

```
  flex-wrap: wrap-reverse;
  align-content: center;
  height: 300px;
  border: 1px solid #777;
}
```

So there's a lot going on here, and it's hard to tell exactly what, but one thing we can say is we are centered horizontally:

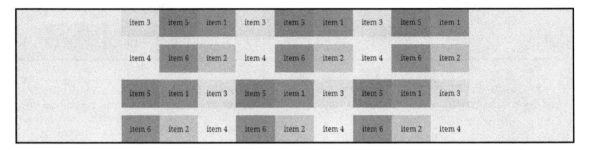

Let's simplify this a little to comprehend what's happening. First, let's change `flex-wrap` from `wrap-reverse` back to just `wrap`:

```
.flex-container {
    margin-top: 200px;
    display: flex;
    justify-content: space-between;
    flex-direction: column;
    flex-wrap: wrap;
    align-content: center;
    height: 300px;
    border: 1px solid #777;
}
```

In `flexbox.html`, we'll reduce the number of flex items considerably:

```
<section class='flex-container'>
    <div class="flex-item flex-item1">item 1</div>
    <div class="flex-item flex-item2">item 2</div>
    <div class="flex-item flex-item3">item 3</div>
    <div class="flex-item flex-item4">item 4</div>
    <div class="flex-item flex-item5">item 5</div>
    <div class="flex-item flex-item1">item 6</div>
</section>
```

Now, it's a little easier to see that `flex-direction` is `column`, which forces two vertical columns because `flex-wrap` is set to `wrap` and we are out of available space for all 6 flex items:

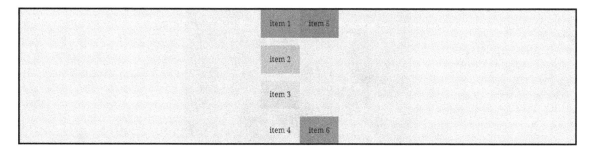

Our `space-between` setting for `justify-content` is redistributing the extra space between each flex item. Notice how both the columns are getting their extra space redistributed independently, as shown in the following diagram.

When there is extra space along the cross axis and multiple rows, `align-content` is used to arrange rows along the cross axis. And as we know the cross axis runs from top to bottom when `flex-direction` is row.

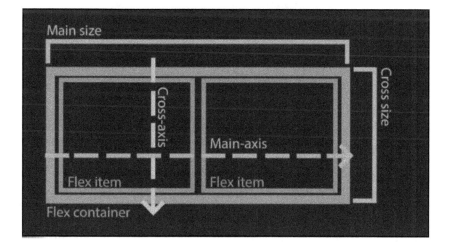

And, the cross axis runs from left to right when `flex-direction` is column:

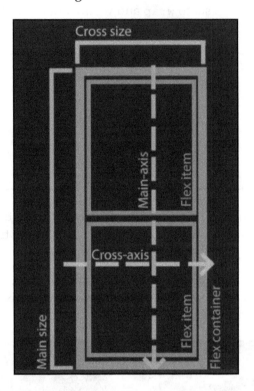

 My apologies, if I'm starting to sound like a broken record, but I feel it's important to over-communicate things that are important to how flexbox operates.

Using the flex-flow shorthand

Previously, we looked at how the `flex` shorthand combined `flex-grow`, `flex-shrink`, and `flex-basis` together. Let's introduce another shorthand, `flex-flow`, which will allow us to cut down on our properties a bit by combining `flex-direction` and `flex-wrap` together. Anyway, this simplifies our CSS a little bit:

```
.flex-container {
  margin-top: 200px;
  display: flex;
  justify-content: space-between;
  flex-flow: column wrap;
```

```
    align-content: center;
    height: 300px;
    border: 1px solid #777;
}
```

Nothing changes, which is exactly what we want when we refactor using a shorthand:

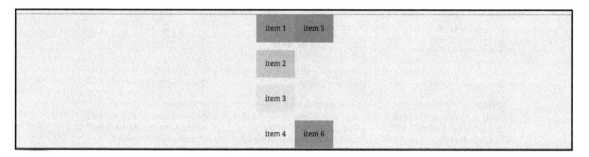

Given how closely dependent `align-content` is on `flex-wrap`, I would expect `align-content` to be part of the `flex-flow` shorthand. However, `align-content` isn't part of the `flex-flow` shorthand with `flex-direction` and `flex-wrap`.

In this section, you learned how `flex-wrap` allows us to create multiple streams—or rows—of content, while `align-items` positions those multiple rows within their container along the cross axis.

Changing the display order of flex items

In this section, we'll talk about how we can change the display order of flex items and how this can be helpful for responsive web design. We'll also talk about how this impacts web accessibility.

At wider screen widths, the content is displayed horizontally: first with the octopus, then the crab, and then the whale:

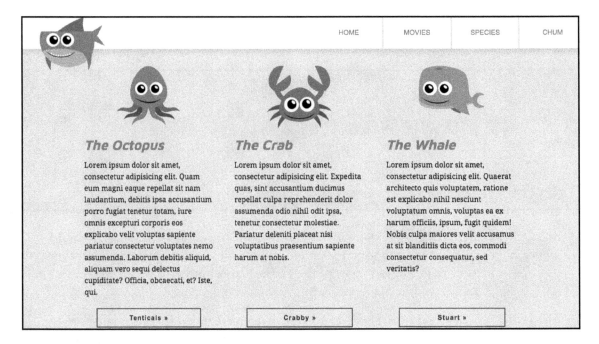

At narrower device widths, the content is displayed in the same order, just vertically, as shown in the following screenshot:

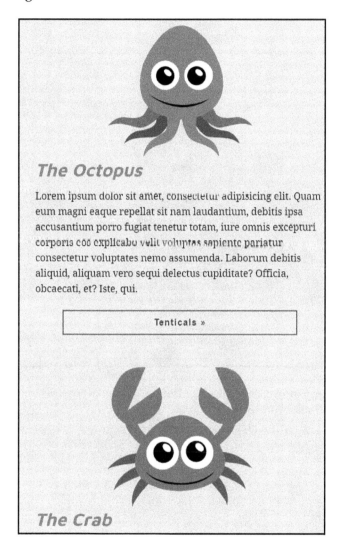

In both the cases, the display order is identical to the source order, and this makes sense in this scenario.

Let's do something different here. Let's say we're working with a designer who wants to feature the crab this week and give it visual priority over the octopus and whale. That's what we have done here. I've added a little extra to the HTML and CSS to achieve this new featured treatment:

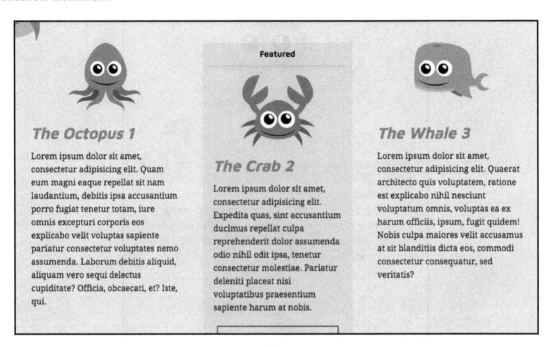

In the markup, I added a number to the headline of each column so we can easily remember the source order when viewing in the browser. Then, for the crab, I added a class called `featured` and a `div` tag with a class called `ribbon`.

```
<div class="column">
    <figure>
        <img src="images/octopus-icon.svg" alt="Octopus">
    </figure>
    <h2>The Octopus 1</h2>
    <p>Lorem ipsum dolor...</p>
    <a href="#" class="button">Tenticals &raquo;</a>
</div>
<div class="column featured">
    <div class="ribbon">Featured</div>
    <figure>
        <img src="images/crab-icon.svg" alt="Crab">
    </figure>
    <h2>The Crab 2</h2>
    <p>Lorem ipsum dolor...</p>
```

```
    <a href="#" class="button">Crabby &raquo;&lt;/a>
</div>
<div class="column">
    <figure>
        <img src="images/whale-icon.svg" alt="Whale">
    </figure>
    <h2>The Whale 3</h2>
    <p>Lorem ipsum dolor sit...</p>
    <a href="#" class="button">Stuart &raquo;</a>
 </div>
```

I've added some CSS to style the ribbon:

```
/*featured column*/
.featured {
  padding: 0 0 20px 0;
  background-color: #d3d3d3;
  overflow: hidden;
}
.featured h2,
.featured p {
  margin-left: 20px;
  margin-right: 20px;
}
.ribbon {
    background-color: #ffc0cb;
    padding: 10px 50px;
    margin-bottom: 20px;
    align-self: stretch;
    text-align: center;
    font-family: 'Maven Pro', Arial, sans-serif;
    font-weight: bold;
    box-shadow: #b7b7b7 0px 2px 15px 0px;
}
```

You may have noticed that the featured ribbon was stretched across the top; this was done using align-self: stretch. As we already discussed, align- self aligns flex items along the cross axis, which in our case runs from left to right since flex-direction is set to column. The align-self property is like align-items, except that it's used on a flex item and overrides the align-items property.

On the desktop or a wider view, our business partners and designers are really happy when they see this. But on a mobile, they are saying, *"Mmmmm, I don't know, the crab is still showing second."* And they might be right, it's the featured content, so it should not only be visually featured, it should also appear first. Well, if our content was coming from a database, we could update it so the crab would appear first; alternatively, we could use some JavaScript to rearrange our featured content to put the crab first. Both of these solutions are, at a minimum, not ideal.

Flexbox comes to the rescue here. In our media query for smaller devices we can use a property for flex items called `order`:

```
@media screen and (max-width: 1023px){
  .intro-content {
    width: auto;
    float: none;
    padding-bottom: 0;
    margin-bottom: 30px;
  }
  .go-premium {
    width: auto;
    float: none;
    margin-top: 0;
  }
  .columns {
    flex-direction: column;
  }
  .column {
    flex-basis: auto;
    margin-bottom: 50px;
  }
  .featured {
    order: -1;
  }
}/* end of media query */
```

Alright, when I refresh the browser, it instantly moves our crab to the first position, as shown in the following screenshot:

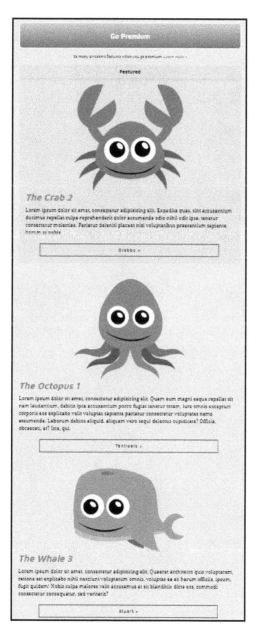

By default, all flex items are given an `order` of 0, so providing `-1` moved the crab to the top. The order of items runs with the main axis; the lowest-ordered flex item will be at the start of the main axis, while the highest-ordered flex items will appear at the end of the main axis.

Again, in our case, since `flex-direction` is `column`, the main axis runs from top to bottom. Let's change the `order` to 1:

```
@media screen and (max-width: 1023px){
  .intro-content {
    width: auto;
    float: none;
    padding-bottom: 0;
    margin-bottom: 30px;
  }
  .go-premium {
    width: auto;
    float: none;
    margin-top: 0;
  }
  .columns {
    flex-direction: column;
  }
  .column {
    flex-basis: auto;
    margin-bottom: 50px;
  }
  .featured {
    order: 1;
  }
}/* end of media query */
```

This moves the crab to the bottom because since both the octopus and whale are, by default, `0` - and, we've specified the crab as `1`—so now it's placed at the end:

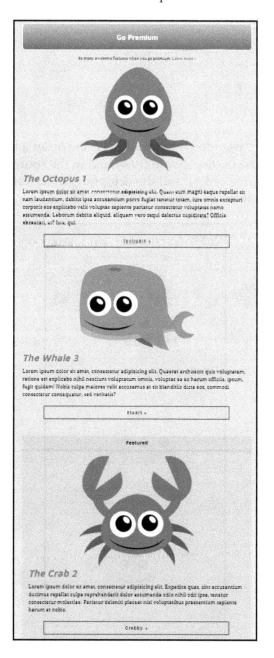

Alright, let's add two more rulesets:

```
.column:nth-child(1) {
  order: 3;
}
.featured {
  order: 1;
}
.column:nth-child(3) {
  order: 2;
}
```

We're using the `nth-child` pseudo classes to mix up the order a bit. When we refresh the browser now, the crab is first in display order (second in the source order), the whale is second (but third in the source order), and the octopus is third (but first in the source order). This is what it should look like:

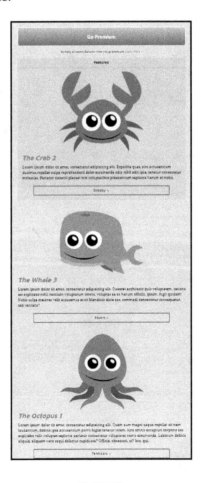

So I can also put them in reverse order. I already have the first one as third, and I can make the second one second, and the third one first:

```
.column:nth-child(1) {
  order: 3;
}
.featured {
  order: 2;
}
.column:nth-child(3) {
  order: 1;
}
```

This is what we should see:

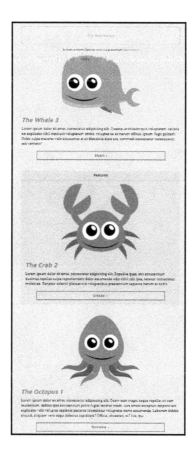

Now we have the third as the first, second as second, and the first as third. Reverse order. But remember, I have an easier way to do this; I can actually just get rid of all three of these rulesets and just specify `flex-direction` as `column-reverse`:

```
@media screen and (max-width: 1023px){
  .intro-content {
    width: auto;
    float: none;
    padding-bottom: 0;
    margin-bottom: 30px;
  }
  .go-premium {
    width: auto;
    float: none;
    margin-top: 0;
  }
  .columns {
    flex-direction: column-reverse;
  }
  .column {
    flex-basis: auto;
    margin-bottom: 50px;
  }
}/* end of media query */
```

Now when I refresh the browser, they're still in reverse order:

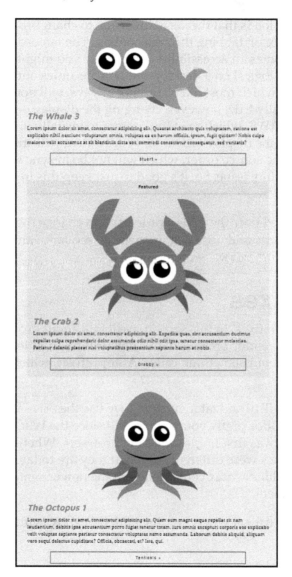

Accessibility impact

One thing I want to mention is that there's a downside to changing the display order that you may want to be aware of: tabbing through content. The tab order is still based on the source order, which becomes an accessibility issue. Now you might be thinking that in our example, the tab order is logical on a desktop but only becomes out of logic on smaller devices, such as phones, which most likely, but not always, will not be tabbing through fields. Perhaps that's mostly true; however, changing the display order is also a problem for screen readers, such as JAWS, which read the content to visually impaired users based on the source order and not the display order. So, your content will still be announced by the screen reader based on the source order, which will not be in sync with the visual order. This could be an accessibility issue. So, it's good to just keep this in mind if changing the order.

In this section, you learned how the `order` property can change the display order of flex items within a flex container and how that impacts tab sequence and accessibility.

Vendor prefixes

Let's talk about vendor prefixes. In this section, we'll talk about browser support for flexbox and how we should add vendor prefixes to our flexbox CSS in order to get deeper flexbox support. We'll also talk about something called **Autoprefixer**, which helps us add those prefixes.

Flexbox support starts at IE10 and later version if we use the `-ms-` vendor prefix. But this might not be the only vendor prefix you want to add since the W3C specification has actually changed since it was first implemented in browsers. When it was implemented, the syntax and property names were different from that they are today. To get deep browser support, we can use an older syntax combined with the newer syntax to support some of the early adopting browsers.

Let's update our original ruleset where we first added flexbox, which was our `.columns`:

```
.columns {
  display: -webkit-box;
  display: -webkit-flex;
  display: -ms-flexbox;
  display: flex;
  -webkit-box-pack: justify;
  -webkit-justify-content: space-between;
  -moz-box-pack: justify;
  -ms-flex-pack: justify;
```

```
        justify-content: space-between;
    }
```

Wow! There's a ton going on here. We're not just adding -ms-, -moz-, and -webkit- to the beginning of the property. We're adding the vendor prefix to the start of the value when it comes to the values for the display property. And the values themselves aren't very different from our non-prefixed version. And there's 2 -webkit- values! Chrome and Safari were really early adopters of flexbox, so there's actually two different prefixes that WebKit browsers were supporting: -webkit-box and -webkit-flex. So, that's a lot of prefixes and a lot of memorizing and it looks just as crazy for the justify-content property. This is a lot. The tricky part is learning and remembering the older syntax, especially since it's not obvious which prefixes are still needed.

Autoprefixer

Here's where a tool such as Autoprefixer CSS online (https://autoprefixer.github.io/) can be super helpful. It provides the prefixes we need based on the total market share of the browsers and the number of versions we want to go back for each browser. Let's update this filter to .01%:

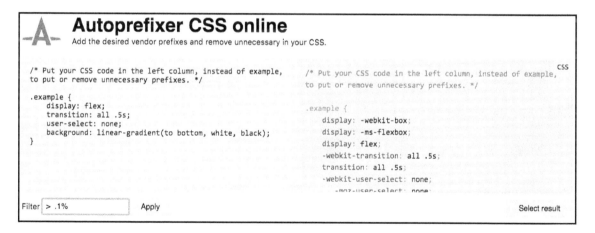

Let's get rid of all these prefixes and just copy and paste this ruleset to the left box of the Autoprefixer tool:

On the right-hand side, it provides the prefixes we should use:

Let's copy that back over to our CSS:

```
.columns {
  display: -webkit-box;
  display: -ms-flexbox;
  display: flex;
  -webkit-box-pack: justify;
      -ms-flex-pack: justify;
          justify-content: space-between;
}
```

This is pretty sweet and much easier than memorizing the different syntaxes of all the flexbox properties. It would be nice if there were some way to automatically add vendor prefixes for us, without us having to do all this copying and pasting. One thing we can do is we can use a preprocessor, such as **Sass**, to write something called a **mixin** to add vendor prefixes for us, so we don't have to think about this as much. We'll look at Sass mixins in the next chapter

Gulp

Now I want to mention something that you may have heard of: Gulp.

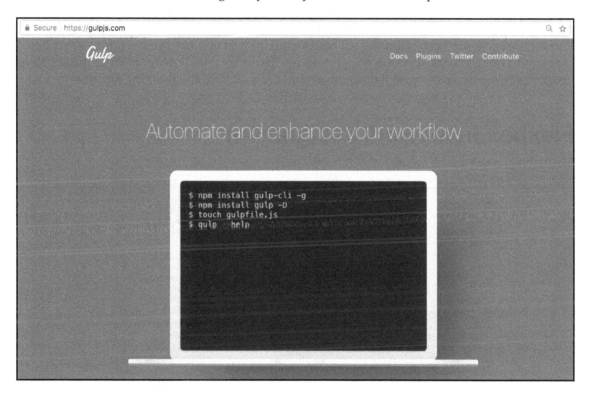

Gulp (https://gulpjs.com/), and its friend Grunt(https://gruntjs.com/), allow us to create build processes that things like minify our CSS and JavaScript files, compile Sass into CSS, and even add vendor prefixes to CSS automatically, using Autoprefixer. Gulp runs on Node and requires you to download it and then download Gulp. You can then download individual tasks, such as Autoprefixer. Learning Gulp is far out of the scope of this book, but Gulp is really useful and I really like it a lot. In order to get started with it, I highly recommend that you read *Getting Started with Gulp, Travis Maynard, Packt Publishing*, which does an excellent job of explaining how to install Gulp, set it up, and use it. This is how I learned how to use Gulp, by reading this book.

Gulp is a *command line* tool that you can configure to run Autoprefixer every time you save your CSS file. So if I write a flexbox property in my CSS and do a *Ctrl + S*, Gulp will be watching my file for any deltas and if it detects a change, it will tell Autoprefixer to run and update my CSS file with the necessary vendor prefixes. I know that sounds weird—update my CSS file with vendor prefixes—but technically, what it does is it creates a new CSS file that will have all the vendor prefixes. There's more to it than what I've explained here, but check out Travis Maynard's book to get it set up. This way, you'll never have to think about vendor prefixes again because Autoprefixer and Gulp will do the thinking for you.

Flexbox homework assignment

We've built one heck of a site:

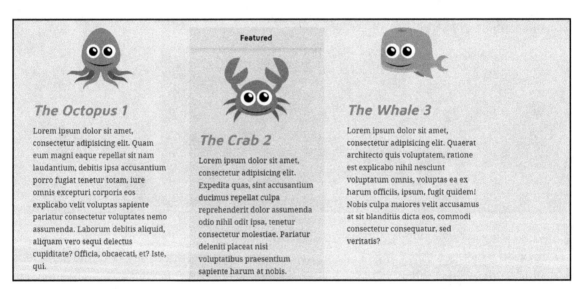

However, it is not without its problems. One thing you may have noticed is, in the product listing section, when we shrink down our browser, it starts to look a little wonky, as shown in the following screenshot:

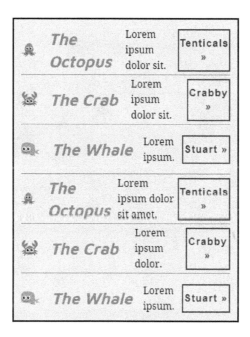

One final take-home test for you would be to update the CSS inside a media query to make the display look good here in smaller device sizes.

In this section, we talked about how we need to add vendor prefixes to our flexbox properties in order to get deeper browser support. Vendor prefixes, though, can be tricky, and it's best to leave prefixing to a tool such as Autoprefixer. Better yet, it's best to automate Autoprefixer so it is executed every time you save your CSS file. You can use a task runner, such as Gulp or Grunt, for this.

Summary

That completes our journey through flexbox. We've now seen every single one of the properties associated with it, and put them into practice building a new product listing for our site. In the next chapter, we'll look at the next steps for advancing your skillset and tooling around CSS in the finale: Chapter 11, *Wrapping Up*.

11
Wrapping Up

Welcome to the last chapter of this book. As we're at the end of this journey, I wanted to walk you through some steps in your web development learning progression as well as go through some links and resources for more information on everything you've learned up to this point.

The next steps

The next logical progression when learning CSS is moving to a CSS preprocessor, like Sass or Less. CSS preprocessors allow you to write CSS using programming features like nesting, imports, variables, and mixins that get compiled down to regular CSS. Another logical step in front end development is learning JavaScript. First though, let's talk about the CSS preprocessor, Sass.

CSS preprocessors

I've used both *Less* and *Sass*, but I've been using Sass for a while now. When I started to create the course materials for this book I had almost forgotten what it was like to write CSS without Sass. Needless to say, writing CSS is much easier using Sass. It keeps your code much more organized and clean, and I highly recommend it. Let's go over some of the notable features of Sass.

Variables

One simple yet powerful feature of Sass is variables. Let's set up variables called `$blue`, and `$red` which respectively equal the colors I've been using throughout the site for basically anything you saw that was blue or red:

```
//colors
$blue: #0072AE;
$red: #EB2428;
```

Now when I need to put enter the hard-to-remember hex value of `#0072AE`, I can just type in `$blue` and Sass magically takes care of it. An equally good use of variables is they with fonts, and that's where I think it really gets powerful. With fonts, you can usually type in a `font-family` and then create a stack of fonts. But, this can get lengthy and repetitive. So plugging all of this information into a variable, a very simple one such as `$maven` or `$droid`, makes it really easy to use fonts quickly and at any time you need to:

```
//fonts
$serif: 'Times New Roman', Georgia, serif;
$sans: Arial, Helvetica, sans-serif;
$maven: 'Maven Pro', $sans;
$droid: 'Droid Serif', $serif;
```

Then I can use those variables anywhere I set a `font-family`:

```
h1, h2 {
  font-family: $maven;
}
p {
  font-family: $droid;
}
```

This will be compiled into this whole string:

```
h1, h2 {
  font-family: 'Maven Pro', Arial, Helvetica, sans-serif;;
}
p {
  font-family: 'Droid Serif', 'Times New Roman', Georgia, serif;
}
```

Mixins

There's an even better feature in Sass called **mixins**. Basically, they are a method for abstracting out repetition. For instance, it's a drag to type in vendor prefixes for CSS3, but I can declare a mixin using the `@mixin` keyword and then create a template chock-full of vendor prefixes. Here, I have declared a mixin named `transition`:

```
@mixin transition($property: all, $duration: .25s, $timing-function: ease)
{
    -webkit-transition: $property $duration $timing-function;
    transition: $property $duration $timing-function;
}
```

The mixin has parenthesis with arguments inside of it, `$property`, `$duration`, and `$timing-function`. Each argument has a default assigned to it, `all`, `.25s`, and `ease`. Then I have the -webkit- prefixed transition property and the un-prefixed verison. Both have the arguments of the mixin as their values.

This allows me to go into my CSS and, if I want to use a transition, just add the `@include transition`:

```
.button {
    @include transition();
}
```

This compiles down to:

```
.button {
  -webkit-transition: all .25s ease;
  transition: all .25s ease;
}
```

Another thing I can do is update the default values of this mixin anytime I call it:

```
.button {
    @include transition(background-color, .5s, ease-in-out);
}
```

This will compile down to:

```
.button {
  -webkit-transition: background-color .5s ease-in-out;
  transition: background-color .5s ease-in-out;
}
```

SASS nesting

Beyond variables and mixins, there's nesting, which on the surface may not seem too powerful but is extremely convenient. Instead of writing descendant selectors, you can nest selectors inside of each other. You can see in the following CSS code that I've actually nested the `focus` and `hover` selectors inside of `.button`:

```
.button {
  &:focus,
  &:hover {
    background-color: #333;
    color: #fff;
    transform: scale(1, 1) translate(0, -5px);
  }
}
```

This compiles down in to the following:

```
.button:focus,
.button:hover {
  background-color: #333;
  color: #fff;
  transform: scale(1, 1) translate(0, -5px);
}
```

As a rule of thumb, don't nest if you don't have to because the selector gets more specific and weighs more each time you nest. The trick to modular CSS is keeping your selectors lightweight. For more information on nesting and using the special ampersand character in Sass check out my article I wrote for CSS-Tricks.com entitled, *The Sass Ampersand* (`https://css-tricks.com/the-sass-ampersand/`).

Creating and importing partial files with SASS

In the *Font kits and font services* section in `Chapter 7`, *Web Fonts*, we also discussed that Sass allows you to create partial files for different parts of your CSS and import them into your main Sass file:

```
//Imports
@import '_variables.scss';
@import '_mixins.scss';
@import '_icons.scss';
@import '_reset.scss';
@import '_modular.scss';
@import '_modal.scss';
```

Sass will compile all partial Sass files into one main CSS file. So I have my CSS broken down into smaller chunks. They all compile down into `style.css`.

The best part about having these multiple organized files is that they compile down into one file, so that means just one HTTP request instead of multiple requests. That's a performance gain right there. Not to mention it keeps my CSS very organized.

So these are just a few of the very nice features of a preprocessor, specifically Sass. Using Sass or Less is definitely the most logical step at this point. The Sass style sheet you write will need to go through a compiler though that turns it into regular old CSS; otherwise, the browsers won't understand the Sass code. For compiling, you have a few options. You can install Ruby and Sass and use your command line to watch for any changes made to the Sass files. You could also check out software like CodeKit to do the same. Or you can use a task runner like Gulp, as we talked about at the end of the last section.

To learn more about SASS, I recommend *Brock Nunn's Rapid SASS* video course in the Packt library:

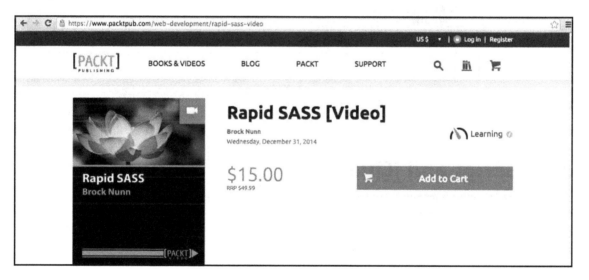

Also, check out *SASS for Web Designers* by *Dan Cederholm*. This book does a really great job at explaining Sass in simple terms, and it's a quick read:

JavaScript and jQuery

Another logical step for front end developers is to learn JavaScript if you haven't done so already. With CSS, we can add interactivity through the hover and focus states, but we can't have the on-click or swipe feature or anything like that. Enter JavaScript and jQuery. I recommend that you learn the basics of JavaScript; however, if you want to get a springboard in it, you can start out by learning jQuery.

So let's say we want to do something like display a modal when we click on the **Learn more >>** link:

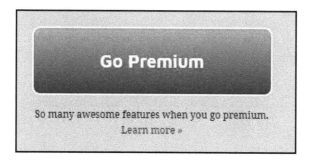

We could have a modal that shows:

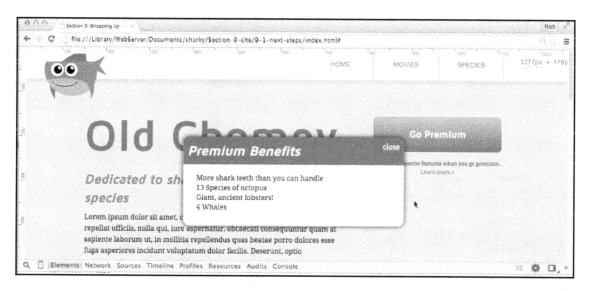

So we have an animation that will fade in and out. Therefore, it is relatively easier to set up animations with jQuery than JavaScript. The idea is to create a modal in HTML and CSS as if it has been there always. I created the modal and put that HTML at the very bottom of the HTML file:

```
<div class="modal modal-learn-more">
    <span class="close-modal">close</span>
    <h2>Premium Benefits</h2>
    <ul>
        <li>More shark teeth than you can handle</li>
        <li>13 Species of octopus</li>
```

```
            <li>Giant, ancient lobsters!</li>
            <li>4 Whales</li>
        </ul>
    </div>
```

Then I have a Sass partial file called `modal.scss`, which styles the modal and positions it where it's supposed to be:

```
//learn more modal
.modal {
  display: none;
  width: 40%;
  margin: 0 auto;
  position: absolute;
  top: 200px;
  left: 50%;
  @include translateX(-50%);
  background: #fff;
  @include box-shadow;
  @include border-radius;
  overflow: hidden;
  .close-modal {
    position: absolute;
    right: 10px;
    top: 10px;
    color: #fff;
    cursor: pointer;
    text-decoration: underline;
  }
  h2 {
    background: $blue;
    color: #fff;
    padding: 10px;
  }
  ul {
    padding: 10px 30px 30px 30px;
  }
}
```

The `.modal` class is also set to `display: none`, so by default, it's not present. It's like our drop-down menu; by default, it's hidden.

Here we have some jQuery to open the modal:

```
//open modal//
$(".learn-more").on("click", function(event){
    event.preventDefault();
    $(".modal-learn-more").fadeIn();
});
```

This basically watches for a click on the link with a class of `learn-more`, then fade in the element with the class of `modal-learn-more`. If we go back to the HTML, we'll see that we have the `modal-learn-more` class on the outermost parent `div` of the modal:

```
<div class="modal modal-learn-more">
    <span class="close-modal">close</span>
    <h2>Premium Benefits</h2>
    <ul>
        <li>More shark teeth than you can handle</li>
        <li>13 Species of octopus</li>
        <li>Giant, ancient lobsters!</li>
        <li>4 Whales</li>
    </ul>
</div>
```

This is readable and a very small amount of jQuery. The same thing goes if we want to tell the modal that we want to close it when we click on the **close** link:

```
//close modal//
$(".close-modal").on("click", function(event){
    event.preventDefault();
    $(".modal-learn-more").fadeOut();
});
```

We're basically saying when you click on the **close** modal, we're going to have `modal-learn-more` fade out. jQuery handles the animation of fading in and fading out through predefined methods that they have created. Selecting the `div` that we want to fade out and selecting the item or the element that we want to click on is very easy in jQuery. To learn more about jQuery, I recommend checking out the jQuery books in the Packt library, particularly *jQuery for Designers: Beginner's Guide*.

Sass and jQuery are the next logical steps going forward. Sass takes CSS authoring to the next level, and jQuery will give you the ability to add functionality and deeper interaction to your website. Not to mention that it will round you out as a front end developer. In the next section, I'm going to wrap up by recapping everything we've discussed and point out a few good resources you can use to get more information.

Conclusion and links

Thank you for reading *Mastering CSS*. I truly enjoyed putting this book together. We covered a lot of ground, so I'm going to do a recap of the things we've learned and point you in the direction of where you can get more information on the topics.

The box model and block versus inline elements

We started this book by reviewing the basics, such as the box model, and the difference between block and inline elements. A great place to learn more about these two important, fundamental topics is on Sitepoint's A to Z CSS screencasts. For block vs inline elements: `https://www.sitepoint.com/atoz-css-screencast-display/` and for the box model `https://www.sitepoint.com/atoz-css-screencast-box-model/`. Here you can view some really helpful box models and display videos.

Floats

We also talked a lot about floats and how to use them to create a multicolumn layout, as we did on our home page:

We talked about the problems created by floats, such as collapse, and other content flowing around the float. We also discussed different ways, such as using the `clear-fix`, to avoid these problems. To learn more about floats, I'm going to point you right back to Sitepoint's A to Z CSS, and the short six-minute video (`https://www.sitepoint.com/atoz-css-screencast-float-and-clear/`) that covers the basics of floats and how to get used to their quirks.

Modular CSS

Next you learned how to create modular CSS. We didn't want to style one piece of our site and then redo all those styles again if we felt like styling another similar piece of our site. We wanted to be able to reuse the CSS we had already created by employing modular techniques. I emphasized this when we built our buttons using modular classes. To learn more about modular CSS, you can get smacked over at **SMACSS (Scalable and modular architecture for CSS)**; refer to the `smacss.com` website.

CSS3

We ended up using a lot of CSS3 at this point for our buttons. We used a lot of hover effects throughout the site. On the movies page, we added a hover effect to one of the movie images. If you want to learn more about CSS3, there's a great book in the Packt library called *Designing Next Generation Web Projects with CSS3* by *Sandro Paganotti*.

Also, you might want to check out *CSS3 for Web Designers, second edition* by *Dan Cederholm*, available through `abookapart.com`.

Creating the navigation

We went on to build one heck of navigation that was in a fixed position to the top with our content scrolled underneath it. It had a nice drop-down menu that animated downward nicely using CSS animations:

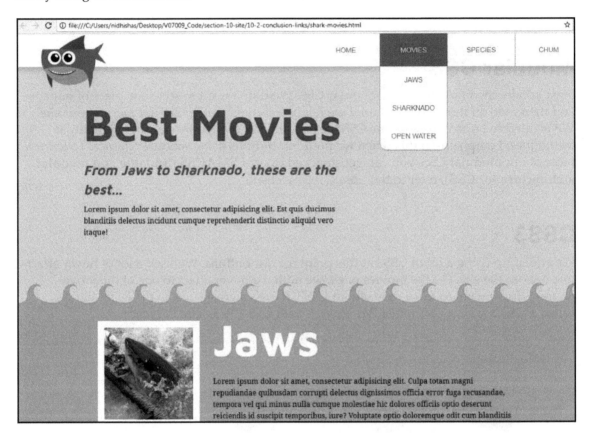

We also had our shark animate upon browser refresh; we made it look like it was swimming, and that was a lot of fun. I'm proud of an article I wrote on CSS animations: `http://www.richfinelli.com/css-animations-arent-that-tough/`. In this article, I get into all the animation properties in detail and slowly progress to creating a rather complex animation:

I find myself constantly referring to the **Mozilla Developer Network** (**MDN**) website for a quick reference on animation properties. I think MDN is a very reliable and deep resource for all things web:

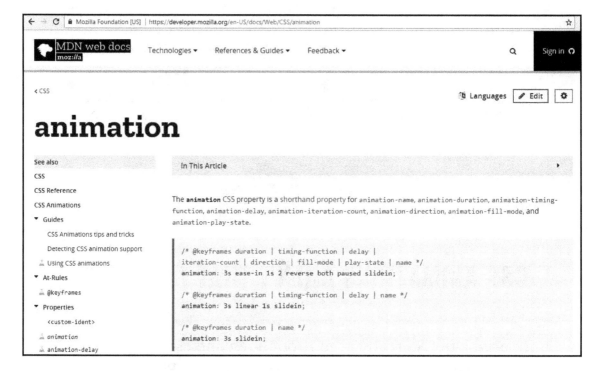

Making the site responsive

We did a great job in making our site responsive, especially when we completely transformed our menu into a small screen to accommodate mobile devices:

In my opinion, the best place to learn more about responsive web design is from the man who invented it himself-Ethan Marcotte. Check out the ground breaking book that started it all – *Responsive Web Design.* The second edition of the book was released at the end of 2014.

Web fonts

In `Chapter 7`, *Web Fonts*, we talked about web fonts and icon fonts. We learned how a good font can really make a site look great. Back to the `abookapart.com` website, there is a very good book you can use to learn how to set and pair type phases. It's called *On Web Typography* by *Jason Santa Maria.*

HiDPI devices

Finally, in `Chapter 8`, *Workflow for HiDPI Devices*, we got our site "retina ready" by learning what we needed to do with images in order to make them look crisp on double density displays such as the iPad Retina. We looked at a number of approaches to account for Retina. One of the things I'm most excited about in web development is SVG. It really solves some of the glaring problems of Retina. Chris Coyier of CSS tricks (`https://css-tricks.com`) has written a few great articles that sum up SVG and how to use it, including the one titled – Using SVG.

Also for more information on the `srcset` attribute I wrote two articles on that topic. One on the W descriptor and `sizes` attribute (`http://www.richfinelli.com/srcset-part-2/`) and another on the X descriptor (`http://www.richfinelli.com/srcset-part-1/`).

Flexbox

Flexbox is so much fun! We converted our 3 column float-based layout to a flexbox-based layout and built a new section, our product listing, using flexbox. For more information on flexbox I recommend checking out Wes Bos' video course, *What the Flexbox! at* flexbox.io or for a quick and comprehensive reference to all flexbox properties check out *CSS Tricks' A Complete Guide to Flexbox* at `https://css-tricks.com/snippets/css/a-guide-to-flexbox/`.

Final tidbit of advice: Audio Podcasts are terrific

If you're like me and have a strong desire to learn and a long drive to work, audio podcasts can be a great resource. Two of my favorite podcasts on front end development are Shoptalk (`http://shoptalkshow.com/`) and Syntax (`https://syntax.fm/`). Both are very fun and informative. Listening to podcasts on my way to work is my way of staying up to date in what's happening in web development and what's new out there to learn.

Summary

In the end, I think we created one heck of a little site here, learning a lot about CSS and web development. So once again thanks for reading. I really did have a lot of fun putting it together. I wish you much success and hope that you continue to hone your CSS skills.

Index

@

@font-face property
  about 295
  font files, adding to site folder 296

A

absolute positioning
  about 183
  fixed positioning, used for nav bar 188
  shark 183, 184, 186
accessibility impact 480
action button
  HTML, adding 146, 148
  styling 144, 151, 152, 153, 155
align-content
  about 455
  using 460, 461, 463, 465, 466
align-items
  using 436, 438, 440, 441, 442, 443, 444, 445,
    447, 448, 449
align-self flexbox property
  using 451, 452, 455
automatic margins
  using 431, 432, 433, 434
Autoprefixer 480, 481
Autoprefixer CSS online
  reference link 481

B

basic HTML list
  creating 189
block element modifier (BEM) 71
block elements
  versus inline elements 496
block level elements 21, 22, 24, 26
box model 17, 496

box-shadow
  adding 221, 223, 224
browser shrinking 401
button
  creating, with modular CSS 102
  standard buttons, building 104, 105, 107, 108,
    110
  types 102

C

Chrome DevTools, for troubleshooting HTML and
    CSS
  reference link 55
Chrome DevTools
  about 46
  console, used to find errors 53, 55
  CSS, changing inside the inspector 50, 53
  opening 46, 48
classes
  about 57, 59
  multiple elements, classifying 60
clear method
  using 93
code suggestion 35
collapsed containers 91
companion CSS
  implementing, to web font 300
content management system (CMS) 315, 460
CSS animations
  about 201, 209
  additional keyframes, setting 205
  animation-delay 215
  fill-mode 209, 213
  iteration-count 209, 215
CSS foundations
  disclaimer 11
CSS gradient generator

reference link 156
CSS preprocessors
  about 487
  mixins 489
  partial files, creating with SASS 490, 491
  partial files, importing with SASS 490
  SASS nesting 490
  SASS variables 488
CSS reset
  about 36
  customizing 43, 44
  examining 40, 42
  loading 36, 38, 39
  reference link 36
CSS tricks
  references 502
CSS3 497
CSS
  used, for positioning 147

D

descendant selectors
  about 63
  BEM 71
  child elements 64
  creating 65, 67, 69
  parent elements 64
  selector weight, calculating 70, 71
  sibling elements 64
display order
  changing, of flex items 467, 468, 469, 474, 479
div tag
  centering 84
drop-down menu
  building 189
  hiding, off screen hidden trick used 199
  styles maintaining, overflow hidden approach
    used 197
  styling 193, 194, 195

E

elements
  classes 57, 59
  classes or IDs, using 63
  IDs 61

renaming 56
embedded style sheet 14, 15
external style sheet 13

F

flex 403
flex container 384
flex items
  about 384
  display order, changing 467, 468, 469, 474, 479
flex shorthand
  using 417, 419, 420
flex terminology
  about 383
  align-items 385
  cross axis 385
  cross size 384, 385
  justify-content 385
  main axis 385
  main size 384, 385
flex-basis
  about 403
  using 408, 409, 410, 411, 412, 413
flex-direction
  browser shrinking 401
  changing 395, 397, 398, 399, 400
flex-flow shorthand
  using 466
flex-grow
  about 403
  using 403, 404, 405, 406, 407, 408
flex-shrink
  about 403
  using 413, 414, 416, 417
flex-wrap
  using 455, 459, 460
flexbox homework assignment 485
flexbox
  automatic margins, used 431, 432, 433, 434
  justify-content property, used 421, 422, 423,
    424, 425, 426, 428
  layout 420
  nesting flexboxes 428, 429, 430, 431
  positioning 420
  turning, display used 391, 393, 394, 395

flexible box layout module
  overview 383
flexible images 239, 241, 242, 243, 244, 245
float-related properties
  removing, from columns section 386, 389, 390
floating columns 86, 87, 89
floats
  about 73, 74, 75, 76, 78, 496
  clear method, used 93
  clear property, used for solving basic issues 79,
    80
  clearfix hack 98
  float method 97
  issues, solving 93
  overflow_hidden 96
  to flexbox 386
fluid grid
  about 227
  on shark movies page 237
  pixels, converting to percentages 228, 229
font foundries
  fonts, adding to site 316, 320
  fonts, selecting from Typekit 312, 315
  subscription 311
fonts
  adding, to site 316, 318
  applying, in CSS 296, 299
  defining, in CSS 296, 299
  selecting, from Typekit 315
foundation icon 328

G

Google Web Fonts
  about 301
  applying, in CSS 308
  finding 301, 302, 308
  URL 301
gradients
  about 155
  CSS gradient generator, output 161
  CSS gradient generator, using 156, 157, 160
Grunt
  URL 483
Gulp
  about 483, 484

URL 483

I

icon fonts
  about 321
  adding, to website 326, 330
  downloading, from Zurb foundation 324, 326
  footer, building 321, 323
  styling 332, 333, 335
inline elements
  versus block elements 496
inline style sheet 14, 15

J

JavaScript 492, 494
jQuery
  about 492, 494, 495
  using, to trigger menu on click 283, 285, 289
justify-content property
  using 421, 422, 423, 424, 425, 426, 427, 428

M

media queries
  about 250, 251
  columns, adding 259
  iPads, considering 258
  mobile first approach 265
  navigation, building for narrower widths 266, 267
  tablet dimensions, considering 258
  writing 252, 254
micro clearfix 98
mixins 482, 489
mobile menu
  about 270
  hiding 282
  icon, adding 279, 281
  mobile nav, styling in open state 272, 274, 276
mobile nav
  styling, in open state 272, 274, 276
Modular CSS 497
modular CSS
  button, creating 102
Mozilla Developer Network (MDN) 500
multicolumn layout
  .column targeting, pseudo class used 89

collapsed containers 91
creating 82, 84
floating columns 86, 87, 89
multiple classes
about 110
border, changing 114
button, positioning 115, 116, 118
button, width changing 112
font colors, changing of button 114
multiple cursors 33
multiple elements
classifying 60

N

navigation
box-shadow, adding 221, 223, 224
creating 498, 500
CSS, used for styling 168, 169, 171, 172
semantic HTML, for building menu 166
starting 165
Z index issue, fixing 218, 219, 220
nesting flexboxes 428, 429, 430, 431

O

off screen hidden trick 199
overflow_hidden
using 96

P

pixels
converting, to percentages 228, 229
padding, changed to percentage 237
target/content equals result 230, 231, 234, 235
product listing
align-items, used 436, 438, 440, 441, 442, 443,
444, 445, 447, 448, 449
align-self flexbox property, used 451, 452, 455
building 436
pseudo class
used, for targeting .column 89
pseudo classes
first child 176, 178
last child 179
nth child class 179
nth of type 182

using 175

R

rule set
anatomy 12
dissecting 12

S

Sass 482
Scalable and modular architecture for CSS
(SMACSS)
about 497
URL 497
semantic HTML
for building menu 166
shrinking images
on shark movies page 246, 247, 248, 250
site responsive
creating 500
snippets 30, 32, 33
specificity rules
about 119
important declaration 123, 124
selectors, weights 119, 120, 121, 123
universal selector 125, 126
standard buttons
building 107, 108, 110
style sheets
embedded style sheets 15
external style sheet 13, 14
inline style sheet 15
types 12
sublime packages
URL, for installation 32
syntax highlighting 34

T

text editors
about 29, 30
code suggestion 35
multiple cursors 33
snippets 30, 32, 33
syntax highlighting 34
transforms
about 133

rotate value, using 136, 137, 139, 141
scale, applying to button 134
translate function, using 135
vendor prefixes, adding 143
transitions
  about 128
  hover state, creating 129
  transition property, using 130
  vendor prefixes 133

V

vendor prefixes
  about 480
  Autoprefixer 481
  flexbox homework assignment 484, 485

Gulp 483, 484
viewport meta tag
  about 290
  anatomy 293
  responsive design, testing on mobile device 290, 292

W

web fonts 501

Z

Z index issue
  fixing 218, 219, 220
Zurb foundation
  icon font, downloading 326

www.ingramcontent.com/pod-product-compliance
Lightning Source LLC
Chambersburg PA
CBHW060639060326
40690CB00020B/4457